MEMOI

OF THE AUTHOR OF A VINDICATION OF THE RIGHTS OF WOMAN

MEMOIRS

OF THE AUTHOR OF A VINDICATION OF THE RIGHTS OF WOMAN

William Godwin

edited by Pamela Clemit
& Gina Luria Walker

broadview literary texts

Canadian Cataloguing in Publication Data

Godwin, William, 1756-1836
        Memoirs of the author of A vindication of the rights of woman

(Broadview literary texts)
Includes bibliographical references.
ISBN 1-55111-259-0

1. Wollstonecraft, Mary, 1759-1797. 2. Authors, English — 18th century — Biography. 3. Feminists — Great Britain — Biography. I. Clemit, Pamela. II. Walker, Gina Luria. III. Title. IV. Series.

PR5841.W8Z714 2001   828'.609   C00-932554-9

Broadview Press Ltd., is an independent, international publishing house, incorporated in 1985.

North America:
P.O. Box 1243, Peterborough, Ontario, Canada K9J 7H5
3576 California Road, Orchard Park, NY 14127
TEL: (705) 743-8990; FAX: (705) 743-8353;
E-MAIL: customerservice@broadviewpress.com

United Kingdom:
Turpin Distribution Services Ltd.,
Blackhorse Rd., Letchworth, Hertfordshire SG6 1HN
TEL: (1462) 672555; FAX (1462) 480947; E-MAIL: turpin@rsc.org

Australia:
St. Clair Press, P.O. Box 287, Rozelle, NSW 2039
TEL: (02) 818-1942; FAX: (02) 418-1923

www.broadviewpress.com

Broadview Press gratefully acknowledges the financial support of the Book Publishing Industry Development Program, Ministry of Canadian Heritage, Government of Canada.

Broadview Press is grateful to Professor Eugene Benson for advice on editorial matters for the Broadview Literary Texts series.

Text design and composition by George Kirkpatrick

PRINTED IN CANADA

Contents

Acknowledgements

We should like to thank the following publishers for permission to reproduce sections of text: Oxford University Press, for extracts from James Boswell's *Life of Johnson*, edited by G.B. Hill, revised by L.F. Powell (1934-50); Penguin Books, for extracts from Rousseau's *The Confessions*, translated by J.M. Cohen (1953); Pickering and Chatto, for extracts from volumes 3 and 5 of *Political and Philosophical Writings of William Godwin*, general editor, Mark Philp (1993); the University of Kansas Press, for extracts from *Godwin & Mary: Letters of William Godwin and Mary Wollstonecraft*, edited by Ralph M. Wardle (1967). We are grateful to Lord Abinger for permission to transcribe and publish manuscript letters held in the Abinger Collection in the Bodleian Library, Oxford; to the Pierpont Morgan Library, New York, for permission to transcribe and publish manuscript annotations to one of their editions of Godwin's *Memoirs*; to the Carl H. Pforzheimer Collection of Shelley and His Circle, New York Public Library, Astor, Lenox, and Tilden Foundations, for permission to quote from the unpublished correspondence of Mary Hays. John Whale kindly gave us permission to reproduce his poem, "Elegy: for Mary Wollstonecraft" (1997).

We acknowledge our debts to the scholarship of previous editors of the *Memoirs*, W. Clark Durant, Richard Holmes, and Mark Philp. We are grateful for the kind assistance of the following librarians: Bruce Barker-Benfield and the staff of the Bodleian Library; the staff of the Elmer Holmes Bobst Library, New York University; Gail Persky, University Librarian, and the staff of the Raymond Fogelman Library, New School University; and Stephen Wagner, Curator of the Pforzheimer Collection. We should like to thank Barbara Conolly, Judith Earnshaw, and Julia Gaunce of Broadview Press for their aid in seeing this volume through the press. Special thanks are due to the following colleagues and friends, who provided help of various kinds: Pamela Sue Anderson, Eugene Benson, Liz Brown, T.W. Craik, Kate Godin, Gary Kelly, Jeanne Moskal, Michael Rossington, Alexander Stein, Irene Sullivan, and, above all, Doucet Devin Fischer.

Pamela Clemit's part in this book was completed during her tenure, mainly for other purposes, of a Research Fellowship of the Leverhulme Trust and of a Fellowship at the New York Public Library's Center for Scholars and Writers. She gratefully acknowledges the material support of both institutions in this and in other areas of her research. Gina Luria Walker thanks the New School and New School University for a Faculty Development Grant for 1999-2000. She dedicates her part in this book to Chauncey L. Walker.

Abbreviations

The following abbreviations are used throughout this edition.

G&M: *Godwin & Mary: Letters of William Godwin and Mary Wollstonecraft.* Ed. Ralph M. Wardle. London and Lincoln: University of Nebraska Press / London: Constable, 1967.

LJ: James Boswell, *Life of Johnson.* Ed. G.B. Hill. Rev'd. L.F. Powell. 6 vols. Oxford: Clarendon Press, 1934-50.

LMW: *Collected Letters of Mary Wollstonecraft.* Ed. Ralph M. Wardle. Ithaca and London: Cornell University Press, 1979.

NM: *Collected Novels and Memoirs of William Godwin.* Gen. ed. Mark Philp. 8 vols. London: Pickering and Chatto, 1992.

PPW: *Political and Philosophical Writings of William Godwin.* Gen. ed. Mark Philp. 7 vols. London: Pickering and Chatto, 1993.

PW: *Posthumous Works of the Author of a Vindication of the Rights of Woman.* Ed. William Godwin. 4 vols. London: J. Johnson, 1798.

WMW: *The Works of Mary Wollstonecraft.* Ed. Janet Todd and Marilyn Butler. 7 vols. London: Pickering and Chatto, 1989.

Mary Wollstonecraft Godwin.

London, Published Jan. 1, 1798, by J. Johnson, St Pauls Church Yard.

Frontispiece of the first edition, engraved by James Heath (1757–1834) after the 1797 painting by John Opie (1761–1807). Reproduced by kind permission of The Carl H. Pforzheimer Collection of Shelley and His Circle, The New York Public Library, Astor, Lenox and Tilden Foundations.

Introduction

The publication of William Godwin's *Memoirs of the Author of a Vindication of the Rights of Woman* in January 1798 provoked widespread hostility from the conservative press. Issuing from the pen of the leading radical political philosopher of the 1790s, and memorializing his intellectual associate, lover, and wife, the feminist writer Mary Wollstonecraft, the *Memoirs* was a work of unprecedented biographical frankness. It included candid discussion of every phase of Wollstonecraft's unconventional career: her friendship with the married artist, Henry Fuseli, her liaison with the American merchant Gilbert Imlay – to whom she bore a daughter, Fanny – her two attempts at suicide, her relationship with Godwin, and her slow and painful death after the birth of her second daughter, Mary.[1]

From Godwin's point of view, such directness was an attempt to enact in the public sphere the revolutionary doctrine of sincerity he had advocated in *An Enquiry concerning Political Justice* (1793), a major treatise of philosophical anarchism, and had previously sought to demonstrate in *Cursory Strictures* (1794), a pamphlet defending twelve leading radicals charged with high treason. Contemporary reviewers, however, were shocked rather than liberated by what they perceived as callous revelations of Wollstonecraft's immorality (see Appendix D.1). Godwin quickly became notorious for, in the words of his former disciple Robert Southey, "the want of all feeling in stripping his dead wife naked."[2] The strength of conservative reaction was such that Godwin's publication of a revised edition of the *Memoirs* in August 1798 went virtually unnoticed. The popular counter-revolutionary interpretation of the *Memoirs* as a work which yoked radicalism, feminism, and sexual

---

1   For an analysis of the medical circumstances of Wollstonecraft's death, see Vivien Jones, "The Death of Mary Wollstonecraft," *British Journal for Eighteenth-Century Studies*, 20: 2 (Autumn 1997): 187-205.

2   Robert Southey to William Taylor, 1 July 1804, *A Memoir of the Life and Writings of William Taylor of Norwich*, ed. J.W. Robberds, 2 vols. (London: John Murray, 1824) 1: 507.

immorality continued to shape attitudes to the lives and writings of both authors well into the nineteenth century.

The notoriety of the *Memoirs* suggests one of the main reasons for its subsequent neglect as a work in its own right. Though the work appeared in abridged form in a nineteenth-century edition of Wollstonecraft's *Vindication of the Rights of Woman* (1844), it was not until the twentieth century that it was republished separately. In 1927 W. Clark Durant produced a limited edition of 700 copies, in which he attempted a comprehensive rehabilitation of both the work and its subject. Durant's text of the *Memoirs* was republished in Constable's Miscellany, with a preface by John Middleton Murry (1928). More recently, Richard Holmes edited the *Memoirs* in a Penguin Classics volume alongside Wollstonecraft's *Letters Written during a Short Residence in Sweden, Norway and Denmark* (1987). A scholarly edition of the *Memoirs* appeared in the first collected edition of Godwin's novels (1992). Yet critics still tend to view the *Memoirs* either as a mere source of information about Wollstonecraft's life, or as an explanation for the nineteenth-century backlash against her arguments for female equality. It is to be hoped that the present edition, by providing access to contemporary political, intellectual, and literary contexts, will establish the *Memoirs* as one of the most significant biographical documents in Revolutionary and Romantic writing.

1. Godwin's Theory of Biography

Godwin was brought up in the traditions of eighteenth-century English Protestant Dissent, and became a lifelong critic of the established political and social order. In addition to *Political Justice*, he wrote novels, works of educational theory, children's books, biographies, plays, essays, and political pamphlets. The generic diversity of his writings shows him to be engaged in a lasting reform programme, in which he sought to convey his progressive vision to different readerships by exploiting a wide variety of literary forms. Among these forms, the increasingly popular modes of biography and "self-biography" or autobiography – a term first used in the early nineteenth century[1] – occupied a special place. In the *Memoirs* he brought these two forms together to create the first of several philosophical biographies, in which he aimed to foster gradual social change by transforming the moral consciousness of his readers.

Godwin set out his claims for the importance of biography as an agent of reform in an essay of 1797 called "Of History and Romance." Here he dismisses the history of mass movements in favour of "individual history," or biography, which contributes to progress of mind by providing scope for the study of the intricacies of mental life: "It will be necessary for us to scrutinise the nature of man, before we can pronounce what it is of which social man is capable.... It is thus, and thus only, that we shall be enabled to add, to the knowledge of the past, a sagacity that can penetrate into the depths of futurity" (*PPW* 5: 293; see Appendix B.3). For Godwin, the reformist potential of biography lies in its ability to depict the individual in a social context, and the best subjects for biography are historical individuals who contributed to moral and social improvement in their own time. By demonstrating how social forces act on such individuals, and how they, in turn, had an impact on society, Godwin argues, biography has the power to inspire the reader with an analogous spirit of reform.

This view of "individual history" as an agent of historical change leads Godwin to advocate a particular approach to writing biography. In studying a character in history, he declares, it is not enough to observe him "upon the public stage": "I would follow him into his closet. I would see the friend and the father of a family, as well as the patriot.... I should rejoice to have ... a journal of his ordinary and minutest actions" (ibid., 294). This emphasis on private behaviour as an index of public morality brings to mind Samuel Johnson's classic statement on the importance of domestic minutiae as a source of historical truth in *The Rambler*, No. 60.[2] This state-

---

1 Laura Marcus, *Auto/biographical Discourses: Criticism, Theory, Practice* (Manchester and New York: Manchester UP, 1994) 11-12.

2 *The Rambler*, No. 60, 13 Oct. 1750, in *The Rambler*, ed. W.J. Bate and Albrecht B. Strauss, Yale Edition of the Works of Samuel Johnson (New Haven and London: Yale UP, 1969) 3: 318-23.

ment gained currency in the revolutionary decade after it was quoted by James Boswell at the start of his *Life of Johnson* (1791) to justify his method of gathering "minute particulars" concerning Johnson's private life in order to explain his public character (*LJ* 1: 33; see Appendix A.2).

Yet Godwin's biographical theory involves more than the standard eighteenth-century view of life-writing as a valuable form of historical enquiry: he argued that the analysis of individual lives also had a political purpose. In *Political Justice*, he emphasizes the liberating power of total sincerity: "If every man to-day would tell all the truth he knows, three years hence there would be scarcely a falsehood of any magnitude remaining in the civilised world" (*PPW* 3: 137). This belief in the duty of truth-telling was based on the Dissenting principle of "candour," which might best be described as the disposition to form impartial judgements in all affairs.[1] Such a principle was central to Godwin's theory of anarchism, in which the exercise of rational judgement will lead to individual men and women gradually becoming wiser, until government withers away because it is no longer necessary. As he wrote in a chapter called "Mode of Effecting Revolutions": "The revolutions of states ... consist principally in a change of sentiments and dispositions in the members of those states. The true instruments for changing the opinions of men are argument and persuasion" (*PPW* 3: 115). In addition, sincere delineation of character has a particular role to play in effecting gradual political change. "If truth were universally told of men's dispositions and actions," Godwin declares, "gibbets and wheels might be dismissed from the face of the earth" (ibid., 345). Candid truth-telling, by transforming the moral consciousness of its audience, points the way to institutional reform.

Moreover, Godwin turned to life-writing at a particular moment in his career. By the summer of 1797, many who had initially welcomed the French Revolution had become disillusioned by its excesses and alarmed by the escalating political

---

1   See Mark Philp, *Godwin's Political Justice* (London: Duckworth, 1986) 15-37.

crisis at home.[1] The government campaign to stop the spread of radicalism, which had begun in mid-1792 and culminated in the outlawing of the reform societies in 1799, led to the increasing fragmentation of the reform movement from the mid-1790s. At the same time, there developed a flourishing counter-radical culture, in which educated radicals were subjected to a campaign of popular abuse orchestrated by members of their own class. These changes in public mood prompted Godwin to a revaluation of his reforming aims and methods. This reassessment began in *Considerations on Lord Grenville's and Mr Pitt's Bills* (1795), a pamphlet protesting against the Two Acts prohibiting seditious meetings and unlawful assemblies, in which Godwin directly criticized leaders of the democratic reform movement for attempting to incite popular tumult through public lectures. However, this should not be read as an abandonment of the radical cause: the point at issue was the appropriate method of political education. In the preface to his next work, *The Enquirer: Reflections on Education, Manners, and Literature* (1797), Godwin announced a programme of aesthetic education designed to appeal to those who, like himself, were committed to individual reform rather than collective action. While maintaining "as ardent a passion for innovation as ever," he declares his conviction that "the cause of political reform, and the cause of intellectual and literary refinement, are inseparably connected" (*PPW* 5: 79). Additionally, he rejects the method of systematic enquiry pursued in *Political Justice* in favour of "an incessant recurrence to experiment and actual observation" (ibid., 77). This heightened interest in moral and intellectual development underpins his biographical and auto-biographical writings of the late 1790s.

Godwin's increased emphasis on gradual reform, through the agencies of education, manners, and literature, was accompanied by important changes in his ethical views.[2] In the first

---

1   For a fuller account, see Clive Emsley, *British Society and the French Wars, 1793-1815* (London and Basingstoke: Macmillan, 1979) 41-64; Albert Goodwin, *The Friends of Liberty: The English Democratic Movement in the Age of the French Revolution* (London: Hutchinson, 1979) 171-415, 451-99.

2   See Philp, 154-67, 202-09.

edition of *Political Justice*, his anarchism is premissed on the belief that reason can become the sole determinant of human action. Yet the central role accorded to feeling in the final chapters of *Caleb Williams* (1794) indicates that he recognized the inadequacy of this account almost at once, even though he did not formulate it until he revised *Political Justice* during 1795.[1] In the second edition (1796), as in the third (1798), he places increasing emphasis on sympathy and feeling in moral judgements. As he wrote in *The Enquirer:* "Not only the passions of men, but their very judgments, are to a great degree the creatures of sympathy" (*PPW* 5: 106). Godwin's searching revaluation of his philosophical position also led him to examine his own development. He began writing his first and longest autobiographical piece on 1 August 1797, two days after completing his revisions for the third edition of *Political Justice*.[2]

Godwin's intellectual reassessment gained further impetus from his relationship with Mary Wollstonecraft. Though it is sometimes asserted that she was the principal cause of his philosophical revisions,[3] there is little evidence to support this view. When Godwin met Wollstonecraft again on 8 January 1796 at the house of a mutual friend, Mary Hays (see 103, and note 1), he had already published the second edition of *Political Justice*. Yet he was in part attracted to Wollstonecraft because her most recent book, *Letters from Norway*, exemplified the synthesis of reason and sympathy for which he was searching.[4] As he wrote in the *Memoirs:* "If ever there was a book calculated to make a man in love with its author, this appears to me to be the book. She speaks of her sorrows, in a way that fills us with melancholy, and dissolves us in tenderness, at the same

---

1   Pamela Clemit, *The Godwinian Novel: The Rational Fictions of Godwin, Brockden Brown, Mary Shelley* (Oxford: Clarendon P, 1993) 66-69.

2   The dates of composition of these works are recorded in Godwin's unpublished diary, Abinger Manuscripts, Bodleian Library, Dep. e. 203.

3   See Don Locke, *A Fantasy of Reason: The Life and Thought of William Godwin* (London: Routledge and Kegan Paul, 1980) 139.

4   On Wollstonecraft's synthesizing design, see Peter Swaab, "Romantic Self-Representation: The Example of Mary Wollstonecraft's *Letters in Sweden*," *Mortal Pages, Literary Lives: Studies in Nineteenth-Century Autobiography*, ed. Vincent Newey and Philip Shaw (Aldershot: Scholar P, 1996) 13-30.

time that she displays a genius which commands all our admiration" (95). Here Godwin recognizes that Wollstonecraft's use of an autobiographical mode, in the words of Gregory Dart, "does not offer a repudiation or rejection of the project of social perfectibility, but a tactical manipulation of it."[1] Wollstonecraft's "calculation" lies in her deliberate exploitation of the language of sensibility in order to educate the reader in domestic affections as the foundation of moral, and hence political, improvement. This project of revolutionary instruction is rendered doubly efficacious because it is based on letters sent to a real-life correspondent, her employer and former lover Imlay, in whom she sought to inculcate domestic sympathies as an alternative to what she saw as the corrupting spirit of commerce. It is Godwin's admiration for this project of indirect political education that underlies his preference for *Letters from Norway* over the insistently polemical *Vindication of the Rights of Woman*, not his wish to promote "the feeling woman over the radical thinker," as had been suggested.[2] Similarly, he presents his own emphasis on intellectual and literary cultivation in *The Enquirer* as an advance on the deductive method of *Political Justice*.

Godwin's relationship with Wollstonecraft proved a catalyst for further changes in his thought. As their intimacy developed, the educative project of *Letters from Norway* became the basis for a more successful revolutionary domesticity than Wollstonecraft had enjoyed with Imlay.[3] While she and Godwin worked apart, reading and criticizing each other's works in progress, *The Wrongs of Woman* (1798) and *The Enquirer*, they "woo[ed] philosophy" together in their conversations and letters (*G&M* 35; see Appendix C.2.viii). Under Wollstonecraft's tutelage, Godwin was drawn to the literature of sensibility which had proved so influential on her later thought – and

---

1 Gregory Dart, *Rousseau, Robespierre and English Romanticism* (Cambridge: Cambridge UP, 1999) 131.
2 Mary A. Favret, *Romantic Correspondence: Women, Politics and the Fiction of Letters* (Cambridge: Cambridge UP, 1993) 130.
3 On Wollstonecraft's quest for what he calls a "revolutionary, vanguardist domesticity," see Gary Kelly, *Revolutionary Feminism: The Mind and Career of Mary Wollstonecraft* (London: Macmillan, 1992, reprinted 1996) 140-70 (141).

which he was to exploit in memorializing her.[1] In particular, he re-read some of Rousseau's writings, notably the two works that had provided a model for her politicized language of sensibility in *Letters from Norway*: the epistolary novel, *Julie, or The New Eloise* (1761), which presents romantic love as the source of public virtue, and *Reveries of a Solitary Walker* (1782), from which she drew her socially detached, reflective pose. At the same time, Godwin's re-reading of Rousseau's *The Confessions* (1782-89) and Goethe's *The Sorrows of Young Werther* (1774) focused his growing interest in self-exploration. Work on a narrative of his own life was interrupted by Wollstonecraft's death on 10 September 1797, following the birth of their daughter Mary ten days earlier, but resumed shortly afterwards, when he began writing the *Memoirs*.

2. *Memoirs of the Author of a Vindication of the Rights of Woman*

Analysis of an individual life, whether his own or someone else's, was never purely inward-looking or private for Godwin. Though he has been routinely criticized for presenting a depoliticized, sentimental image of Wollstonecraft in the *Memoirs*,[2] the very title of the work suggests his radical aims. *Memoirs of the Author of a Vindication of the Rights of Woman* is not only a portrait of a loved individual, but also a vindication of a woman's entitlement to the type of moral and political education advocated by Wollstonecraft in her public writings. Moreover, Godwin's preparation of a four-volume companion edition, *Posthumous Works of the Author of a Vindication of the Rights of Woman*, demonstrates the same synthesizing aim as the *Memoirs*: in both projects, public and private concerns are inseparable. For example, as editor Godwin chose to include some of

---

1 Godwin's reading is documented in his diary, Abinger MSS, Dep. e. 202-03.

2 See Claire Tomalin, *The Life and Death of Mary Wollstonecraft* (Harmondsworth: Penguin Books, 1977) 294-95; Janet Todd, "Mary Wollstonecraft and the Rights of Death," *Gender, Art and Death* (Cambridge: Polity P, 1993) 116; Mary Jacobus, "In Love with a Cold Climate: Travelling with Wollstonecraft," *First Things: The Maternal Imaginary in Literature, Art, and Psychoanalysis* (New York and London: Routledge, 1995) 64-65; Barbara Caine, *English Feminism, 1780-1980* (Oxford: Oxford UP, 1997) 40-43.

Wollstonecraft's private love-letters to Imlay, advertising their "striking resemblance to the celebrated romance of Werter," but left out her manuscript comedy based in part "upon the incidents of her own story" (*WMW* 6: 367; 101). Though, from a modern editorial view, it is regrettable that Godwin did not publish the totality of Wollstonecraft's manuscripts, his editorial choices scarcely constitute a disavowal of her radicalism.[1] On the contrary, his selection and arrangement of her surviving papers reinforce his biographical conception of her as a "female Werter" whose innovative "culture of the heart" (88, *WMW* 1: 116) forms an indictment of present-day social corruption.

Godwin's depiction of Wollstonecraft as a harbinger of revolutionary change further involves his reworking of existing biographical traditions which represented private experience as inseparable from public character. For example, to give authority to his project he aligns his research methods with those of Boswell's representation of an eighteenth-century "manly" subject in the *Life of Johnson*.[2] Just as Boswell bases his claims to biographical authenticity on Johnson's direct communication of "the incidents of his early years," so too Godwin declares that the facts in his narrative "are principally taken from the mouth of the person to whom they relate" (*LJ* 1: 26; see Appendix A.2; 43-44). While Boswell describes his assiduity in keeping records of his conversations with Johnson, Godwin explains how he made notes on his discussions with Wollstonecraft. Again, Boswell's claim to have made use of "the most liberal communications by his [Johnson's] friends" is echoed in Godwin's account of his "industrious enquiry" among Wollstonecraft's acquaintances (*LJ* 1: 26; see Appendix A.2; 44). This yielded informative letters from the publisher Joseph Johnson (see Appendix C.3.ii), among others, though some acquaintances, such as Fuseli and Wollstonecraft's sisters, Eliza and Everina, withheld information.[3] Yet Godwin is not

---

1 For a different view, see Favret, 130-31.

2 On Boswell's "manly" subjects, see Felicity A. Nussbaum, *The Autobiographical Subject: Gender and Ideology in Eighteenth-Century England* (Baltimore and London: Johns Hopkins UP, 1989) 117-26.

3 Tomalin, 286-87.

concerned with the formation of character for its own sake, and, unlike Boswell, he does not present the integration of public and private experience as the exclusive property of a male subject. Instead he documents his female subject's history as "the fairest source of animation and encouragement to those who would follow [her] in the same career" (43).

In addition, Godwin's biographical project should be read in the context of the association between subjectivity and social change in the 1790s. Following Wollstonecraft in *Letters from Norway*, he was especially drawn to Rousseau's autobiographical writings, notably the *Confessions* and *Reveries of a Solitary Walker*, which presented a mythical figure of male virtue thwarted by an unjust social order.[1] These works were written as exercises in self-justification and self-analysis. In them, Rousseau presents sincere self-examination as the key to his vision of humanity freed from modern social corruption.[2] In order to restore a harmonious relationship with the physical and social world, he argues, the thinker of good faith must first look for it within himself. By exploring the depths of his own being, the individual will discover not only his own nature, and how it has been distorted by social circumstances, but also the nature of man himself. In this way, self-analysis forms a way of rethinking social and political relations. Yet Godwin's construction of Wollstonecraft's revolutionary consciousness forms an advance on Rousseau's thought, since it demonstrates the inseparability of individual and social experience in a woman's life, as well as in a man's.

Moreover, by using Rousseau's writings as a means of shaping "individual history," Godwin established a link between Wollstonecraft's career and those of French revolutionary figures, both male and female, whose memoirs began to appear in English translation from 1794 onwards. The most significant of these memoirs were produced by leaders of the Gironde, the moderate faction in the French National Assembly, after they

---

1   Carol Blum, *Rousseau and the Republic of Virtue: The Language of Politics in the French Revolution* (Ithaca and London: Cornell UP, 1986) 27–132.

2   Ronald Grimsley, *Rousseau and the Religious Quest* (Oxford: Clarendon P, 1968) 40–45.

were proscribed in the early summer of 1793, several of whom Wollstonecraft met in Paris (see 84, and Appendix C.3.iv). Their justificatory self-representations were written while they were awaiting trial and facing almost certain death, as in the cases of Jacques-Pierre Brissot and Manon Roland, or while they were on the run, as in the case of Jean-Baptiste Louvet de Couvray.[1] As suggested by the title of Manon Roland's *An Appeal to Impartial Posterity* (1795), these figures turned to memoir-writing in order to vindicate their political conduct and beliefs – just as Godwin did with regard to Wollstonecraft. Moreover, they all gave candid first-person accounts of their conversion to revolutionary principles, which were based on the themes and techniques of Rousseau's autobiographical writings and fiction.[2] In some cases, they directly identified with the "sublime and virtuous Rousseau" as a fellow-victim of public hostility for "having been also the friend of the people."[3]

For Godwin, the main appeal of Rousseau lay not in co-incidences of fact between his life and Wollstonecraft's, but in the way that he interpreted his early life so as to elucidate the foundations of his adult beliefs. Similarly, Godwin is concerned with the formation of Wollstonecraft's identity as a woman intellectual, and this involves the organization of her life into a coherent pattern. Adopting the structural principle of the *Confessions*, Godwin depicts Wollstonecraft's history as a series of "revolutions" or turning-points which threaten to alienate her from society, but in fact lead to a growth in moral and political awareness. For example, he presents her response to her father's violence towards her mother, in which, like the young Jean-Jacques (*Confessions* 21; see Appendix A.1), she would "throw

---

1 According to his diary, Godwin read *The Life of J.P. Brissot ... Written by Himself* (London: J. Debrett, 1794), *An Appeal to Impartial Posterity, by Citizenness Roland,* 2 vols (London: J. Johnson, 1795), and *Narrative of the Dangers to which I have been Exposed, since the 31st of May, 1793 ... By John Baptiste Louvet* (London: J. Johnson, 1795), in September 1794, September 1795, and August 1795 respectively (Abinger MSS, Dep. e. 201-02).

2 Blum, 139-43; see also Robert Darnton, "A Spy in Grub Street," *The Literary Underground of the Old Regime* (Cambridge, Mass., and London: Harvard UP, 1982) 68-69, and Dart, 127-30.

3 Louvet, *Narrative,* 228.

herself between the despot and his victim" (46), as giving rise to an indignation against tyranny rather than a sense of oppression. Again, he describes how her zealous altruism repeatedly met with opposition and rendered her "the victim of a desire to promote the benefit of others" (55). Yet the difficulties of her early life lead not to demoralization but to an expanded sense of her own potential: "scarcely any thing she desired, appeared hard to perform" (58). Moreover, it is central to Godwin's view of Wollstonecraft as a revolutionary figure that she is not fundamentally damaged by personal and social disappointments. Though the collapse of her relationship with Imlay – which Godwin presents as the most extreme instance of the clash between her advanced moral idealism and present-day social corruption – leads her to attempt suicide, he describes this as an act of "cool and deliberate firmness" (97), which recalls the principled suicides of the proscribed Girondins.[1] After this experience, she remains "fraught with that generous confidence, which, in a great soul, is never extinguished" (105).

For Godwin this "generous confidence" not only provides the key to Wollstonecraft's own improvement, but also makes her an agent of change in others, including himself. In describing Wollstonecraft's endless capacity to assimilate change, he also tells the story of her catalytic effect on his own development. Significantly, in a manuscript analysis of his own character, begun while he was writing the *Memoirs*, he attributes to himself the same Rousseauvian capacity for mental transformation that he found in Wollstonecraft: "Every four or five years I gain some new perception, or become intimately sensible to some valuable circumstance, that introduces an essential change of many of my preconceived notions and determinations" (*NM* 1: 59). The "essential change" that Wollstonecraft introduces in Godwin is the main subject of the last two chapters of the *Memoirs*. Here his autobiographical impulse becomes explicit as he traces the growth of their egalitarian affection. He describes how he was gradually initiated through her love for him into

---

1   Simon Schama, *Citizens: A Chronicle of the French Revolution* (Harmondsworth: Penguin Books, 1989) 803-04; a different reading is proposed by Todd, 102-19. For Godwin's early views on suicide, see Appendix B.1.i.

new modes of thinking and feeling, which became the basis of a shared "experiment" in revolutionary domesticity, untrammelled by legal institutions (104-06). However, in the first edition of the *Memoirs*, this re-educative process is abruptly curtailed by her death. Godwin's sense of loss comes to the fore in his self-representation as a Rousseauvian solitary walker whose access to love as a source of moral improvement has been blocked: "This light was lent to me for a very short period, and is now extinguished for ever!" (122).

Godwin revisited the question of Wollstonecraft's educative influence in his revisions for the second edition of the *Memoirs* (see Appendix E). As Mitzi Myers notes, these changes "are not recantations, but expansions of his vision of human possibility."[1] While writing them in June 1798, he drew inspiration from *The New Eloise*, in which Rousseau had forged a link between private feeling and the public sphere by representing Julie's sublimated love for her former tutor, St Preux, as the basis of civic virtue.[2] This Rousseauvian rehabilitation of the affections as a source of political change gives a particular resonance to Godwin's revised account of Wollstonecraft's aesthetic education: "Her taste awakened mine; her sensibility determined me to a careful development of my feelings" (217). The underlying connection between private feeling and public benevolence is made explicit in a long addition justifying Wollstonecraft's conduct during her relationship with Fuseli. Here Godwin presents the "exercise of the affections" as the key to social sympathy:

> True wisdom will recommend to us individual attachments; for with them our minds are more thoroughly maintained in activity and life than they can be under the privation of them, and it is better that man should be a living being, than a stock or a stone. True virtue will sanction this recommendation, since it is the object of virtue to produce happiness, and since the man who lives

---

1 Mitzi Myers, "Godwin's *Memoirs* of Wollstonecraft: The Shaping of Self and Subject," *Studies in Romanticism* 20 (Fall 1981): 315.

2 Godwin's diary, Abinger MSS, Dep. e. 203; see Dart, 123-24.

in the midst of domestic relations, will have many opportunities of conferring pleasure, minute in the detail, yet not trivial in the amount, without interfering with the purposes of general benevolence. (208)

This passage was quoted by Godwin in his next two works, *St Leon* (1799) and *Thoughts: Occasioned by the Perusal of Dr Parr's Spital Sermon* (1801), as a public testimony to the transformative impact of Wollstonecraft's "culture of the heart" on his ethical and political views (see *NM* 4: 11; *PPW* 2: 179). Yet his revisions were not confined to formal philosophical statements: they also include new passages of psychological analysis which strengthen his defence of her conduct. Such additions form an advance on the conclusions of the first edition of the *Memoirs* by demonstrating Godwin's fulfilment of the lessons he had learned from Wollstonecraft. In this way she is conceptualized as not only the embodiment but also the agent of the gradual social revolution they both sought to further, in their lives as in their writings.

3. "Wooing Philosophy": Theory and Practice

After Wollstonecraft's return to London in early October 1795 from her Scandinavian travels on Imlay's behalf, a small circle of like-minded men and women rallied to encourage her recovery from his duplicity. Among these, the radical intellectual Mary Hays, "a professed admirer" of Wollstonecraft and a student of Godwin's, invited Godwin, Wollstonecraft, and Thomas Holcroft for tea in her rooms on Friday, 8 January 1796 (see 103, note 1).[1] Hays later explained her motives in reuniting her two friends, who had first met in November 1791 and disliked each other (79-81): "Their acquaintance was now renewed, in consequence of a meeting at the apartments of a common friend (the writer of the present narrative), who had forwarded the interview, with a view of removing their prejudices, and of diverting

---

1   Mary Hays to William Godwin, 20 November 1795, MH 9, Mary Hays Correspondence and Manuscripts, the Carl H. Pforzheimer Collection of Shelley & His Circle, New York Public Library, Astor, Lenox and Tilden Foundations.

the melancholy of a woman whose talents and misfortunes had excited in her heart the most affectionate interest."[1] For his part, as Godwin notes in the *Memoirs*, the reunion with Wollstonecraft had "no particular effect, except so far as sympathy in her anguish, added in my mind to the respect I had always entertained for her talents"(103). For Wollstonecraft, however, the gathering revealed Godwin in a different light: Hays reported to him afterwards that Wollstonecraft had commented on his "humane & tender consideration" for Hays, who was suffering, like Wollstonecraft, from a failure in love, marking this as "proof of the sensitivity & goodness of your heart ... she has told me that it has raised you greatly in her esteem."[2] Over the next few months, mutual recognition of each other's humanity and shared beliefs fostered the evolution of an innovative relationship, which Godwin represents as the culmination of the *Memoirs*.

As Wollstonecraft recovered from her second suicide attempt on 10 October 1795, she wrestled with the consequences of her relationship with Imlay in which she had been, by her own reckoning, "strangely deficient in sagacity" (*WMW* 6: 428). She continued to be plagued by that "Despair" which had caused "the withering touch of disappointment" to her body and soul (ibid., 419). In early April 1796, Hays wrote to Godwin that Wollstonecraft's "health appears in a still more declining State ... her heart, I think, is broken."[3] Godwin, by contrast, in describing this episode in the *Memoirs*, retrospectively emphasized Wollstonecraft's resiliency: unlike "ordinary persons under extreme anguish of mind," she did not "sink into listlessness and debility," but kept on working (101). She recast the correspondence with Imlay into *Letters from Norway*, published in January 1796, and completed a comedy drawing on her own experiences. Godwin and Wollstonecraft spent more time together after she made an unexpected visit to his apartments in late April, although Godwin frequently saw the actress Elizabeth Inchbald (see 108, note 1) and the pretty, young, aspiring

---

1 [Mary Hays], "Memoirs of Mary Wollstonecraft," *Annual Necrology for 1797-8* (London: R. Phillips, 1800) 453.

2 Hays to Godwin, 11 January 1796, Pforzheimer MSS, MH 11.

3 Hays to Godwin, 4 April 1796, Pforzheimer MSS, MH 19; Tomalin, 193.

author, Amelia Alderson, as well. During July Godwin made his annual trip to Norfolk. While he was away Wollstonecraft moved with her daughter Fanny to No. 16, Judd Place West, on the outskirts of Somers Town, near Godwin, and, despite her uncertainties about the future, settled in. On 13 July, Godwin wrote his first letter to Wollstonecraft. In mid-August, three weeks after he returned to London, they became lovers.

As they wrestled with the dilemmas of alliance and autonomy, Wollstonecraft and Godwin each reached for their pens. "I had rather at this moment talk to you on paper than in any other mode," Godwin wrote early on, "I should feel ashamed in seeing you" (*G&M* 16; see Appendix C.2.ii). He assured Wollstonecraft that, unlike Imlay and the majority of men she had previously encountered, he would be the "friend of [her] mind, the admirer of [her] excellencies" (*G&M* 17). He invoked Hays by way of contrast: "Be happy. Resolve to be happy," he urged Wollstonecraft: "You deserve to be so. Every thing that interferes with it, is weakness & wandering; & a woman, like you, can, must, shall, shake it off. Afford, for instance, no food for the morbid madness, & no triumph to the misanthropical gloom, of your afternoon visitor. Call up, with firmness, the energies, which, I am sure, you so eminently possess" (ibid.). In contrast to the protean Wollstonecraft, Godwin represented Hays as a self-absorbed, dependent woman, who despite her serious intellectual competence was unable to move beyond the personal to develop a philosophical understanding of her frustrations in the search for an enlightened man with whom to share "domestic affections" (89). Godwin feared that Hays's despair might prove contagious to the still-vulnerable Wollstonecraft, that she might withdraw into the guise of the "Solitary Walker," a persona of social isolation borrowed from Rousseau that Wollstonecraft had previously assumed because men had failed her (*G&M* 15, 17; see Appendix C.2.i, ii). Inexperienced, Godwin responded as best he could, attempting at the same time to register his own feelings. He tried to play ally and friend to Wollstonecraft, but in the interests of "perfect sincerity," he also disclosed his tumultuous passions. "Do you not see, while I exhort you to be a philosopher, how painfully acute are my own feelings? I need some soothing though I cannot ask it from you," he wrote to Wollstonecraft (ibid.).

Such revelations were the very stuff of the "new language" (88; *WMW* 6: 382; see Appendix C.1.i) of male/female collaboration that Wollstonecraft had attempted, and failed, to initiate with Imlay. Even before she learned firsthand the pitfalls of attempting to alter the conventions of romance, she had formulated in the *Vindication of the Rights of Woman* a "wild wish to see the distinction of sex confounded in society, unless where love animates the behaviour" (*WMW* 5:126). To effect this, she called for "a revolution in female manners" that would transform, as well, the practices of men. "I do not chuse to be a secondary object" (*WMW* 6:398), she warned Imlay when he equivocated about the future of their liaison, and Godwin amply demonstrated his willingness to participate in the vibrant interplay she had envisioned. Increasingly buoyed by his reassurances of her importance to him, she prompted communication between them in talk and text about the mutual pleasures of the body, their subjective responses to each other, and the intellectual endeavours in which they were each engaged.

As their relationship progressed, Wollstonecraft and Godwin developed a vision that enlightened intimacy would prove to be the crucible for private, and, therefore, social regeneration. They saw themselves as companions and colleagues as well as lovers. They strove for frankness as the basis for a lasting alliance, but when Godwin, the more formally educated, criticized her writing, Wollstonecraft smarted, arguing that he failed to assess accurately the iconoclastic value of her texts (*G&M* 28; see Appendix C.2.vii). When she acknowledged the self-deprecating side of her growing reliance on him, describing herself as "sometimes painfully humble", Godwin admonished her: "Humble! for heaven's sake, be proud, be arrogant! You are – but I cannot tell what you are. I cannot yet find the circumstance about you that allies you to the frailty of our nature. I will hunt it out" (*G&M* 23). To Imlay Wollstonecraft had voiced her hopelessness at ever finding a sexual partner who would also be a confidant; in Godwin, she encountered the last in the lineage of "benevolent older men in her life,"[1] a reliable champion to stimulate and support her powers to their fullest potential who was also her ardent lover. As an adolescent, Wollstonecraft discerned in herself the "essential characteristics of genius" (58). She portrayed her consequent loneliness – that "solitariness" that Godwin later spoke of (69) – in her first novel, *Mary; A Fiction* (1788), in which "the mind of a woman, who has thinking powers is displayed" (*WMW* 1:5). Isolation dogged her stark insights into the intractableness of the female condition. But despite the vicissitudes of her own life, she struggled to keep hold of the unique combination of introspection, observation, and intense response which comprised the self that Godwin valorized, as he later memorialized her "intuitive perception of intellectual beauty"(121), echoing Wollstonecraft's phrase in the *Vindication of the Rights of Woman*.[2]

For Wollstonecraft, in Barbara Taylor's words, "the cost of womanhood was high – but high also the price of refusing it. Too high for Wollstonecraft herself, who could no more deny her sensuality than repress her intellect – yet the dilemma which she posed loses none of its significance through her own inability to resolve it."[3] Attempting to integrate the disparate aspects of her consciousness, Wollstonecraft accepted Godwin's tutelage. "We must ... woo philosophy *chez vous* ce soir," she wrote, "for I do not like to lose my Philosopher even in the lover" (*G&M* 35; see Appendix C.2.viii). Together, they experimented with existing cultural forms that combined feminine love and masculine learning, trying out variations on the models of the historical Abelard and Héloïse, and the fictional St Preux and Julie of Rousseau's *The New Eloise*. Wollstonecraft and Godwin were each other's mentor and student in their

---

1   Barbara Taylor, "For the Love of God: Religion and the Erotic Imagination in Wollstonecraft's Feminism," *Mary Wollstonecraft and 200 Years of Feminisms*, ed. Eileen Janes Yeo (London and New York: Rivers Oram Press, 1997) 33.

2   Quoted in Nathaniel Brown, *Sexuality and Feminism in Shelley* (Cambridge Mass.: Harvard UP, 1979) 190.

3   Barbara Taylor, "Mary Wollstonecraft and the Wild Wish of Early Feminism," *History Workshop Journal* 33 (1992): 217.

turn. In their pursuit of greater equality and trust, the gendered disparities in their education and experiences seemed to diminish. Godwin felt safe enough to ask for emotional clarification – "you must send me a bill of understanding. How can I always distinguish between your jest & earnest, & know when your satire means too much & when it means nothing? But I will try" (G&M 50).

Bitterly, Wollstonecraft had observed to Imlay that she had not known that "theory and practice could be so different ... that the sentiments of passion, and the resolves of reason, are very distinct" (WMW 6: 402; see Appendix C.1.ii). With Godwin, on the other hand, "theory and practice" coincided, extending, as he attests, to "every ... circumstance that related to our intercourse" (106). This involved living out their most deeply-held convictions. They agreed on the value of hard work and individual freedom, assenting – most of the time – to do their writing apart, and to keep their friendships separate. For Wollstonecraft, solidarity with other women was important, just as Godwin continued to see his male friends.[1] She and Hays visited each other frequently, sharing books, discussing their writing projects, seeing mutual friends like Rebecca Christie, the wife of Imlay's business associate (see 84, note 4); Sarah Siddons, the actress (see 108, note 1); and Maria Reveley, a talented woman with whom Godwin had an enduring friendship. Wollstonecraft and Godwin kept their liaison a secret out of both principle and expedience. In one of the most contentious passages in the first edition of the Memoirs, Godwin writes, "We did not marry" (105), offering as reasons their philosophical objections to the institution under prevailing English law, Wollstonecraft's financial difficulties, and her wariness about becoming, again, an object of public criticism.

After what Godwin described as an "experiment of seven months of as intimate an intercourse as our respective modes of living would admit" (106), the love affair became marriage on 29 March 1797, after Wollstonecraft discovered she was pregnant (despite their attempts at a primitive rhythm method of

---

1 Ibid., 207.

contraception). They took tea at the writer Mary Robinson's with Joseph Johnson, the painter John Opie, and Hays, among others on 2 April,[1] but said nothing of their new relationship. However, Godwin announced the union to some of their friends by letter after he and Wollstonecraft had moved into new lodgings together.[2] To the surprise and chagrin of the couple, lawful wedlock produced additional social discomforts: it confirmed that Wollstonecraft had been Imlay's mistress, not his wife, and that Fanny Imlay was therefore illegitimate. According to Godwin, Mrs Inchbald and Mrs Siddons were among the disaffected (108). On 19 April Wollstonecraft and Godwin attended the theatre where Mrs Inchbald insulted Wollstonecraft. Godwin's note to Wollstonecraft the next morning suggests that she held him partly responsible for the incident. "I am pained by the recollection of our conversation last night," he wrote, reminding her that at the outset of their liaison, in addition to her vigorous intelligence, he had also "found a wounded heart, &, as that heart cast itself upon me, it was my ambition to heal it. Do not let me be wholly disappointed" (G&M 75). Later, in reconstructing this episode in the *Memoirs*, Godwin represents Wollstonecraft's best self: "Mary felt a transitory pang," he writes, at learning of the rejection of her new status by other women, but with the indomitable spirit that he so admired, "she disdained to sink under the injustice … of the supercilious and the foolish" (109).

Now came the practical challenge of transmuting ardour and insecurity into the rhythms of daily domesticity. Husband and wife agreed to continue working on their writing projects in separate locations and to dine out with friends independently. Once they settled into a common home at the Polygon, household business intruded. In the frequent notes they exchanged, with Wollstonecraft's servant Mary as the go-between, Wollstonecraft complained that "my spirits have been harassed" by "the state of the sink &c do you know you plague me (a little) by not speaking more determinately to the Landlord" (G&M 74). The care and feeding of "little Fannikin" required further

---

1   Godwin's diary, Abinger MSS, Dep e. 203.
2   Godwin to Hays, 10 April 1797, Pforzheimer MSS, MH 321.

cooperation from "Man" (*G&M* 13, 30). When Godwin visited Etruria with Basil Montague in June 1797 (see 51, note 1, and 114, note 2),[1] their letters began to misfire towards the end of his absence: he wrote sprightly accounts of his adventures, while she concentrated on the new life within – "I begin to love this little creature, and to anticipate his birth as a fresh twist to a knot, which I do not wish to untie" (*G&M* 82).

As it evolved, Godwin and Wollstonecraft's experimental mode of living proved intellectually productive for both partners. Wollstonecraft was at work on her second novel, the first composition, according to Godwin, that she wrote "slowly and with mature consideration" (111). At this time she was, as Mary Hays described her, "a wife, a mother, surrounded by tender, admiring, intelligent friends … her powers acquired new vigour, life brightened, and futurity opened a prospect beaming with hope and promise."[2] In this situation Wollstonecraft felt secure enough to bear down imaginatively to portray "the wrongs of woman," her most deliberate project, in which her talents were, according to Godwin, finally to "effect what they were capable of effecting" (111). Reciprocally, Godwin turned to consideration of the "culture of the heart" that Wollstonecraft advocated.

When Wollstonecraft died on 10 September, following the birth of her second daughter on 30 August, the first death notice was written by Hays, but published without attribution in the *Monthly Magazine* for September 1797. In her obituary Hays attempted to capture Wollstonecraft's unique amalgam of generous character and strong convictions, emphasizing her proud feminism. Anticipating Godwin, Hays depicted Wollstonecraft's history as a continuum of "heroic fortitude" over adversity because of her "ardent, ingenuous, unconquerable spirit."[3] Though in the October issue of the *Monthly Magazine* Hays claimed authorship of the obituary, she indicated that she

---

1   Peter H. Marshall, *William Godwin* (New Haven and London: Yale UP, 1984) 188.
2   [Mary Hays], Obituary of Mary Wollstonecraft, *Monthly Magazine* 4 (September 1797), 233.
3   Ibid. There were other obituaries as well: see Tomalin, 234-35; *Wollstonecraft*, ed. Harriet Devine Jump, *Lives of the Great Romantics III* (London: Pickering and Chatto, 1999) 2: 1-3.

was "not at liberty" to add more information about Woll-stonecraft, "as they will probably, within a short period, be given to the public by a far abler hand" – that of Godwin, who was already at work on the *Memoirs*.[1]

4. Reactions

Godwin's *Memoirs* and the *Posthumous Works* were published in January 1798 to intense public and private reaction. The *Memoirs* provoked heated debate about the philosophical theories and practical issues Godwin and Wollstonecraft had wrestled with, separately and together: the power of individual judge-ment and "perfect sincerity"; the validity of prevailing morality; and relations between the sexes as revealed in contemporary assumptions about marriage, divorce, and suicide. The *Analytical Review* (see 69, note 1) criticized the *Memoirs* for failing to fulfil the "chief use of biography [which] is to teach us to attain to eminence in virtue and knowledge," citing particularly the absence of a "correct history of the formation of Mrs. G.'s mind" (see Appendix D.1.i). Predicting the charge of "*immorality*" for her unconventional attitude towards marriage, the review pointed to the revolutionary context for Woll-stonecraft's theories and originality as a thinker, but blamed her imprudent conduct and "*indelicacy*" towards Fuseli and, espe-cially, Imlay. As a mother, her two suicide attempts were judged by their emotional quotient: "we can only say, that we possess not the scale of suffering by which to estimate what every one ought to endure before he seeks relief in death." The review concluded by echoing Godwin's intentions: "We wish her char-acter and conduct to be seriously and candidly examined, and we would protect it, if we could, from the freedom of licentious tongues. She appears to us another Heloise; and it is a reflection upon men, that Abelard should have possessed the first, and Imlay the second of these illustrious women" (ibid.).

The hope of protection from "licentious tongues" proved

---

1 Mary Hays, "Letter to the Editor," *Monthly Magazine*, 4 (October 1797): 1.

unrealistic. The conservative *Anti-Jacobin Review* (July 1798) took issue with the assessment in the *Analytical Review*, condemning the *Memoirs* which, in their view, "exemplify and illustrate JACOBIN MORALITY" in both theory and practice (see Appendix D.1.ii). The reviewer conflated the personal history of the "philosopher Godwin" as biographer and his "lady" with their presumed beliefs about organized religion, the institution of marriage, the perils of divorce, and the blasphemy of suicide. The *Monthly Review* (November 1798) appeared less partisan and more empathetic, but no kinder: it questioned the wisdom of Godwin's judgement in telling Wollstonecraft's story so completely (see Appendix D.1.iii): "Blushes would suffuse the cheeks of most husbands, if they were *forced* to relate those anecdotes of their wives which Mr. Godwin voluntarily proclaims to the world." The reviewer deplored Godwin's self-referential interpretations, concluding that too great detail was given about Wollstonecraft's premature death, but adding, "Mr. G.'s feelings on the occasion do him credit, and it is impossible not to feel with him."

The *New Annual Register for 1798* (1799) puzzled over Godwin's decision to publicize those elements of Wollstonecraft's life "which were whispered concerning her while living, but which the good natured part of mankind were willing to resolve into scandal and calumny. This appears to us to be a very extraordinary method of doing honour to her memory" (see Appendix D.1.iv). By the time the New York *Lady's Monitor* completed their series of excerpts from the *Memoirs* and the *Posthumous Works* with a summary review (1801), they were inclined to be more forgiving: with Imlay, Wollstonecraft had "erred fatally – but it is an error too common with her sex: and to which women of sensibility and intellect are peculiarly liable." That failed connection excited the reviewer's pity, while the relationship with Godwin was dismissed as "a *rational* love; for the heart does not admit of many real ones." The reviewer esteemed Wollstonecraft as "a woman of high genius" whose "deviations from propriety, have been mistaken for her principles of action" (see Appendix D.1.v). Theory and practice, the biographer and his subject, the individuals and their ideas, continued to be confused with one another.

In the same year that the *Memoirs* appeared, the Reverend Richard Polwhele issued a 68-page mock epic poem, *The Unsex'd Females* (1798), cataloguing the main feminine offenders to orthodoxy and patriotism, with Wollstonecraft as their leader, and displaying Polwhele's familiarity with many of his subjects' published texts, as well as with the *Memoirs* (see Appendix D.2.ii). *The Unsex'd Females* was one of several satires that conflated the personal history of Wollstonecraft and Godwin with their principles. Notable among these was C. Kirkpatrick Sharpe's "The Vision of Liberty" (1801), a Spenserian poem, published anonymously in the *Anti-Jacobin Review*, which chronicled a grotesque parade of Jacobins, including Godwin, who was pilloried for writing the *Memoirs* in the apparently mistaken belief that Wollstonecraft's "whoredoms were not known enough,/Till fairly printed off in black and white" (see Appendix D.2.v). In contrast to such hostile views, in a private letter written in April 1798, the celebrated poet Anna Seward confided that she believed the *Memoirs* did "justice to the memory of a deceased wife." In her eyes, the great fault in the work was Godwin's attempt to involve Wollstonecraft in his own religious scepticism, "since he allows she was habitually and fervently devout" (see Appendix D.2.i). Mary Hays responded to the invective of the reviews with a second, fifty-page obituary of Wollstonecraft in the *Annual Necrology for 1797-8* (1800) that took the *Memoirs* as its model, implicitly corroborating Godwin's conceptions, while more explicitly articulating Wollstonecraft's feminism (see Appendix D.2.iii). Around the same time, John Fenwick, Godwin's close friend and husband of Eliza Fenwick (see 117, note 3), published a "public character" of Godwin in which he emphasized the educative force of "conversation with persons of superior talents," such as Wollstonecraft, in Godwin's intellectual development. Linking the *Memoirs* with Rousseau's *Confessions*, Fenwick suggested that adverse public reaction was evidence of each work's far-sighted significance (see Appendix D.2.iv).

Throughout the nineteenth century, Wollstonecraft remained a potent, if publicly unacknowledged, presence.[1] An anonymous "Ode to the Memory of Mary Wollstonecraft" (1804) paid respect to her talents, warned that these had not provided protection for her against life's disappointments, and commended to female readers a more conventional, if mundane, existence (see Appendix D.2.vi). Amelia Alderson, now married to the painter John Opie, joined the company of former associates who had turned against Wollstonecraft and Godwin in her novel *Adeline Mowbray; or, The Mother and the Daughter: A Tale* (1805), illustrating the dangers of scepticism about the institution of marriage (see Appendix D.2.vii). Leigh Hunt noted reactions from both ends of the contemporary spectrum on a copy of the *Memoirs*, now in the Pierpont Morgan Library, on which he transcribed the most notorious stanza from the cynical polemic, *The Spirit of Anti-Jacobinism*, beginning "William hath penned a wagonload of stuff," along with an anecdote concerning Elizabeth Benger, the novelist, who, it was said, had thrown herself on Wollstonecraft's grave at St Pancras, pouring forth an eulogy on the departed.

Hostile criticism was further answered in both private and public spheres by supportive responses among kindred spirits. In early February 1798, Godwin's sister Hannah responded with enthusiasm to the copy of the *Memoirs* that he sent her, praising the authenticity of his depiction of Wollstonecraft (see Appendix C.3.v). Eliza Fenwick, in the letter that Godwin requested she write to Everina Wollstonecraft, bore witness to the success of their marriage: "No woman was ever more happy in marriage than Mrs Godwin," she wrote, balancing this with Wollstonecraft's last words, "He is the kindest best man in the world" (see Appendix C.3.iii). For later generations the early Modernist Virginia Woolf invoked the marriage of Wollstonecraft and Godwin as Godwin painted it, as "an experiment, as Mary's life had been an experiment from the start, an attempt to make human conventions conform more closely to

---

1   For differing views see Caine, 40–41; Taylor, "For the Love of God"; Alice O. Browne, *The Eighteenth-Century Feminist Mind* (Detroit: Wayne State UP, 1987) 170–72; G.J. Barker-Benfield, *The Culture of Sensibility: Sex and Society in Eighteenth-Century Britain* (Chicago and London: U of Chicago P, 1992) 368–95.

human needs" (see Appendix D.2.viii). And, at end of the twentieth century, in his "Elegy: for Mary Wollstonecraft" (1997), John Whale, a British Romantics scholar, recreated Godwin's experience of the moment of Wollstonecraft's death for yet another generation (see Appendix D.2.ix).

Godwin wrote the *Memoirs* for posterity. He believed that the story of Wollstonecraft's career, in combination with her texts, would ineluctably galvanize future social reformers. He was correct in this judgement. In the two centuries since the events he memorialized, Wollstonecraft's life and ideas have been interpreted in various ways. Writing of the *Vindication of the Rights of Woman*, Godwin proposed that Wollstonecraft "performed more substantial service for the cause of her sex, than all the other writers, male or female, that ever felt themselves animated in the behalf of oppressed and injured beauty" (76). At the new millennium, as scholars co-operate to reassess Wollstonecraft's place in cultural history and feminist thought, the *Memoirs* are both praised and repudiated for colouring subsequent understanding of her contributions. Celebrating *Mary Wollstonecraft and 200 Years of Feminisms*, Joan W. Scott points to the crucial function of "the imaginative identifications women make with the past" as a means of creating feminist traditions out of disparate experiences: "the history of Wollstonecraft as a feminist, from this perspective, is the history of the uses made of her by subsequent generations."[1] The *Memoirs* are designed to stimulate us to make new "uses" of Wollstonecraft through its portrayal of her as an agent of reform, through its representations of the contested categories of "male" and "female" as Godwin and Wollstonecraft tried to rethink them, and through its lyrical evocation of their shared "experiment" in living. Whatever the changing prisms through which we view her, Godwin's artefact of Wollstonecraft offers us access to her life and writings, not as the conclusion, but as a beginning.

---

1 Joan W. Scott, "The Imagination of Olympe de Gouges," *Mary Wollstonecraft and 200 Years of Feminisms,* 37.

William Godwin: A Brief Chronology

1756   Birth of William Godwin at Wisbech, Cambridgeshire
       (3 March).
1759   Birth of Mary Wollstonecraft in London (27 April).
1770   Godwin enters Coward's Dissenting Academy, Hoxton
       (September).
1777   Godwin preaches at Yarmouth and Lowestoft
       (June/July).
1778   Godwin graduates from Hoxton Academy (May) and
       becomes minister at Ware in Hertfordshire (June).
1779   The congregration at Ware rejects Godwin (August).
       He moves to London temporarily, then becomes minis-
       ter at Stowmarket in Suffolk (December).
1782   Godwin is dismissed by his church and moves to Lon-
       don temporarily (April). He becomes minister at Bea-
       consfield, Buckinghamshire (December).
1783   Godwin publishes, anonymously, *The History of the Life
       of William Pitt, Earl of Chatham* (January), and *A Defence
       of the Rockingham Party*, his first political pamphlet
       (May). He leaves Beaconsfield, abandons the ministry
       for good, and returns to London to live (June). He
       publishes, anonymously, *An Account of the Seminary*
       (July), a school prospectus, *The Herald of Literature*
       (November), a collection of literary parodies, and
       Sketches of History, in Six Sermons (November).
1784   Godwin publishes, anonymously, the pamphlet *Instruc-
       tions to a Statesman* (January), and three short novels:
       Damon and Delia (January/February), *Italian Letters*
       (July), and *Imogen: A Pastoral Romance* (July). He is
       employed as writer of the "British and Foreign Histo-
       ry" section of the Whig *New Annual Register* (July), a
       job he continues until 1791.
1785   Godwin becomes acting editor of the Whig *Political
       Herald* (August), a post he retains until the journal col-
       lapses in 1787.

1787   Godwin's *History of the Internal Affairs of the United Provinces* is published anonymously (September).

1790   Godwin's *The English Peerage* is published anonymously.

1791   Godwin gives up his post on the *New Annual Register* and signs a contract with the publisher George Robinson for a book on "Political Principles" (July). He meets Mary Wollstonecraft at Joseph Johnson's (November).

1793   Godwin publishes *An Enquiry concerning Political Justice* (February).

1794   Birth of Fanny Imlay (May). Godwin publishes *Things As They Are; or, The Adventures of Caleb Williams* (May), and, anonymously, *Cursory Strictures*, first in the *Morning Chronicle* and then as a pamphlet (October). He attends the treason trials (November-December).

1795   Godwin meets Mary Hays (May). He publishes, anonymously, *Considerations on Lord Grenville's and Mr Pitt's Bills* (November). A second, revised edition of *Political Justice* appears (November, dated 1796).

1796   Godwin meets Wollstonecraft again at Mary Hays's (January). His intimacy with Wollstonecraft begins to develop after she calls on him (April), and they become lovers (August).

1797   Godwin publishes *The Enquirer* (February). He and Wollstonecraft marry (March) and together move into 29, The Polygon, Somers Town; he also takes separate rooms at 17 Evesham Buildings, Chalton Street (April). He publishes, anonymously, a translation of *Memoirs of the Life of Simon Lord Lovat* (April). Birth of Mary Wollstonecraft Godwin (30 August). Wollstonecraft dies (10 September). A third, revised edition of *Political Justice* appears (November, dated 1798).

1798   The publication of Godwin's *Memoirs of the Author of a Vindication of the Rights of Woman* (January, second edition, corrected, August) and *Posthumous Works of the Author of a Vindication of the Rights of Woman* (January) gives rise to a hostile critical reaction.

1799   Godwin publishes *St Leon* (December).

1800 Godwin's play *Antonio* is performed at Drury Lane Theatre (13 December) and subsequently published.

1801 Godwin publishes *Thoughts: Occasioned by the Perusal of Dr Parr's Spital Sermon* (April). He meets Mary Jane Clairmont (May) and marries her (December). Her two children, Charles and Jane (Claire), join the Godwin household.

1802 Mrs Godwin has a miscarriage or a still-born baby (January). Godwin, as William Scolfield, publishes *Bible Stories*, his first children's book.

1803 William Godwin, Jr. born (March). Godwin publishes *Life of Geoffrey Chaucer* (October).

1805 Godwin publishes *Fleetwood* (February). During the summer he and his wife establish a shop and publishing house, the Juvenile Library, at Hanway Street. He publishes, as Edward Baldwin, *Fables, Ancient and Modern*, and, as Theophilus Marcliffe, *The Looking-Glass*, a biography of the artist William Mulready (both October).

1806 Godwin publishes, as Marcliffe, *Life of Lady Jane Grey*; and, as Baldwin, *The History of England* (June), and *The Pantheon* (December).

1807 The Godwins open a new shop at 41 Skinner Street, Snow Hill, Holborn (May). Godwin's play *Faulkener* is performed at Drury Lane (16-19 December).

1809 Godwin publishes *Essay on Sepulchres*; and, as Baldwin, *The History of Rome: From the Building of the City to the Ruin of the Republic* (July), and *Mylius's School Dictionary of the English Language*.

1812 Mary Godwin elopes to the Continent with Percy Bysshe Shelley, accompanied by Claire Clairmont (July), returning six weeks later.

1815 Godwin publishes *Lives of Edward and John Philips, Nephews and Pupils of Milton* (May). His first "Letter of Verax" appears in the *Morning Chronicle* (25 May). It is republished with a second letter as a pamphlet (June), withdrawn by Godwin when he hears of Napoleon's defeat at Waterloo.

1816 Fanny Imlay commits suicide (October). Following the

suicide of his first wife Harriet, Shelley marries Mary Godwin (December).

1817　Godwin publishes *Mandeville* (December).

1818　Godwin's *Letter of Advice to a Young American* appears in Constable's *Edinburgh Magazine* (March) and is reprinted by Godwin as a pamphlet for private distribution. Godwin receives notice to quit Skinner Street because of non-payment of rent (June), marking the start of a legal battle.

1820　Godwin publishes *Of Population* (November).

1821　Godwin publishes, as Baldwin, *History of Greece*.

1822　A writ of eviction is served upon the Godwins (May), who leave Skinner Street and re-establish the Juvenile Library at 195, The Strand (July). Death of Shelley (July).

1823　Mary Shelley returns to London from Italy (August).

1824　Godwin publishes *History of the Commonwealth*, Volume 1 (February).

1825　The Juvenile Library is declared bankrupt (March), and the Godwins move to 44 Gower Place (May).

1826　Godwin publishes *History of the Commonwealth*, Volume 2 (April).

1827　Godwin publishes *History of the Commonwealth*, Volume 3 (June).

1828　Godwin publishes *History of the Commonwealth*, Volume 4 (October).

1830　William Godwin, Jr. and Emily Eldred marry (February). Godwin publishes *Cloudesley; A Tale* (March).

1831　Godwin publishes *Thoughts on Man* (February). William Godwin, Jr. dies of cholera (September).

1833　Godwin publishes "Fragment of a Romance" in the *New Monthly Magazine* (January) and *Deloraine* (February). Grey's Whig ministry appoints Godwin Office Keeper and Yeoman Usher of the Receipt of the Exchequer, a post that carries a salary of £200 per annum (April). The Godwins move to free accommodation in New Palace Yard, adjoining the Houses of Parliament (May).

1834   Godwin publishes *Lives of the Necromancers* (June).

1835   Godwin publishes "Memoirs of the Author, by his Father," in *Transfusion*, by William Godwin, Jr. The Godwins move to Exchequer Building, Whitehall Yard (November).

1836   Godwin dies (7 April).

A Note on the Text

The present text is based on the first edition of *Memoirs of the Author of a Vindication of the Rights of Woman*, published by J. Johnson and G.G. and J. Robinson in January 1798. Although a second, revised edition appeared in August 1798, the first edition is preferred because it provides Godwin's frankest vindication of Mary Wollstonecraft's beliefs and conduct. Substantive variants in the second edition are listed in Appendix E, not only to provide a record of Godwin's final intentions, but also to stimulate critical debate concerning the significance of his revisions. In reproducing the text, the idiosyncrasies of the original spelling, capitalization, and punctuation have been retained, even where these involve inconsistencies, except for the correction of printer's errors, the discarding of the long "s," and the regularization of quotation marks. The same editorial principles have been followed in the case of documents from published sources included in the appendices. In the case of documents transcribed from manuscript in the appendices, false starts have been silently omitted, editorial additions required for sense completion are set in square brackets, and inconsistencies of spelling and punctuation have been retained.

MEMOIRS.

CHAP. I.

1759–1775.

It has always appeared to me, that to give to the public some account of the life of a person of eminent merit deceased, is a duty incumbent on survivors. It seldom happens that such a person passes through life, without being the subject of thoughtless calumny, or malignant misrepresentation. It cannot happen that the public at large should be on a footing with their intimate acquaintance, and be the observer of those virtues which discover themselves principally in personal intercourse. Every benefactor of mankind is more or less influenced by a liberal passion for fame; and survivors only pay a debt due to these benefactors, when they assert and establish on their part, the honour they loved. The justice which is thus done to the illustrious dead, converts into the fairest source of animation and encouragement to those who would follow them in the same career. The human species at large is interested in this justice, as it teaches them to place their respect and affection, upon those qualities which best deserve to be esteemed and loved. I cannot easily prevail on myself to doubt, that the more fully we are presented with the picture and story of such persons as the subject of the following narrative, the more generally shall we feel in ourselves an attachment to their fate, and a sympathy in their excellencies. There are not many individuals with whose character the public welfare and improvement are more intimately connected, than the author of A Vindication of the Rights of Woman.[1]

The facts detailed in the following pages, are principally

---

1   *Vindication of the Rights of Woman: With Strictures on Political and Moral Subjects* (1792).

taken from the mouth of the person to whom they relate; and of the veracity and ingenuousness of her habits, perhaps no one that was ever acquainted with her, entertains a doubt. The writer of this narrative, when he has met with persons, that in any degree created to themselves an interest and attachment in his mind, has always felt a curiosity to be acquainted with the scenes through which they had passed, and the incidents that had contributed to form their understandings and character. Impelled by this sentiment, he repeatedly led the conversation of Mary to topics of this sort; and, once or twice, he made notes in her presence, of a few dates calculated to arrange the circumstances in his mind. To the materials thus collected, he has added an industrious enquiry among the persons most intimately acquainted with her at the different periods of her life.

Mary Wollstonecraft was born on the 27th of April 1759. Her father's name was Edward John, and the name of her mother Elizabeth, of the family of Dixons of Ballyshannon in the kingdom of Ireland:[1] her paternal grandfather was a respectable manufacturer in Spitalfields, and is supposed to have left to his son a property of about 10,000l.[2] Three of her brothers and two sisters are still living; their names, Edward, James, Charles, Eliza, and Everina.[3] Of these, Edward only was older than herself; he resides in London.[4] James is in Paris, and Charles in or near Philadelphia in America.[5] Her sisters have for some years been engaged in the office of governesses in private families, and are both at present in Ireland.

1   Edward John Wollstonecraft (?1737-1803); Elizabeth Dickson (misspelled by Godwin) (d. 1782).
2   Edward Wollstonecraft (1688-1765) was a successful silk weaver in Spitalfields, the cloth manufacturing area on the eastern edge of the City of London; his fortune was worth about £940,000 according to 1998 figures.
3   Edward Bland Wollstonecraft (c.1758-1807); James Wollstonecraft (1768-1806); Charles Wollstonecraft (1770-1818); Elizabeth (Eliza) Wollstonecraft, later Bishop (1763-1833); Everina Wollstonecraft (1765-1841).
4   Edward Wollstonecraft became a successful lawyer in the City of London.
5   For the careers of James and Charles Wollstonecraft, see 70, note 2, and 71, note 1.

I am doubtful whether the father of Mary was bred to any profession;[1] but, about the time of her birth, he resorted, rather perhaps as an amusement than a business, to the occupation of farming. He was of a very active, and somewhat versatile disposition, and so frequently changed his abode, as to throw some ambiguity upon the place of her birth.[2] She told me, that the doubt in her mind in that respect, lay between London, and a farm upon Epping Forest,[3] which was the principal scene of the five first years of her life.

Mary was distinguished in early youth, by some portion of that exquisite sensibility, soundness of understanding, and decision of character, which were the leading features of her mind through the whole course of her life. She experienced in the first period of her existence, but few of those indulgences and marks of affection, which are principally calculated to sooth the subjection and sorrows of our early years. She was not the favourite either of her father or mother. Her father was a man of quick, impetuous disposition, subject to alternate fits of kindness and cruelty. In his family he was a despot, and his wife appears to have been the first, and most submissive of his subjects. The mother's partiality was fixed upon the eldest son, and her system of government relative to Mary, was characterized by considerable rigour. She, at length, became convinced of her mistake, and adopted a different plan with her younger daughters. When, in the Wrongs of Woman, Mary speaks of "the petty cares which obscured the morning of her heroine's life; continual restraint in the most trivial matters; unconditional submission to orders, which, as a mere child, she soon discovered to be unreasonable, because inconsistent and contradictory; and the being often obliged to sit, in the presence of her parents, for three or four hours together, without daring to utter a word;"[4] she is, I believe, to be considered as copying the outline of the first period of her own existence.

---

1 In fact Edward John Wollstonecraft was a master weaver.
2 Wollstonecraft was born in Primrose Street, off Bishopsgate, in Spitalfields.
3 An area about fifteen miles north of London, in Essex.
4 *The Wrongs of Woman; or Maria: A Fragment* (first published in *PW*, vols. 1-2), *WMW* 1: 124-25 (adapted).

But it was in vain, that the blighting winds of unkindness or indifference, seemed destined to counteract the superiority of Mary's mind. It surmounted every obstacle; and, by degrees, from a person little considered in the family, she became in some sort its director and umpire. The despotism of her education cost her many a heart-ache. She was not formed to be the contented and unresisting subject of a despot; but I have heard her remark more than once, that, when she felt she had done wrong, the reproof or chastisement of her mother, instead of being a terror to her, she found to be the only thing capable of reconciling her to herself. The blows of her father on the contrary, which were the mere ebullitions of a passionate temper, instead of humbling her, roused her indignation. Upon such occasions she felt her superiority, and was apt to betray marks of contempt. The quickness of her father's temper, led him sometimes to threaten similar violence towards his wife. When that was the case, Mary would often throw herself between the despot and his victim, with the purpose to receive upon her own person the blows that might be directed against her mother.[1] She has even laid whole nights upon the landing-place near their chamber-door, when, mistakenly, or with reason, she apprehended that her father might break out into paroxysms of violence. The conduct he held towards the members of his family, was of the same kind as that he observed towards animals. He was for the most part extravagantly fond of them; but, when he was displeased, and this frequently happened, and for very trivial reasons, his anger was alarming. Mary was what Dr. Johnson would have called, "a very good hater."[2] In some instance of passion exercised by her father to one of his dogs, she was accustomed to speak of her emotions of abhorrence, as having risen to agony. In a word, her conduct during her girlish years, was such, as to extort some portion of affection from her mother, and to hold her father in considerable awe.

---

1 Cf. Jean-Jacques Rousseau, *The Confessions* 21 (see Appendix A.1.i).

2 Samuel Johnson (1709-84), writer, critic, lexicographer, and conversationalist, quoted in Hester Lynch Piozzi, *Anecdotes of the Late Samuel Johnson LL. D., During the Last Twenty Years of his Life* (1786) 83.

In one respect, the system of education of the mother appears to have had merit. All her children were vigorous and healthy. This seems very much to depend upon the management of our infant years. It is affirmed by some persons of the present day, most profoundly skilled in the sciences of health and disease, that there is no period of human life so little subject to mortality, as the period of infancy. Yet, from the mismanagement to which children are exposed, many of the diseases of childhood are rendered fatal, and more persons die in that, than in any other period of human life. Mary had projected a work upon this subject, which she had carefully considered, and well understood. She has indeed left a specimen of her skill in this respect in her eldest daughter,[1] three years and a half old, who is a singular example of vigorous constitution and florid health. Mr. Anthony Carlisle,[2] surgeon, of Soho-square, whom to name is sufficiently to honour, had promised to revise her production. This is but one out of numerous projects of activity and usefulness, which her untimely death has fatally terminated.

The rustic situation in which Mary spent her infancy, no doubt contributed to confirm the stamina of her constitution. She sported in the open air, and amidst the picturesque and refreshing scenes of nature, for which she always retained the most exquisite relish. Dolls and the other amusements usually appropriated to female children, she held in contempt; and felt a much greater propensity to join in the active and hardy sports of her brothers, than to confine herself to those of her own sex.

About the time that Mary completed the fifth year of her age, her father removed to a small distance from his former habitation, and took a farm near the Whalebone[3] upon Epping Forest, a little way out of the Chelmsford road. In Michaelmas

---

1 Frances (Fanny) Imlay (1794-1816), brought up by Godwin as his own child after Wollstonecraft's death, committed suicide at the age of twenty-two.
2 Anthony Carlisle (1768-1840), surgeon to Westminster Hospital from 1793 to 1840, became friendly with Godwin in 1795 and attended Wollstonecraft during her pregnancy and final illness (see 117-20), after which the two men maintained social contact for several years. Carlisle became professor of anatomy at the Royal Academy in 1808 and was knighted in 1820.
3 Probably the Sun and Whalebone Inn, three miles beyond the village of Epping.

1765, he once more changed his residence, and occupied a convenient house behind the town of Barking in Essex, eight miles from London. In this situation some of their nearest neighbours were, Bamber Gascoyne, esquire,[1] successively member of parliament for several boroughs, and his brother, Mr. Joseph Gascoyne. Bamber Gascoyne resided but little on this spot; but his brother was almost a constant inhabitant, and his family in habits of the most frequent intercourse with the family of Mary. Here Mr. Wollstonecraft remained for three years. In September 1796, I accompanied my wife in a visit to this spot. No person reviewed with greater sensibility, the scenes of her childhood. We found the house uninhabited, and the garden in a wild and ruinous state. She renewed her acquaintance with the market-place, the streets, and the wharf, the latter of which we found crowded with barges, and full of activity.

In Michaelmas 1768, Mr. Wollstonecraft again removed to a farm near Beverley in Yorkshire. Here the family remained for six years, and consequently, Mary did not quit this residence, till she had attained the age of fifteen years and five months. The principal part of her school-education passed during this period; but it was not to any advantage of infant literature, that she was indebted for her subsequent eminence; her education in this respect was merely such, as was afforded by the day-schools of the place, in which she resided. To her recollections Beverley appeared a very handsome town, surrounded by genteel families, and with a brilliant assembly. She was surprized, when she visited it in 1795,[2] upon her voyage to Norway, to find the reality so very much below the picture in her imagination.

Hitherto Mr. Wollstonecraft had been a farmer; but the restlessness of his disposition would not suffer him to content himself with the occupation in which for some years he had been engaged, and the temptation of a commercial speculation of

---

1 Bamber Gascoyne (1725-91) was successively MP for Malden from 1761 to 1763, Midhurst from 1765 to 1770, Weobly from 1770 to 1774, Truro from 1774 to 1784, and Bossiney from 1784 to 1786.
2 For Wollstonecraft's account of this visit, see "Letters to Imlay," XLV (14 June [1795]) (first published in *PW*, vols. 3-4), *WMW* 6: 410-11.

some sort being held out to him, he removed to a house in Queen's-Row, in Hoxton near London, for the purpose of its execution. Here he remained for a year and a half; but, being frustrated in his expectations of profit, he, after that term, gave up the project in which he was engaged, and returned to his former pursuits. During this residence at Hoxton, the writer of these memoirs inhabited, as a student, at the dissenting college in that place.[1] It is perhaps a question of curious speculation to enquire, what would have been the amount of the difference in the pursuits and enjoyments of each party, if they had met, and considered each other with the same distinguishing regard in 1776, as they were afterwards impressed with in the year 1796. The writer had then completed the twentieth, and Mary the seventeenth year of her age. Which would have been predominant; the disadvantages of obscurity, and the pressure of a family; or the gratifications and improvement that might have flowed from their intercourse?

One of the acquaintances Mary formed at this time was with a Mr. Clare,[2] who inhabited the next house to that which was tenanted by her father, and to whom she was probably in some degree indebted for the early cultivation of her mind. Mr. Clare was a clergyman, and appears to have been a humourist of a very singular cast. In his person he was deformed and delicate; and his figure, I am told, bore a resemblance to that of the celebrated Pope.[3] He had a fondness for poetry, and was not destitute of taste. His manners were expressive of a tenderness and benevolence, the demonstrations of which appeared to have been somewhat too artificially cultivated. His habits were those of a perfect recluse. He seldom went out of his drawing-room, and he showed to a friend of Mary a pair of shoes, which had served him, he said, for fourteen years. Mary frequently spent days and weeks together, at the house of Mr. Clare.

---

1 Godwin attended Coward's Dissenting Academy at Hoxton, a village on the northern outskirts of London, from September 1773 to May 1778.
2 Not further identified.
3 The poet and critic Alexander Pope (1688-1744), whose growth was stunted by a tubercular infection of the spine contracted at the age of twelve.

CHAP. II.

1775–1783.

BUT a connection more memorable originated about this time, between Mary and a person of her own sex, for whom she contracted a friendship so fervent, as for years to have constituted the ruling passion of her mind. The name of this person was Frances Blood;[1] she was two years older than Mary. Her residence was at that time at Newington Butts, a village near the southern extremity of the metropolis; and the original instrument for bringing these two friends acquainted, was Mrs. Clare, wife of the gentleman already mentioned, who was on a footing of considerable intimacy with both parties. The acquaintance of Fanny, like that of Mr. Clare, contributed to ripen the immature talents of Mary.

The situation in which Mary was introduced to her, bore a resemblance to the first interview of Werter with Charlotte.[2] She was conducted to the door of a small house, but furnished with peculiar neatness and propriety. The first object that caught her sight, was a young woman of a slender and elegant form, and eighteen years of age, busily employed in feeding and managing some children, born of the same parents, but considerably inferior to her in age. The impression Mary received from this spectacle was indelible; and, before the interview was concluded, she had taken, in her heart, the vows of an eternal friendship.

Fanny was a young woman of extraordinary accomplishments. She sung and played with taste. She drew with exquisite fidelity and neatness; and, by the employment of this talent, for some time maintained her father, mother, and family, but ulti-

---

1   Frances Blood, later Skeys (1757–85), who was a skilled painter of flowers and illustrator of botanical works.
2   Cf. Johann Wolfgang von Goethe, *The Sorrows of Werter [sic]: A German Story* (English translation, 1779), Book 1, letter dated 16 June.

mately ruined her health by her extraordinary exertions. She read and wrote with considerable application; and the same ideas of minute and delicate propriety followed her in these, as in her other occupations.

Mary, a wild, but animated and aspiring girl of sixteen, contemplated Fanny, in the first instance, with sentiments of inferiority and reverence. Though they were much together, yet, the distance of their habitation being considerable, they supplied the want of more frequent interviews by an assiduous correspondence. Mary found Fanny's letters better spelt and better indited than her own, and felt herself abashed. She had hitherto paid but a superficial attention to literature. She had read, to gratify the ardour of an inextinguishable thirst of knowledge; but she had not thought of writing as an art. Her ambition to excel was now awakened, and she applied herself with passion and earnestness. Fanny undertook to be her instructor; and, so far as related to accuracy and method, her lessons were given with considerable skill.

It has already been mentioned that, in the spring of the year 1776, Mr. Wollstonecraft quitted his situation at Hoxton, and returned to his former agricultural pursuits. The situation upon which he now fixed was in Wales, a circumstance that was felt as a severe blow to Mary's darling spirit of friendship. The principal acquaintance of the Wollstonecrafts in this retirement, was the family of a Mr. Allen, two of whose daughters are since married to the two elder sons of the celebrated English potter, Josiah Wedgwood.[1]

Wales however was Mr. Wollstonecraft's residence for little more than a year. He returned to the neighbourhood of London; and Mary, whose spirit of independence was unalterable, had influence enough to determine his choice in favour of the

---

1 John Bartlett Allen (1733-1803) of Cresselly, in Wales, had nine daughters. In 1793 the eldest, Elizabeth (Bessy) Allen (1764-1846), married Josiah Wedgwood II (1769-1843), the eldest son of the Staffordshire potter Josiah Wedgwood (1730-95), founder-owner of a large pottery works and model village called Etruria. Shortly afterwards her sister Louisa Jane Allen (1771-1836) married John Wedgwood (1766-1844), the second Wedgwood son. (Godwin, who was a friend of Josiah's youngest son Thomas Wedgwood (1771-1805), visited Etruria in June 1797: see G&M 78-106.)

village of Walworth,[1] that she might be near her chosen friend. It was probably before this, that she had once or twice started the idea of quitting her parental roof, and providing for herself. But she was prevailed upon to resign this idea, and conditions were stipulated with her, relative to her having an apartment in the house that should be exclusively her own, and her commanding the other requisites of study. She did not however think herself fairly treated in these instances, and either the conditions abovementioned, or some others, were not observed in the sequel, with the fidelity she expected. In one case, she had procured an eligible situation, and every thing was settled respecting her removal to it, when the intreaties and tears of her mother led her to surrender her own inclinations, and abandon the engagement.

These however were only temporary delays. Her propensities continued the same, and the motives by which she was instigated were unabated. In the year 1778, she being nineteen years of age, a proposal was made to her of living as a companion with a Mrs. Dawson of Bath,[2] a widow lady, with one son already adult. Upon enquiry she found that Mrs. Dawson was a woman of great peculiarity of temper, that she had had a variety of companions in succession, and that no one had found it practicable to continue with her. Mary was not discouraged by this information, and accepted the situation, with a resolution that she would effect in this respect, what none of her predecessors had been able to do. In the sequel she had reason to consider the account she had received as sufficiently accurate, but she did not relax in her endeavours. By method, constancy and firmness, she found the means of making her situation tolerable; and Mrs. Dawson would occasionally confess, that Mary was the only person that had lived with her in that situation, in her treatment of whom she had felt herself under any restraint.

With Mrs. Dawson she continued to reside for two years, and only left her, summoned by the melancholy circumstance

---

1 A village just south of Newington Butts.
2 Sarah Dawson, *née* Regis (d. 1812), the widow of William Dawson, a prosperous London merchant.

of her mother's rapidly declining health. True to the calls of humanity, Mary felt in this intelligence an irresistible motive, and eagerly returned to the paternal roof, which she had before resolutely quitted. The residence of her father at this time, was at Enfield near London. He had, I believe, given up agriculture from the time of his quitting Wales, it appearing that he now made it less a source of profit than loss, and being thought advisable that he should rather live upon the interest of his property already in possession.

The illness of Mrs. Wollstonecraft was lingering, but hopeless. Mary was assiduous in her attendance upon her mother. At first, every attention was received with acknowledgments and gratitude; but, as the attentions grew habitual, and the health of the mother more and more wretched, they were rather exacted, than received. Nothing would be taken by the unfortunate patient, but from the hands of Mary; rest was denied night or day, and by the time nature was exhausted in the parent, the daughter was qualified to assume her place, and become in turn herself a patient. The last words her mother ever uttered were, "A little patience, and all will be over!" and these words are repeatedly referred to by Mary in the course of her writings.[1]

Upon the death of Mrs. Wollstonecraft, Mary bid a final adieu to the roof of her father. According to my memorandums, I find her next the inmate of Fanny at Walham Green, near the village of Fulham. Upon what plan they now lived together I am unable to ascertain; certainly not that of Mary's becoming in any degree an additional burthen upon the industry of her friend. Thus situated, their intimacy ripened; they approached more nearly to a footing of equality; and their attachment became more rooted and active.

Mary was ever ready at the call of distress, and, in particular, during her whole life was eager and active to promote the welfare of every member of her family. In 1780 she attended the death-bed of her mother; in 1782 she was summoned by a not

---

1 See Wollstonecraft to Godwin, 30 August 1797, *G&M* 120 (see Appendix C.2.xi); *WMW* 1: 132, 183.

less melancholy occasion, to attend her sister Eliza, married to a
Mr. Bishop, who, subsequently to a dangerous lying-in, remained for some months in a very afflicting situation.[1] Mary
continued with her sister without intermission, to her perfect
recovery.

---

1 Meredith Bishop was the son of a prosperous shipwright in Bermondsey, south
   London. Godwin's dates are incorrect: Eliza gave birth to a daughter, Elizabeth
   Mary Frances Bishop (1783-84), in August 1783, ten months after her wedding, and
   Bishop summoned Wollstonecraft to attend his wife the following November.

CHAP. III.

1783-1785.

MARY was now arrived at the twenty-fourth year of her age. Her project, five years before, had been personal independence; it was now usefulness. In the solitude of attendance on her sister's illness, and during the subsequent convalescence, she had had leisure to ruminate upon purposes of this sort. Her expanded mind led her to seek something more arduous than the mere removal of personal vexations; and the sensibility of her heart would not suffer her to rest in solitary gratifications. The derangement of her father's affairs daily became more and more glaring; and a small independent provision made for herself and her sisters, appears to have been sacrificed in the wreck. For ten years, from 1782 to 1792, she may be said to have been, in a great degree, the victim of a desire to promote the benefit of others. She did not foresee the severe disappointment with which an exclusive purpose of this sort is pregnant; she was inexperienced enough to lay a stress upon the consequent gratitude of those she benefited; and she did not sufficiently consider that, in proportion as we involve ourselves in the interests and society of others, we acquire a more exquisite sense of their defects, and are tormented with their untractableness and folly.

The project upon which she now determined, was no other than that of a day-school, to be superintended by Fanny Blood, herself, and her two sisters.

They accordingly opened one in the year 1783, at the village of Islington; but in the course of a few months removed it to Newington Green.[1] Here Mary formed some acquaintances who influenced the future events of her life. The first of these

---

1 Islington and Newington Green, the latter known for its thriving Dissenting community, were villages on the northern outskirts of London.

in her own estimation, was Dr. Richard Price,[1] well known for his political and mathematical calculations, and universally esteemed by those who knew him, for the simplicity of his manners, and the ardour of his benevolence. The regard conceived by these two persons for each other, was mutual, and partook of a spirit of the purest attachment. Mary had been bred in the principles of the church of England, but her esteem for this venerable preacher led her occasionally to attend upon his public instructions. Her religion was, in reality, little allied to any system of forms; and, as she has often told me, was founded rather in taste, than in the niceties of polemical discussion. Her mind constitutionally attached itself to the sublime and the amiable. She found an inexpressible delight in the beauties of nature, and in the splendid reveries of the imagination. But nature itself, she thought, would be no better than a vast blank, if the mind of the observer did not supply it with an animating soul. When she walked amidst the wonders of nature, she was accustomed to converse with her God. To her mind he was pictured as not less amiable, generous and kind, than great, wise and exalted. In fact, she had received few lessons of religion in her youth, and her religion was almost entirely of her own creation. But she was not on that account the less attached to it, or the less scrupulous in discharging what she considered as its duties. She could not recollect the time when she had believed the doctrine of future punishments. The tenets of her system were the growth of her own moral taste, and her religion therefore had always been a gratification, never a terror, to her. She expected a future state; but she would not allow her ideas of that future state to be modified by the notions of judgment and retribution. From this sketch, it is sufficiently evident, that the pleasure she took in an occasional attendance upon the sermons of Dr. Price, was not accompanied with a superstitious adherence to his doctrines. The fact

---

1   The leading Dissenting preacher, moralist, and economist Richard Price (1723-91) was minister at Newington Green from 1758 to 1783, and continued to live there until 1786. During his acquaintance with Wollstonecraft, he was working on revisions for the third edition (1787) of his best-known work, *A Review of the Principal Questions and Difficulties in Morals* (1758).

is, that, as far down as the year 1787, she regularly frequented public worship, for the most part according to the forms of the church of England. After that period her attendance became less constant, and in no long time was wholly discontinued. I believe it may be admitted as a maxim, that no person of a well furnished mind, that has shaken off the implicit subjection of youth, and is not the zealous partizan of a sect, can bring himself to conform to the public and regular routine of sermons and prayers.

Another of the friends she acquired at this period, was Mrs. Burgh, widow of the author of the Political Disquisitions,[1] a woman universally well spoken of for the warmth and purity of her benevolence. Mary, whenever she had occasion to allude to her, to the last period of her life, paid the tribute due to her virtues. The only remaining friend necessary to be enumerated in this place, is the rev. John Hewlet,[2] now master of a boarding-school at Shacklewel near Hackney, whom I shall have occasion to mention hereafter.

I have already said that Fanny's health had been materially injured by her incessant labours for the maintenance of her family. She had also suffered a disappointment, which preyed upon her mind. To these different sources of ill health she became gradually a victim; and at length discovered all the symptoms of a pulmonary consumption. By the medical men that attended her, she was advised to try the effects of a southern climate; and, about the beginning of the year 1785, sailed for Lisbon.

The first feeling with which Mary had contemplated her friend, was a sentiment of inferiority and reverence; but that, from the operation of a ten years' acquaintance, was considerably changed. Fanny had originally been far before her in literary attainments; this disparity no longer existed. In whatever

---

1 Sarah Burgh, *née* Harding (d. 1788), was known as a vigorous advocate of the opinions of her husband, the Dissenting author and schoolmaster James Burgh (1714-75), whose works included *Political Disquisitions* (1774-75), a three-volume compilation of statistics concerning electoral reform.

2 Properly, Hewlett (1762-1844), an Anglican clergyman and biblical scholar, at whose school Godwin placed his cousin and ward Thomas Abthorpe Cooper (1776-1849) in 1788.

degree Mary might endeavour to free herself from the delusions of self-esteem, this period of observation upon her own mind and that of her friend, could not pass, without her perceiving that there were some essential characteristics of genius, which she possessed, and in which her friend was deficient. The principal of these was a firmness of mind, an unconquerable greatness of soul, by which, after a short internal struggle, she was accustomed to rise above difficulties and suffering. Whatever Mary undertook, she perhaps in all instances accomplished; and, to her lofty spirit, scarcely any thing she desired, appeared hard to perform. Fanny, on the contrary, was a woman of a timid and irresolute nature, accustomed to yield to difficulties, and probably priding herself in this morbid softness of her temper. One instance that I have heard Mary relate of this sort, was, that, at a certain time, Fanny, dissatisfied with her domestic situation, expressed an earnest desire to have a home of her own. Mary, who felt nothing more pressing than to relieve the inconveniences of her friend, determined to accomplish this object for her. It cost her infinite exertions; but at length she was able to announce to Fanny that a house was prepared, and that she was on the spot to receive her. The answer which Fanny returned to the letter of her friend, consisted almost wholly of an enumeration of objections to the quitting her family, which she had not thought of before, but which now appeared to her of considerable weight.

The judgment which experience had taught Mary to form of the mind of her friend, determined her in the advice she gave, at the period to which I have brought down the story. Fanny was recommended to seek a softer climate, but she had no funds to defray the expence of such an undertaking. At this time Mr. Hugh Skeys of Dublin, but then resident in the kingdom of Portugal, paid his addresses to her. The state of her health Mary considered as such as scarcely to afford the shadow of a hope; it was not therefore a time at which it was most obvious to think of marriage. She conceived however that nothing should be omitted, which might alleviate, if it could not cure; and accordingly urged her speedy acceptance of the proposal. Fanny accordingly made the voyage to Lisbon; and the marriage took place on the twenty-fourth of February 1785.

The change of climate and situation was productive of little benefit; and the life of Fanny was only prolonged by a period of pregnancy, which soon declared itself. Mary, in the mean time, was impressed with the idea that her friend would die in this distant country; and, shocked with the recollection of her separation from the circle of her friends, determined to pass over to Lisbon to attend her. This resolution was treated by her acquaintance as in the utmost degree visionary; but she was not to be diverted from her point. She had not money to defray her expences: she must quit for a long time the school, the very existence of which probably depended upon her exertions.

No person was ever better formed for the business of education; if it be not a sort of absurdity to speak of a person as formed for an inferior object, who is in possession of talents, in the fullest degree adequate to something on a more important and comprehensive scale. Mary had a quickness of temper, not apt to take offence with inadvertencies, but which led her to imagine that she saw the mind of the person with whom she had any transaction, and to refer the principle of her approbation or displeasure to the cordiality or injustice of their sentiments. She was occasionally severe and imperious in her resentments; and, when she strongly disapproved, was apt to express her censure in terms that gave a very humiliating sensation to the person against whom it was directed. Her displeasure however never assumed its severest form, but when it was barbed by disappointment. Where she expected little, she was not very rigid in her censure of error.

But, to whatever the defects of her temper might amount, they were never exercised upon her inferiors in station or age. She scorned to make use of an ungenerous advantage, or to wound the defenceless. To her servants there never was a mistress more considerate or more kind. With children she was the mirror of patience. Perhaps, in all her extensive experience upon the subject of education, she never betrayed one symptom of irascibility. Her heart was the seat of every benevolent feeling; and accordingly, in all her intercourse with children, it was kindness and sympathy alone that prompted her conduct. Sympathy, when it mounts to a certain height, inevitably begets affection in the person towards whom it is exercised; and I have heard her say, that she never was concerned in the education of one child, who was not personally attached to her, and earnestly concerned not to incur her displeasure. Another eminent advantage she possessed in the business of education, was that she was little troubled with scepticism and uncertainty. She saw, as it were by intuition, the path which her mind determined to pursue, and had a firm confidence in her own power to effect what she desired. Yet, with all this, she had scarcely a tincture of obstinacy. She carefully watched symptoms as they rose, and the success of her experiments; and governed herself accordingly. While I thus enumerate her more than maternal qualities, it is impossible not to feel a pang at the recollection of her orphan children!

Though her friends earnestly dissuaded her from the journey to Lisbon, she found among them a willingness to facilitate the execution of her project, when it was once fixed. Mrs. Burgh in particular, supplied her with money, which however she always conceived came from Dr. Price. This loan, I have reason to believe, was faithfully repaid.

It was during her residence at Newington Green, that she was introduced to the acquaintance of Dr. Johnson, who was at that time considered as in some sort the father of English literature. The doctor treated her with particular kindness and attention, had a long conversation with her, and desired her to repeat her visit often. This she firmly purposed to do; but the news of his last illness, and then of his death, intervened to prevent her making a second visit.

Her residence in Lisbon was not long. She arrived but a short time before her friend was prematurely delivered, and the event was fatal to both mother and child. Frances Blood, hitherto the chosen object of Mary's attachment, died on the twenty-ninth of November 1785.

It is thus that she speaks of her in her Letters from Norway, written ten years after her decease. "When a warm heart has received strong impressions, they are not to be effaced. Emotions become sentiments; and the imagination renders even transient sensations permanent, by fondly retracing them. I cannot, without a thrill of delight, recollect views I have seen, which are not to be forgotten, nor looks I have felt in every nerve, which I shall never more meet. The grave has closed over a dear friend, the friend of my youth; still she is present with me, and I hear her soft voice warbling as I stray over the heath."[1]

---

1   *Letters Written during a Short Residence in Sweden, Norway and Denmark* (1796), Letter
VI, *WMW* 6: 271–72.

CHAP. IV.

1785–1787.

No doubt the voyage to Lisbon tended considerably to enlarge the understanding of Mary. She was admitted into the best company the English factory[1] afforded. She made many profound observations on the character of the natives, and the baleful effects of superstition. The obsequies of Fanny, which it was necessary to perform by stealth and in darkness, tended to invigorate these observations in her mind.

She sailed upon her voyage home about the twentieth of December. On this occasion a circumstance occurred, that deserves to be recorded. While they were on their passage, they fell in with a French vessel, in great distress, and in daily expectation of foundering at sea, at the same time that it was almost destitute of provisions. The Frenchman hailed them, and intreated the English captain, in consideration of his melancholy situation, to take him and his crew on board. The Englishman represented in reply, that his stock of provisions was by no means adequate to such an additional number of mouths, and absolutely refused compliance. Mary, shocked at his apparent insensibility, took up the cause of the sufferers, and threatened the captain to have him called to a severe account, when he arrived in England. She finally prevailed, and had the satisfaction to reflect, that the persons in question possibly owed their lives to her interposition.

When she arrived in England, she found that her school had suffered considerably in her absence. It can be little reproach to any one, to say that they were found incapable of supplying her place. She not only excelled in the management of the children, but had also the talent of being attentive and obliging to the parents, without degrading herself.

---

1 "An establishment for traders carrying on business in a foreign country" (*OED*).

The period at which I am now arrived is important, as conducting to the first step of her literary career. Mr. Hewlet had frequently mentioned literature to Mary as a certain source of pecuniary produce, and had urged her to make trial of the truth of his judgment. At this time she was desirous of assisting the father and mother of Fanny in an object they had in view, the transporting themselves to Ireland; and, as usual, what she desired in a pecuniary view, she was ready to take on herself to effect. For this purpose she wrote a duodecimo pamphlet of one hundred and sixty pages, entitled, Thoughts on the Education of Daughters.[1] Mr. Hewlet obtained from the bookseller, Mr. Johnson in St. Paul's Church Yard,[2] ten guineas for the copy-right of this manuscript, which she immediately applied to the object for the sake of which the pamphlet was written.

Every thing urged Mary to put an end to the affair of the school. She was dissatisfied with the different appearance it presented upon her return, from the state in which she left it. Experience impressed upon her a rooted aversion to that sort of cohabitation with her sisters, which the project of the school imposed. Cohabitation is a point of delicate experiment, and is, in a majority of instances, pregnant with ill-humour and unhappiness.[3] The activity and ardent spirit of adventure which characterized Mary, were not felt in an equal degree by her sisters, so that a disproportionate share of every burthen attendant upon the situation, fell to her lot. On the other hand, they could scarcely perhaps be perfectly easy, in observing the superior degree of deference and courtship, which her merit extorted from almost every one that knew her. Her kindness for them was not diminished, but she resolved that the mode of its exertion in future should be different, tending to their benefit, without intrenching upon her own liberty.

---

1   *Thoughts on the Education of Daughters: With Reflections on Female Conduct, in the More Important Duties of Life* (1787).

2   The Unitarian publisher and bookseller Joseph Johnson (1738-1809) published all of Wollstonecraft's works. In the 1780s and 1790s his premises at No. 72, St Paul's Churchyard, became the centre of a closely-knit group of political reformers, artisans, scientists, and theologians, many of whose books he published.

3   For further statements of Godwin's views on cohabitation, see Appendix B.1.ii and B.2.

Thus circumstanced, a proposal was made her, such as, regarding only the situations through which she had lately passed, is usually termed advantageous. This was, to accept the office of governess to the daughters of lord viscount Kingsborough, eldest son to the earl of Kingston of the kingdom of Ireland.[1] The terms held out to her were such as she determined to accept, at the same time resolving to retain the situation only for a short time. Independence was the object after which she thirsted, and she was fixed to try whether it might not be found in literary occupation. She was desirous however first to accumulate a small sum of money, which should enable her to consider at leisure the different literary engagements that might offer, and provide in some degree for the eventual deficiency of her earliest attempts.

The situation in the family of lord Kingsborough, was offered to her through the medium of the rev. Mr. Prior, at that time one of the under masters of Eton school. She spent some time at the house of this gentleman, immediately after her giving up the school at Newington Green. Here she had an opportunity of making an accurate observation upon the manners and conduct of that celebrated seminary, and the ideas she retained of it were by no means favourable. By all that she saw, she was confirmed in a very favourite opinion of her's, in behalf of day-schools, where, as she expressed it, "children have the opportunity of conversing with children, without interfering with domestic affections, the foundation of virtue."[2]

Though her residence in the family of lord Kingsborough continued scarcely more than twelve months, she left behind her, with them and their connections, a very advantageous impression. The governesses the young ladies had hitherto had, were only a species of upper servants, controlled in every thing

---

1   Robert King, Viscount Kingsborough (1754-99, second Earl of Kingston following the death of his father Edward King, first Earl of Kingston, in 1797) was MP for County Cork in 1783, 1790, and 1798. Wollstonecraft was employed as governess to his three eldest daughters at their home at Michelstown Castle, County Cork.

2   Wollstonecraft to Godwin, [31 December 1796], G&M 59 (adapted). For Wollstonecraft's strictures on the English public school system, see *Vindication of the Rights of Woman*, WMW 5: 229-50; Godwin set out his own views on the subject in *The Enquirer* (1797), PPW 5: 106-09.

by the mother; Mary insisted upon the unbounded exercise of her own discretion. When the young ladies heard of their governess coming from England, they heard in imagination of a new enemy, and declared their resolution to guard themselves accordingly. Mary however speedily succeeded in gaining their confidence, and the friendship that soon grew up between her and Margaret King, now countess Mount Cashel,[1] the eldest daughter, was in an uncommon degree cordial and affectionate. Mary always spoke of this young lady in terms of the truest applause, both in relation to the eminence of her intellectual powers, and the ingenuous amiableness of her disposition. Lady Kingsborough, from the best motives, had imposed upon her daughters a variety of prohibitions, both as to the books they should read, and in many other respects. These prohibitions had their usual effects; inordinate desire for the things forbidden, and clandestine indulgence. Mary immediately restored the children to their liberty, and undertook to govern them by their affections only. The consequence was, that their indulgences were moderate, and they were uneasy under any indulgence that had not the sanction of their governess. The salutary effects of the new system of education were speedily visible; and lady Kingsborough soon felt no other uneasiness, than lest the children should love their governess better than their mother.

Mary made many friends in Ireland, among the persons who visited lord Kingsborough's house, for she always appeared there with the air of an equal, and not of a dependent. I have heard her mention the ludicrous distress of a woman of quality, whose name I have forgotten, that, in a large company, singled out Mary, and entered into a long conversation with her. After the conversation was over, she enquired whom she had been talking with, and found, to her utter mortification and dismay, that it was Miss King's governess.

---

1 Margaret King (1773-1835) became Lady Mount Cashel on her marriage in 1791 to Stephen Moore, the second Earl of Mount Cashell. (In 1805 she separated from her husband and went to live in Italy with George William Tighe, where they became known as "Mr and Mrs Mason," a name based on that of the instructress in Wollstonecraft's *Original Stories from Real Life: With Conversations, Calculated to Regulate the Affections, and Form the Mind to Truth and Goodness* (1788).)

One of the persons among her Irish acquaintance, whom Mary was accustomed to speak of with the highest respect, was Mr. George Ogle,[1] member of parliament for the county of Wexford. She held his talents in very high estimation; she was strongly prepossessed in favour of the goodness of his heart; and she always spoke of him as the most perfect gentleman she had ever known. She felt the regret of a disappointed friend, at the part he has lately taken in the politics of Ireland.[2]

Lord Kingsborough's family passed the summer of the year 1787 at Bristol Hot-Wells,[3] and had formed the project of proceeding from thence to the continent, a tour in which Mary purposed to accompany them. The plan however was ultimately given up, and Mary in consequence closed her connection with them, earlier than she otherwise had purposed to do.

At Bristol Hot-Wells she composed the little book which bears the title of Mary, a Fiction.[4] A considerable part of this story consists, with certain modifications, of the incidents of her own friendship with Fanny. All the events that do not relate to that subject are fictitious.

This little work, if Mary had never produced any thing else, would serve, with persons of true taste and sensibility, to establish the eminence of her genius. The story is nothing. He that looks into the book only for incident, will probably lay it down with disgust. But the feelings are of the truest and most exquisite class; every circumstance is adorned with that species of imagination, which enlists itself under the banners of delicacy and sentiment. A work of sentiment, as it is called, is too often another name for a work of affectation. He that should imagine that the sentiments of this book are affected, would indeed be entitled to our profoundest commiseration.

---

1 George Ogle (1742-1814), MP for County Wexford from 1768 to 1796, and for Dublin from 1798 to 1800, favoured legislative independence for Ireland but was strongly opposed to Catholic Emancipation.
2 Ogle had openly denounced the Catholic Relief Bill of 1793.
3 A city and spa resort on the Avon river, in the south west of England.
4 Published in 1788.

CHAP. V.

1787-1790.

BEING now determined to enter upon her literary plan, Mary came immediately from Bristol to the metropolis. Her conduct under this circumstance was such as to do credit both to her own heart, and that of Mr. Johnson, her publisher, between whom and herself there now commenced an intimate friendship.[1] She had seen him upon occasion of publishing her Thoughts on the Education of Daughters, and she addressed two or three letters to him during her residence in Ireland.[2] Upon her arrival in London in August 1787, she went immediately to his house, and frankly explained to him her purpose, at the same time requesting his advice and assistance as to its execution. After a short conversation, Mr. Johnson invited her to make his house her home, till she should have suited herself with a fixed residence. She accordingly resided at this time two or three weeks under his roof. At the same period she paid a visit or two of similar duration to some friends,[3] at no great distance from the metropolis.

At Michaelmas 1787, she entered upon a house in George street, on the Surry side of Black Friar's Bridge,[4] which Mr. Johnson had provided for her during her excursion into the country. The three years immediately ensuing, may be said, in the ordinary acceptation of the term, to have been the most active period of her life. She brought with her to this habitation, the novel of Mary, which had not yet been sent to the

---

1   Godwin's account of this period of Wollstonecraft's life is based on Johnson's "A Few Facts" (see Appendix C.3.ii).

2   See Wollstonecraft to Johnson, 5 December [1786] and 14 April [1787], *LMW* 129-30, 148.

3   Wollstonecraft visited her sisters Everina, now a teacher at a school at Henley, and Eliza Bishop, who taught at a school at Market Harborough in Leicestershire, in September 1787.

4   A bridge crossing the Thames from the City of London.

press, and the commencement of a sort of oriental tale, entitled, the Cave of Fancy,[1] which she thought proper afterwards to lay aside unfinished. I am told that at this period she appeared under great dejection of spirits, and filled with melancholy regret for the loss of her youthful friend. A period of two years had elapsed since the death of that friend; but it was possibly the composition of the fiction of Mary, that renewed her sorrows in their original force. Soon after entering upon her new habitation, she produced a little work, entitled, Original Stories from Real Life, intended for the use of children. At the commencement of her literary career, she is said to have conceived a vehement aversion to the being regarded, by her ordinary acquaintance, in the character of an author, and to have employed some precautions to prevent its occurrence.

The employment which the book-seller suggested to her, as the easiest and most certain source of pecuniary income, of course, was translation. With this view she improved herself in her French, with which she had previously but a slight acquaintance, and acquired the Italian and German languages. The greater part of her literary engagements at this time, were such as were presented to her by Mr. Johnson. She new-modelled and abridged a work, translated from the Dutch, entitled, Young Grandison: she began a translation from the French, of a book, called, the New Robinson; but in this undertaking, she was, I believe, anticipated by another translator: and she compiled a series of extracts in verse and prose, upon the model of Dr. Enfield's Speaker, which bears the title of the Female Reader; but which, from a cause not worth mentioning, has hitherto been printed with a different name in the title-page.[2]

---

1   *Extract of the Cave of Fancy: A Tale* (first published in *PW*, vol. 3), *WMW* 1: 191-206.
2   *Young Grandison: A Series of Letters from Young Persons to Their Friends. Translated from the Dutch of Madame de Cambon. With Alterations and Improvements* (1790), was a translation of *De Kleine Grandisson* (1790), by Maria Geertruida van de Werken de Cambon. *The New Robinson Crusoe* (1788) was based on *Le nouveau Robinson* (1783), a French translation, by A. S. d'Arnex, of Joachim Heinrich Campe, *Robinson der jungere* (1779-80). *The Female Reader: or, Miscellaneous Pieces in Prose and Verse; Selected from the Best Writers, and Disposed under Proper Heads; for the Improvement of Young Women* (1789), modelled on William Enfield's *The Speaker, or Miscellaneous Pieces Selected from the Best English Writers* (1774), a popular handbook for young

About the middle of the year 1788, Mr. Johnson instituted the Analytical Review, in which Mary took a considerable share.[1] She also translated Necker on the Importance of Religious Opinions; made an abridgment of Lavater's Physiognomy, from the French, which has never been published; and compressed Salzmann's Elements of Morality, a German production, into a publication in three volumes duodecimo.[2] The translation of Salzmann produced a correspondence between Mary and the author; and he afterwards repaid the obligation to her in kind, by a German translation of the Rights of Woman.[3] Such were her principal literary occupations, from the autumn of 1787, to the autumn of 1790.

It perhaps deserves to be remarked that this sort of miscellaneous literary employment, seems, for the time at least, rather to damp and contract, than to enlarge and invigorate, the genius. The writer is accustomed to see his performances answer the mere mercantile purpose of the day, and confounded with those of persons to whom he is secretly conscious of a superiority. No neighbour mind serves as a mirror to reflect the generous confidence he felt within himself; and perhaps the man never yet existed, who could maintain his enthusiasm to its full vigour, in the midst of this kind of solitariness. He is touched with the torpedo of mediocrity. I believe that nothing which Mary produced during this period, is marked with those daring flights, which exhibit themselves in the little fiction

---

men entering professional life, was edited by Wollstonecraft under the name of "Mr. Cresswick, Teacher of Elocution."

1 The *Analytical Review* (May 1788-June 1799), edited by Thomas Christie (see 84, note 4), represented the political and cultural interests of Johnson's intellectual circle. On the problems of identifying Wollstonecraft's contributions, see Jump 155-56.

2 *On the Importance of Religious Opinions, Translated from the French of Mr Necker* (1788) was a translation of Jacques Necker, *De l'importance des opinions religieuses* (1788). Wollstonecraft's abridgment of Johann Kaspar Lavater, *Physiognomiche Fragmente* (1775-78), may have been withheld from publication because of the appearance of a complete translation by Thomas Holcroft (see 103, note 1), *Essays on Physiognomy Written in German by J. C. Lavater* (1789). *Elements of Morality, for the Use of Children; With an Introductory Address for Parents* (1790-91) was a translation of Christoph Gotthilf Salzmann, *Moralisches elementarbuch* (1782), a fictionalized conduct-book.

3 Salzmann's German translation of *Vindication of the Rights of Woman* appeared in 1793-94. (He also published a German translation of Godwin's *Memoirs* in 1799.)

she composed just before its commencement. Among effusions of a nobler cast, I find occasionally interspersed some of that homily-language, which, to speak from my own feelings, is calculated to damp the moral courage, it was intended to awaken. This is probably to be assigned to the causes above described.

I have already said that one of the purposes which Mary had conceived, a few years before, as necessary to give a relish to the otherwise insipid, or embittered, draught of human life, was usefulness. On this side, the period of her existence of which I am now treating, is more brilliant, than in a literary view. She determined to apply as great a part as possible of the produce of her present employments, to the assistance of her friends and of the distressed; and, for this purpose, laid down to herself rules of the most rigid economy. She began with endeavouring to promote the interest of her sisters. She conceived that there was no situation in which she could place them, at once so respectable and agreeable, as that of governesses in private families. She determined therefore in the first place, to endeavour to qualify them for such an undertaking. Her younger sister she sent to Paris, where she remained near two years. The elder she placed in a school near London, first as a parlour-boarder, and afterwards as a teacher.[1] Her brother James, who had already been at sea, she first took into her house, and next sent to Woolwich for instruction, to qualify him for a respectable situation in the royal navy, where he was shortly after made a lieutenant.[2] Charles, who was her favourite brother, had been articled to the eldest, an attorney in the Minories;[3] but, not being satisfied with his situation, she removed him; and in some time after, having first placed him with a farmer for instruction, she fitted him out for America, where his speculations, founded upon the basis she had provided, are said to have been extremely prosper-

---

1 Eliza Bishop was placed at the school of Madame Bregantz of Putney, where Everina joined her as a teacher on her return from Paris.

2 In 1788 James Wollstonecraft, who first went to sea at the age of twelve, went to study under John Bonnycastle (see 71, note 4) at the Royal Naval Academy, Woolwich, in order to qualify for promotion, though his commission was delayed until 1806. In the intervening years he commanded a merchant vessel and was jailed as a spy in Paris during the French Revolution, then deported to England.

3 A street in the commercial district of the City of London.

ous.[1] The reason so much of this parental sort of care fell upon her, was, that her father had by this time considerably embarrassed his circumstances. His affairs having grown too complex for himself to disentangle, he had intrusted them to the management of a near relation;[2] but Mary, not being satisfied with the conduct of the business, took them into her own hands. The exertions she made, and the struggle into which she entered however, in this instance, were ultimately fruitless. To the day of her death her father was almost wholly supported by funds which she supplied to him. In addition to her exertions for her own family, she took a young girl of about seven years of age under her protection and care, the niece of Mrs. John Hunter, and of the present Mrs. Skeys, for whose mother, then lately dead, she had entertained a sincere friendship.

The period, from the end of the year 1787 to the end of the year 1790, though consumed in labours of little eclat,[3] served still further to establish her in a friendly connection from which she derived many pleasures. Mr. Johnson, the bookseller, contracted a great personal regard for her, which resembled in many respects that of a parent. As she frequented his house, she of course became acquainted with his guests. Among these may be mentioned as persons possessing her esteem, Mr. Bonnycastle, the mathematician, the late Mr. George Anderson, accountant to the board of control, Dr. George Fordyce, and Mr. Fuseli, the celebrated painter.[4] Between both of the two latter and herself, there existed sentiments of genuine affection and friendship.

---

1 Charles Wollstonecraft settled in America in late 1792. After three years as a farmer in Pennsylvania, he was employed by Archibald Hamilton Rowan (see 92, note 2) in a calico printing business at Wilmington, Delaware. In 1798 he enlisted in the United States Army, where he served for the rest of his life, rising to the rank of brevet major just before he died.

2 Edward Wollstonecraft, then a practising lawyer.

3 "Renown" (OED).

4 John Bonnycastle (?1750-1821), professor of mathematics at the Royal Naval Academy, Woolwich; George Anderson (1760-96), who rose from humble origins to become accountant-general of the Board of Control in 1785; George Fordyce, FRS (1736-1802), physician to St Thomas's Hospital from 1770 to 1802, and one of the doctors who attended Wollstonecraft during her last illness (see 113); Henry (Johann Heinrich) Fuseli (Füssli) (1741-1825), Swiss artist and writer who settled in England in 1763, where he became known for the disturbing intensity of his paintings.

CHAP. VI.

─────────

1790-1792.

HITHERTO the literary career of Mary, had for the most part, been silent; and had been productive of income to herself, without apparently leading to the wreath of fame. From this time she was destined to attract the notice of the public, and perhaps no female writer ever obtained so great a degree of celebrity throughout Europe.

It cannot be doubted that, while, for three years of literary employment, she "held the noiseless tenor of her way,"[1] her mind was insensibly advancing towards a vigorous maturity. The uninterrupted habit of composition gave a freedom and firmness to the expression of her sentiments. The society she frequented, nourished her understanding, and enlarged her mind. The French revolution, while it gave a fundamental shock to the human intellect through every region of the globe, did not fail to produce a conspicuous effect in the progress of Mary's reflections. The prejudices of her early years suffered a vehement concussion. Her respect for establishments was undermined. At this period occurred a misunderstanding upon public grounds, with one of her early friends, whose attachment to musty creeds and exploded absurdities, had been increased, by the operation of those very circumstances, by which her mind had been rapidly advanced in the race of independence.

The event, immediately introductory to the rank which from this time she held in the lists of literature, was the publication of Burke's Reflections on the Revolution in France.[2] This

─────────

1 Thomas Gray, "Elegy Written in a Country Church Yard" (1751), l. 76 (adapted).

2 In *Reflections on the Revolution in France, and on the Proceedings in Certain Societies in London Relative to that Event* (1790), Edmund Burke (1729-97), formerly a celebrated Whig parliamentary orator, condemned the French Revolution and defended the British aristocratic system against the Dissenters' demands for constitutional reform.

book, after having been long promised to the world, finally made its appearance on the first of November 1790; and Mary, full of sentiments of liberty, and impressed with a warm interest in the struggle that was now going on, seized her pen in the first burst of indignation, an emotion of which she was strongly susceptible. She was in the habit of composing with rapidity, and her answer,[1] which was the first of the numerous ones that appeared, obtained extraordinary notice. Marked as it is with the vehemence and impetuousness of its eloquence, it is certainly chargeable with a too contemptuous and intemperate treatment of the great man against whom its attack is directed. But this circumstance was not injurious to the success of the publication. Burke had been warmly loved by the most liberal and enlightened friends of freedom, and they were proportionably inflamed and disgusted by the fury of his assault, upon what they deemed to be its sacred cause.

Short as was the time in which Mary composed her Answer to Burke's Reflections, there was one anecdote she told me concerning it, which seems worth recording in this place. It was sent to the press, as is the general practice when the early publication of a piece is deemed a matter of importance, before the composition was finished. When Mary had arrived at about the middle of her work, she was seized with a temporary fit of torpor and indolence, and began to repent of her undertaking. In this state of mind, she called, one evening, as she was in the practice of doing, upon her publisher, for the purpose of relieving herself by an hour or two's conversation. Here, the habitual ingenuousness of her nature, led her to describe what had just past in her thoughts. Mr. Johnson immediately, in a kind and friendly way, intreated her not to put any constraint upon her inclination, and to give herself no uneasiness about the sheets already printed, which he would cheerfully throw aside, if it would contribute to her happiness. Mary had wanted stimulus. She had not expected to be encouraged, in what she well knew to be an unreasonable access of idleness. Her friend's so readily falling in with her ill-humour, and seeming to expect

---

1   *Vindication of the Rights of Men, in a Letter to the Right Honourable Edmund Burke* (1790).

that she would lay aside her undertaking, piqued her pride. She immediately went home; and proceeded to the end of her work, with no other interruptions but what were absolutely indispensible.

It is probable that the applause which attended her Answer to Burke, elevated the tone of her mind. She had always felt much confidence in her own powers; but it cannot be doubted, that the actual perception of a similar feeling respecting us in a multitude of others, must increase the confidence, and stimulate the adventure of any human being. Mary accordingly proceeded, in a short time after, to the composition of her most celebrated production, the Vindication of the Rights of Woman.

Never did any author enter into a cause, with a more ardent desire to be found, not a flourishing and empty declaimer, but an effectual champion. She considered herself as standing forth in defence of one half of the human species, labouring under a yoke which, through all the records of time, had degraded them from the station of rational beings, and almost sunk them to the level of the brutes. She saw indeed, that they were often attempted to be held in silken fetters, and bribed into the love of slavery; but the disguise and the treachery served only the more fully to confirm her opposition. She regarded her sex, in the language of Calista, as

"In every state of life the slaves of men:"[1]

the rich as alternately under the despotism of a father, a brother, and a husband; and the middling and the poorer classes shut out from the acquisition of bread with independence, when they are not shut out from the very means of an industrious subsistence. Such were the views she entertained of the subject; and such the feelings with which she warmed her mind.

The work is certainly a very bold and original production.

---

1 Nicholas Rowe, *The Fair Penitent* (1703), III. i. 41 (adapted); Calista, the play's heroine, is given in marriage by her father to a man she does not love, and eventually commits suicide.

The strength and firmness with which the author repels the opinions of Rousseau, Dr. Gregory, and Dr. James Fordyce, respecting the condition of women,[1] cannot but make a strong impression upon every ingenuous reader. The public at large formed very different opinions respecting the character of the performance. Many of the sentiments are undoubtedly of a rather masculine description. The spirited and decisive way in which the author explodes the system of gallantry, and the species of homage with which the sex is usually treated, shocked the majority. Novelty produced a sentiment in their mind, which they mistook for a sense of injustice. The pretty, soft creatures that are so often to be found in the female sex, and that class of men who believe they could not exist without such pretty, soft creatures to resort to, were in arms against the author of so heretical and blasphemous a doctrine. There are also, it must be confessed, occasional passages of a stern and rugged feature, incompatible with the true stamina of the writer's character. But, if they did not belong to her fixed and permanent character, they belonged to her character *pro tempore*;[2] and what she thought, she scorned to qualify.

Yet, along with this rigid, and somewhat amazonian temper, which characterised some parts of the book, it is impossible not to remark a luxuriance of imagination, and a trembling delicacy of sentiment, which would have done honour to a poet, bursting with all the visions of an Armida and a Dido.[3]

---

1   Three writers who presented a view of women as "naturally" submissive and weak: Jean-Jacques Rousseau (1712-78), philosopher of Geneva, author of *Emilius and Sophia, or: A New System of Education*, translated from French by William Kenrick (1762-63); Dr John Gregory (1724-73), professor of medicine at Edinburgh University, author of *A Father's Legacy to his Daughters* (1774); Dr James Fordyce (1720-96), Dissenting minister and uncle of Wollstonecraft's friend George Fordyce, author of *Sermons to Young Women* (1765).

2   (Latin) for the time being.

3   Two poetic images of women who destroy themselves for love. In Torquato Tasso's *Jerusalem Delivered* (1581), Armida, a beautiful sorceress, falls in love with the Christian knight Rinaldo and lures him into her enchanted garden, but when he escapes she kills herself by rushing into battle. In Virgil's *Aeneid*, Dido, Queen of Carthage, falls in love with Aeneas, who was driven by a storm to her shores, and commits suicide after his departure.

The contradiction, to the public apprehension, was equally great, as to the person of the author, as it was when they considered the temper of the book. In the champion of her sex, who was described as endeavouring to invest them with all the rights of man, those whom curiosity prompted to seek the occasion of beholding her, expected to find a sturdy, muscular, raw-boned virago; and they were not a little surprised, when, instead of all this, they found a woman, lovely in her person, and, in the best and most engaging sense, feminine in her manners.

The Vindication of the Rights of Woman is undoubtedly a very unequal performance, and eminently deficient in method and arrangement. When tried by the hoary and long-established laws of literary composition, it can scarcely maintain its claim to be placed in the first class of human productions. But when we consider the importance of its doctrines, and the eminence of genius it displays, it seems not very improbable that it will be read as long as the English language endures. The publication of this book forms an epocha in the subject to which it belongs; and Mary Wollstonecraft will perhaps hereafter be found to have performed more substantial service for the cause of her sex, than all the other writers, male or female, that ever felt themselves animated in the behalf of oppressed and injured beauty.

The censure of the liberal critic as to the defects of this performance, will be changed into astonishment, when I tell him, that a work of this inestimable moment, was begun, carried on, and finished in the state in which it now appears, in a period of no more than six weeks.

It is necessary here that I should resume the subject of the friendship that subsisted between Mary and Mr. Fuseli, which proved the source of the most memorable events in her subsequent history. He is a native of the republic of Switzerland, but has spent the principal part of his life in the island of Great-Britain. The eminence of his genius can scarcely be disputed; it has indeed received the testimony which is the least to be suspected, that of some of the most considerable of his contemporary artists. He has one of the most striking characteristics of genius, a daring, as well as persevering, spirit of adventure. The work in which he is at present engaged, a series of pictures for the illustration of Milton,[1] upon a very large scale, and produced solely upon the incitement of his own mind, is a proof of this, if indeed his whole life had not sufficiently proved it.

Mr. Fuseli is one of Mr. Johnson's oldest friends, and was at this time in the habit of visiting him two or three times a week. Mary, one of whose strongest characteristics was the exquisite sensations of pleasure she felt from the associations of visible objects, had hitherto never been acquainted, or never intimately acquainted, with an eminent painter. The being thus introduced therefore to the society of Mr. Fuseli, was a high gratification to her; while he found in Mary, a person perhaps more susceptible of the emotions painting is calculated to excite, than any other with whom he ever conversed. Painting, and subjects closely connected with painting, were their almost constant topics of conversation; and they found them inexhaustible. It cannot be doubted, but that this was a species of exercise very conducive to the improvement of Mary's mind.

Nothing human however is unmixed. If Mary derived improvement from Mr. Fuseli, she may also be suspected of having caught the infection of some of his faults. In early life Mr. Fuseli was ardently attached to literature; but the demands of his profession have prevented him from keeping up that extensive and indiscriminate acquaintance with it, that belles-lettres scholars frequently possess. Of consequence, the favourites of his boyish years remain his only favourites. Homer is with Mr. Fuseli the abstract and deposit of every human perfection. Milton, Shakespear, and Richardson,[2] have also engaged much of his attention. The nearest rival of Homer, I believe, if Homer can have a rival, is Jean Jacques Rousseau. A young man embraces entire the opinions of a favourite writer,

---

1 Fuseli's "Milton Gallery," begun in 1790 and exhibited for the first time on 20 May 1799 in Pall Mall, comprised forty pictures based on scenes from Milton's poems, but was not a commercial success.
2 The novelist Samuel Richardson (1689-1761) was known for his use of the epistolary form to achieve a sense of immediacy.

and Mr. Fuseli has not had leisure to bring the opinions of his youth to a revision. Smitten with Rousseau's conception of the perfectness of the savage state, and the essential abortiveness of all civilization, Mr. Fuseli looks at all our little attempts at improvement, with a spirit that borders perhaps too much upon contempt and indifference. One of his favourite positions is the divinity of genius. This is a power that comes complete at once from the hands of the Creator of all things, and the first essays of a man of real genius are such, in all their grand and most important features, as no subsequent assiduity can amend. Add to this, that Mr. Fuseli is somewhat of a caustic turn of mind, with much wit, and a disposition to search, in every thing new or modern, for occasions of censure. I believe Mary came something more a cynic out of the school of Mr. Fuseli, than she went into it.

But the principal circumstance that relates to the intercourse of Mary, and this celebrated artist, remains to be told. She saw Mr. Fuseli frequently; he amused, delighted and instructed her. As a painter, it was impossible she should not wish to see his works, and consequently to frequent his house. She visited him; her visits were returned. Notwithstanding the inequality of their years, Mary was not of a temper to live upon terms of so much intimacy with a man of merit and genius, without loving him. The delight she enjoyed in his society, she transferred by association to his person. What she experienced in this respect, was no doubt heightened, by the state of celibacy and restraint in which she had hitherto lived, and to which the rules of polished society condemn an unmarried woman. She conceived a personal and ardent affection for him. Mr. Fuseli was a married man, and his wife[1] the acquaintance of Mary. She readily perceived the restrictions which this circumstance seemed to impose upon her; but she made light of any difficulty that might arise out of them. Not that she was insensible to the value of domestic endearments between persons of an opposite sex, but that she scorned to suppose, that she could feel a strug-

---

1   Fuseli married Sophia Rawlins, a former artist's model, in 1786.

gle, in conforming to the laws she should lay down to her conduct.

There cannot perhaps be a properer place than the present, to state her principles upon this subject, such at least as they were when I knew her best. She set a great value on a mutual affection between persons of an opposite sex. She regarded it as the principal solace of human life. It was her maxim, "that the imagination should awaken the senses, and not the senses the imagination."[1] In other words, that whatever related to the gratification of the senses, ought to arise, in a human being of a pure mind, only as the consequence of an individual affection. She regarded the manners and habits of the majority of our sex in that respect, with strong disapprobation. She conceived that true virtue would prescribe the most entire celibacy, exclusively of affection, and the most perfect fidelity to that affection when it existed.—There is no reason to doubt that, if Mr. Fuseli had been disengaged at the period of their acquaintance, he would have been the man of her choice. As it was, she conceived it both practicable and eligible, to cultivate a distinguishing affection for him, and to foster it by the endearments of personal intercourse and a reciprocation of kindness, without departing in the smallest degree from the rules she prescribed to herself.

In September 1791, she removed from the house she occupied in George-street, to a large and commodious apartment in Store street, Bedford-square. She began to think that she had been too rigid, in the laws of frugality and self-denial with which she set out in her literary career; and now added to the neatness and cleanliness which she had always scrupulously observed a certain degree of elegance, and those temperate indulgences in furniture and accommodation, from which a sound and uncorrupted taste never fails to derive pleasure.

It was in the month of November in the same year (1791), that the writer of this narrative was first in company with the person to whom it relates. He dined with her at a friend's,

---

1 Probably a loose paraphrase of *Letters to Imlay*, Letter XLIV, *WMW* 6: 408 (see Appendix C.1.iii).

together with Mr. Thomas Paine and one or two other persons.[1] The invitation was of his own seeking, his object being to see the author of the Rights of Man, with whom he had never before conversed.

The interview was not fortunate. Mary and myself parted, mutually displeased with each other. I had not read her Rights of Woman. I had barely looked into her Answer to Burke, and been displeased, as literary men are apt to be, with a few offences, against grammar and other minute points of composition. I had therefore little curiosity to see Mrs. Wollstonecraft, and a very great curiosity to see Thomas Paine. Paine, in his general habits, is no great talker; and, though he threw in occasionally some shrewd and striking remarks; the conversation lay principally between me and Mary. I, of consequence, heard her, very frequently when I wished to hear Paine.

We touched on a considerable variety of topics, and particularly on the characters and habits of certain eminent men. Mary, as has already been observed, had acquired, in a very blameable degree, the practice of seeing every thing on the gloomy side, and bestowing censure with a plentiful hand, where circumstances were in any respect doubtful. I, on the contrary, had a strong propensity, to favourable construction, and particularly, where I found unequivocal marks of genius, strongly to incline to the supposition of generous and manly virtue. We ventilated in this way the characters of Voltaire and others,[2] who have obtained from some individuals an ardent admiration, while the greater number have treated them with

---

1   Godwin met Wollstonecraft at one of Johnson's weekly dinners on 13 November 1791. Thomas Paine (1737-1809) was the author of the openly republican *Rights of Man* (1791-92), for which he was indicted for seditious libel; in September 1792 he fled to Paris, where he became a member of the French National Convention and frequented the moderate Girondin circles that Wollstonecraft joined a year later. The other dinner guest was "Shovet," who has not been further identified. (Godwin's diary, Abinger MSS, Dep. e. 199.)

2   Voltaire, pseudonym of François Marie Arouet (1694-1778), French polymath whose crossing of disciplinary boundaries made him an exemplary Enlightenment intellectual; according to Godwin's diary, the "others" discussed were Samuel Johnson and John Horne Tooke (1736-1812), the veteran radical politician and philologist.

extreme moral severity. Mary was at last provoked to tell me, that praise, lavished in the way that I lavished it, could do no credit either to the commended or the commender. We discussed some questions on the subject of religion, in which her opinions approached much nearer to the received ones, than mine. As the conversation proceeded, I became dissatisfied with the tone of my own share in it. We touched upon all topics, without treating forcibly and connectedly upon any. Meanwhile, I did her the justice, in giving an account of the conversation to a party in which I supped, though I was not sparing of my blame, to yield her the praise of a person of active and independent thinking. On her side, she did me no part of what perhaps I considered as justice.

We met two or three times in the course of the following year, but made a very small degree of progress towards a cordial acquaintance.

In the close of the year 1792, Mary went over to France, where she continued to reside for upwards of two years. One of her principal inducements to this step, related, I believe, to Mr. Fuseli. She had, at first, considered it as reasonable and judicious, to cultivate what I may be permitted to call, a Platonic affection for him; but she did not, in the sequel, find all the satisfaction in this plan, which she had originally expected from it. It was in vain that she enjoyed much pleasure in his society, and that she enjoyed it frequently. Her ardent imagination was continually conjuring up pictures of the happiness she should have found, if fortune had favoured their more intimate union. She felt herself formed for domestic affection, and all those tender charities, which men of sensibility have constantly treated as the dearest band of human society. General conversation and society could not satisfy her. She felt herself alone, as it were, in the great mass of her species; and she repined when she reflected, that the best years of her life were spent in this comfortless solitude. These ideas made the cordial intercourse of Mr. Fuseli, which had at first been one of her greatest pleasures, a source of perpetual torment to her. She conceived it necessary to snap the chain of this association in her mind; and, for that purpose, determined to seek a new climate, and mingle in different scenes.

It is singular, that during her residence in Store street, which lasted more than twelve months, she produced nothing, except a few articles in the Analytical Review. Her literary meditations were chiefly employed upon the Sequel to the Rights of Woman;[1] but she has scarcely left behind her a single paper, that can, with any certainty, be assigned to have had this destination.

---

1 See *Hints*. [Chiefly designed to have been incorporated in the Second Part of the *Vindication of the Rights of Woman*], *PW* 4: 179-95, *WMW* 5: 271-76.

CHAP. VII.

1792-1795.

THE original plan of Mary, respecting her residence in France, had no precise limits in the article of duration; the single purpose she had in view being that of an endeavour to heal her distempered mind. She did not proceed so far as even to discharge her lodging in London; and, to some friends who saw her immediately before her departure, she spoke merely of an absence of six weeks.

It is not to be wondered at, that her excursion did not originally seem to produce the effects she had expected from it. She was in a land of strangers; she had no acquaintance; she had even to acquire the power of receiving and communicating ideas with facility in the language of the country. Her first residence was in a spacious mansion to which she had been invited, but the master of which (monsieur Fillietaz)[1] was absent at the time of her arrival. At first therefore she found herself surrounded only with servants. The gloominess of her mind communicated its own colour to the objects she saw; and in this temper she began a series of Letters on the Present Character of the French Nation, one of which she forwarded to her publisher, and which appears in the collection of her posthumous works.[2] This performance she soon after discontinued; and it is, as she justly remarks, tinged with the saturnine temper which at that time pervaded her mind.

Mary carried with her introductions to several agreeable families in Paris. She renewed her acquaintance with Paine. There also subsisted a very sincere friendship between her and

---

1   Properly, Filliettaz (the son-in-law of Madame Bregantz of Putney), who lived at 22 Rue Meslée.
2   "Letter: Introductory to a Series of Letters on the Present Character of the French Nation," dated 15 February 1793, *PW* 4: 39-51, *WMW* 6: 443-46.

Helen Maria Williams,[1] author of a collection of poems of uncommon merit, who at that time resided in Paris. Another person, whom Mary always spoke of in terms of ardent commendation, both for the excellence of his disposition, and the force of his genius, was a count Slabrendorf, by birth, I believe, a Swede.[2] It is almost unnecessary to mention, that she was personally acquainted with the majority of the leaders in the French revolution.[3]

But the house that, I believe, she principally frequented at this time, was that of Mr. Thomas Christie,[4] a person whose pursuits were mercantile, and who had written a volume on the French revolution. With Mrs. Christie her acquaintance was more intimate than with the husband.

It was about four months after her arrival at Paris in December 1792, that she entered into that species of connection, for which her heart secretly panted, and which had the effect of diffusing an immediate tranquillity and cheerfulness over her manners. The person with whom it was formed (for it would be an idle piece of delicacy, to attempt to suppress a name, which is known to every one whom the reputation of Mary has reached), was Mr. Gilbert Imlay,[5] native of the United States of North America.

1　Helen Maria Williams (1762-1827), chronicler of the French Revolution and author, published a new edition of her popular collected *Poems* (1786) in 1791 and settled in Paris in the summer of the same year.

2　The traveller and author Christoph Georg Gustav, Graf von Schlabrendorf (1750-1824), was in fact born in Stettin, Silesia.

3　In the crisis years of 1797 and 1798 (see Introduction, 14-15), Godwin knew better than to name Wollstonecraft's political contacts; for the evidence on which this claim is based, see I.B. Johnson's letter to Godwin, 13 November 1797, Appendix C.3.iv.

4　Thomas Christie (1761-96) went to Paris in October 1789 as the agent of a London merchant (see 99, note 3), where he wrote *Letters on the Revolution of France and on the New Constitution Established by the French Assembly: Occasioned by the Publications of Edmund Burke and Alexander de Calonne* (1790). In 1792 he married Rebecca Thomson, who became Wollstonecraft's close friend.

5　Gilbert Imlay (?1754-1828), an officer in the American Revolutionary army from 1777 to 1783 and later a land speculator in Kentucky, is thought to have left America around 1786. His two books, *A Topographical Description of the Western Territory of North America* (1792) and *The Emigrants* (1793), a novel set in Kentucky, provided him with the credentials for entry to the circles of French Revolutionary leaders and British expatriates in Paris.

The place at which she first saw Mr. Imlay was at the house of Mr. Christie; and it perhaps deserves to be noticed, that the emotions he then excited in her mind, were, I am told, those of dislike, and that, for some time, she shunned all occasions of meeting him. This sentiment however speedily gave place to one of greater kindness.

Previously to the partiality she conceived for him, she had determined upon a journey to Switzerland, induced chiefly by motives of economy. But she had some difficulty in procuring a passport; and it was probably the intercourse that now originated between her and Mr. Imlay, that changed her purpose, and led her to prefer a lodging at Neuilly, a village three miles from Paris. Her habitation here was a solitary house in the midst of a garden, with no other inhabitants than herself and the gardener, an old man, who performed for her many of the offices of a domestic, and would sometimes contend for the honour of making her bed. The gardener had a great veneration for his guest, and would set before her, when alone, some grapes of a particularly fine sort, which she could not without the greatest difficulty obtain, when she had any person with her as a visitor. Here it was that she conceived, and for the most part executed, her Historical and Moral View of the French Revolution,* into which, as she observes, are incorporated most of the observations she had collected for her Letters, and which was written with more sobriety and cheerfulness than the tone in which they had been commenced. In the evening she was accustomed to refresh herself by a walk in a neighbouring wood, from which her old host in vain endeavoured to dissuade her, by recounting divers horrible robberies and murders that had been committed there.

---

* No part of the proposed continuation of this work, has been found among the papers of the author.[1] [Godwin's note]

---

1 Wollstonecraft proposed such a continuation in the Advertisement to the first volume of *An Historical and Moral View of the French Revolution; and the Effect it has Produced in Europe* (1794) (*WMW* 6: 5), but no further material on this subject appears in *PW*.

The commencement of the attachment Mary now formed, had neither confidant nor adviser. She always conceived it to be a gross breach of delicacy to have any confidant in a matter of this sacred nature, an affair of the heart. The origin of the connection was about the middle of April 1793, and it was carried on in a private manner for four months. At the expiration of that period a circumstance occurred that induced her to declare it. The French convention, exasperated at the conduct of the British government, particularly in the affair of Toulon,[1] formed a decree against the citizens of this country, by one article of which the English, resident in France, were ordered into prison till the period of a general peace. Mary had objected to a marriage with Mr. Imlay, who, at the time their connection was formed, had no property whatever; because she would not involve him in certain family embarrassments to which she conceived herself exposed, or make him answerable for the pecuniary demands that existed against her. She however considered their engagement as of the most sacred nature; and they had mutually formed the plan of emigrating to America, as soon as they should have realized a sum, enabling them to do it in the mode they desired. The decree however that I have just mentioned, made it necessary, not that a marriage should actually take place, but that Mary should take the name of Imlay, which, from the nature of their connection, she conceived herself entitled to do, and obtain a certificate from the American ambassador,[2] as the wife of a native of that country.

Their engagement being thus avowed, they thought proper to reside under the same roof, and for that purpose removed to Paris.

Mary was now arrived at the situation, which, for two or three preceding years, her reason had pointed out to her as affording the most substantial prospect of happiness. She had

---

1 In August 1793 the British Navy assisted a royalist insurrection at Toulon, a seaport town in southern France, which prompted the French National Convention to pass the Law of Suspects (17 September), detaining all British citizens resident in France.

2 Gouverneur Morris (1752–1816), American minister to France from 1792 to 1794 (after which he was recalled at the request of the French authorities).

been tossed and agitated by the waves of misfortune. Her childhood, as she often said, had known few of the endearments, which constitute the principal happiness of childhood. The temper of her father had early given to her mind a severe cast of thought, and substituted the inflexibility of resistance for the confidence of affection. The cheerfulness of her entrance upon womanhood, had been darkened, by an attendance upon the death-bed of her mother, and the still more afflicting calamity of her eldest sister. Her exertions to create a joint independence for her sisters and herself, had been attended, neither with the success, nor the pleasure, she had hoped from them. Her first youthful passion, her friendship for Fanny, had encountered many disappointments, and, in fine, a melancholy and premature catastrophe. Soon after these accumulated mortifications, she was engaged in a contest with a near relation, whom she regarded as unprincipled, respecting the wreck of her father's fortune. In this affair she suffered the double pain, which arises from moral indignation, and disappointed benevolence. Her exertions to assist almost every member of her family, were great and unremitted. Finally, when she indulged a romantic affection for Mr. Fuseli, and fondly imagined that she should find in it the solace of her cares, she perceived too late, that, by continually impressing on her mind fruitless images of unreserved affection and domestic felicity, it only served to give new pungency to the sensibility that was destroying her.

Some persons may be inclined to observe, that the evils here enumerated, are not among the heaviest in the catalogue of human calamities. But evils take their rank, more from the temper of the mind that suffers them, than from their abstract nature. Upon a man of a hard and insensible disposition, the shafts of misfortune often fall pointless and impotent. There are persons, by no means hard and insensible, who, from an elastic and sanguine turn of mind, are continually prompted to look on the fair side of things, and, having suffered one fall, immediately rise again, to pursue their course, with the same eagerness, the same hope, and the same gaiety, as before. On the other hand, we not unfrequently meet with persons, endowed with the most exquisite and delicious sensibility, whose minds seem almost of too fine a texture to encounter the vicissitudes of human affairs, to whom pleasure is transport, and disappointment is agony indescribable. This character is finely pourtrayed by the author of the Sorrows of Werter.[1] Mary was in this respect a female Werter.

She brought then, in the present instance, a wounded and sick heart, to take refuge in the bosom of a chosen friend. Let it not however be imagined, that she brought a heart, querulous, and ruined in its taste for pleasure. No; her whole character seemed to change with a change of fortune. Her sorrows, the depression of her spirits, were forgotten, and she assumed all the simplicity and the vivacity of a youthful mind. She was like a serpent upon a rock, that casts its slough, and appears again with the brilliancy, the sleekness, and the elastic activity of its happiest age. She was playful, full of confidence, kindness and sympathy. Her eyes assumed new lustre, and her cheeks new colour and smoothness. Her voice became chearful; her temper overflowing with universal kindness; and that smile of bewitching tenderness from day to day illuminated her countenance, which all who knew her will so well recollect, and which won, both heart and soul, the affection of almost every one that beheld it.

Mary now reposed herself upon a person, of whose honour and principles she had the most exalted idea. She nourished an individual affection, which she saw no necessity of subjecting to restraint; and a heart like her's was not formed to nourish affection by halves. Her conception of Mr. Imlay's "tenderness and worth, had twisted him closely round her heart;" and she "indulged the thought, that she had thrown out some tendrils, to cling to the elm by which she wished to be supported."[2] This was "talking a new language to her;" but, "conscious that she was not a parasite-plant," she was willing to encourage and foster the luxuriancies of affection. Her confidence was entire;

---

1   See p. 50, note 2.
2   "Letters to Imlay," XVI [14 January 1794], *WMW* 6: 382 (adapted) (see Appendix C.1.i).

her love was unbounded. Now, for the first time in her life she gave a loose to all the sensibilities of her nature.

Soon after the time I am now speaking of, her attachment to Mr. Imlay gained a new link, by finding reason to suppose herself with child.

Their establishment at Paris, was however broken up almost as soon as formed, by the circumstance of Mr. Imlay's entering into business, urged, as he said, by the prospect of a family, and this being a favourable crisis in French affairs for commercial speculations. The pursuits in which he was engaged, led him in the month of September to Havre de Grace, then called Havre Marat, probably to superintend the shipping of goods, in which he was jointly engaged with some other person or persons.[1] Mary remained in the capital.

The solitude in which she was now left, proved an unexpected trial. Domestic affections constituted the object upon which her heart was fixed; and she early felt, with an inward grief, that Mr. Imlay "did not attach those tender emotions round the idea of home,"[2] which, every time they recurred, dimmed her eyes with moisture. She had expected his return from week to week, and from month to month; but a succession of business still continued to detain him at Havre. At the same time the sanguinary character which the government of France began every day more decisively to assume, contributed to banish tranquillity from the first months of her pregnancy. Before she left Neuilly, she happened one day to enter Paris on foot (I believe, by the *Place de Louis Quinze*), when an execution, attended with some peculiar aggravations, had just taken place, and the blood of the guillotine appeared fresh upon the pavement. The emotions of her soul burst forth in indignant exclamations, while a prudent bystander warned her of her danger, and intreated her to hasten and hide her discontents.

---

1 Le Havre, known as Havre de Grace since the sixteenth century, was renamed Havre-Marat in honour of the assassinated radical Revolutionary journalist Jean-Paul Marat (1744-93). Imlay and his Finnish business partner, Elias Backman (1760-1829), were involved in a semi-legal trading business, running the British naval blockade by shipping goods in and out of France via the neutral Baltic ports.

2 "Letters to Imlay," XLII [10 June 1795], *WMW* 6: 407.

She described to me, more than once, the anguish she felt at hearing of the death of Brissot, Vergniaud, and the twenty deputies,[1] as one of the most intolerable sensations she had ever experienced.

Finding the return of Mr. Imlay continually postponed, she determined, in January 1794, to join him at Havre. One motive that influenced her, though, I believe, by no means the principal, was the growing cruelties of Robespierre,[2] and the desire she felt to be in any other place, rather than the devoted[3] city, in the midst of which they were perpetrated.

From January to September, Mr. Imlay and Mary lived together, with great harmony, at Havre, where the child, with which she was pregnant, was born, on the fourteenth of May, and named Frances, in remembrance of the dear friend of her youth, whose image could never be erased from her memory.

In September, Mr. Imlay took his departure from Havre for the port of London. As this step was said to be necessary in the way of business, he endeavoured to prevail upon Mary to quit Havre, and once more take up her abode at Paris. Robespierre was now no more, and, of consequence, the only objection she had to residing in the capital, was removed. Mr. Imlay was already in London, before she undertook her journey, and it proved the most fatiguing journey she ever made; the carriage, in which she travelled, being overturned no less than four times between Havre and Paris.

This absence, like that of the preceding year in which Mr. Imlay had removed to Havre, was represented as an absence that was to have a short duration. In two months he was once again to join her at Paris. It proved however the prelude to an eternal

---

1 Jacques-Pierre Brissot de Warville (1754-93) and Pierre-Victurnien Vergniaud (1753-93) were leaders of the Girondins, the moderate party in the French National Convention. They and twenty of their colleagues were arrested in the *journées* of 31 May-2 June 1793 and guillotined on 16 October 1793.

2 Maximilien-François-Isidore de Robespierre (1758-94), radical Revolutionary politician, helped to institute the Terror (September 1793-July 1794), which ended with the coup of 9 Thermidor (27 July), by which he was overthrown and guillotined.

3 "Doomed" (*OED*).

separation. The agonies of such a separation, or rather desertion, great as Mary would have found them upon every supposition, were vastly increased, by the lingering method in which
it was effected, and the ambiguity that, for a long time, hung
upon it. This circumstance produced the effect, of holding her
mind, by force, as it were, to the most painful of all subjects, and
not suffering her to derive the just advantage from the energy
and elasticity of her character.

The procrastination of which I am speaking was however
productive of one advantage. It put off the evil day. She did not
suspect the calamities that awaited her, till the close of the year.
She gained an additional three months of comparative happiness. But she purchased it at a very dear rate. Perhaps no
human creature ever suffered greater misery, than dyed the
whole year 1795, in the life of this incomparable woman. It was
wasted in that sort of despair, to the sense of which the mind is
continually awakened, by a glimmering of fondly cherished,
expiring hope.

Why did she thus obstinately cling to an ill-starred, unhappy
passion? Because it is of the very essence of affection, to seek to
perpetuate itself. He does not love, who can resign this cherished sentiment, without suffering some of the sharpest strug-
gles that our nature is capable of enduring. Add to this, Mary
had fixed her heart upon this chosen friend; and one of the last
impressions a worthy mind can submit to receive, is that of the
worthlessness of the person upon whom it has fixed all its
esteem. Mary had struggled to entertain a favourable opinion
of human nature; she had unweariedly sought for a kindred
mind, in whose integrity and fidelity to take up her rest. Mr.
Imlay undertook to prove, in his letters written immediately
after their complete separation, that his conduct towards her
was reconcilable to the strictest rectitude; but undoubtedly
Mary was of a different opinion. Whatever the reader may
decide in this respect, there is one sentiment that, I believe, he
will unhesitatingly admit: that of pity for the mistake of the
man, who, being in possession of such a friendship and attachment as those of Mary, could hold them at a trivial price, and,

"like the base Indian, throw a pearl away, richer than all his tribe."*[1]

---

* A person, from whose society at this time Mary derived particular gratification, was Archibald Hamilton Rowan,[2] who had lately become a fugitive from Ireland, in consequence of a political prosecution, and in whom she found those qualities which were always eminently engaging to her, great integrity of disposition, and great kindness of heart. [Godwin's note]

---

1   *Othello*, V. ii. 346-48 (adapted).
2   Archibald Hamilton Rowan (1751-1834), a wealthy radical and secretary of the Dublin Society of United Irishmen, was in 1794 charged with distributing a seditious pamphlet, found guilty, and sentenced to two years' imprisonment, but three months later he escaped to Le Havre. When Wollstonecraft returned to England in April 1795 he took over the tenancy of her house while waiting for a passage to America.

CHAP. VIII.

1795, 1796.

In April 1795, Mary returned once more to London, being requested to do so by Mr. Imlay, who even sent a servant to Paris to wait upon her in the journey, before she could complete the necessary arrangements for her departure. But, notwithstanding these favourable appearances, she came to England with a heavy heart, not daring, after all the uncertainties and anguish she had endured, to trust to the suggestions of hope.

The gloomy forebodings of her mind, were but too faithfully verified. Mr. Imlay had already formed another connection; as it is said, with a young actress from a strolling company of players. His attentions therefore to Mary were formal and constrained, and she probably had but little of his society. This alteration could not escape her penetrating glance. He ascribed it to pressure of business, and some pecuniary embarrassments which, at that time, occurred to him; it was of little consequence to Mary what was the cause. She saw, but too well, though she strove not to see, that his affections were lost to her for ever.

It is impossible to imagine a period of greater pain and mortification than Mary passed, for about seven weeks, from the sixteenth of April to the sixth of June, in a furnished house that Mr. Imlay had provided for her. She had come over to England, a country for which she, at this time, expressed "a repugnance, that almost amounted to horror,"[1] in search of happiness. She feared that that happiness had altogether escaped her; but she was encouraged by the eagerness and impatience which Mr. Imlay at length seemed to manifest for her arrival. When she saw him, all her fears were confirmed. What a picture was she capable of forming to herself, of the overflowing

---

1   "Letters to Imlay," XXXVII (19 February [1795]), *WMW* 6: 403 (adapted).

kindness of a meeting, after an interval of so much anguish and apprehension! A thousand images of this sort were present to her burning imagination. It is in vain, on such occasions, for reserve and reproach to endeavour to curb in the emotions of an affectionate heart. But the hopes she nourished were speedily blasted. Her reception by Mr. Imlay, was cold and embarrassed. Discussions ("explanations" they were called) followed; cruel explanations, that only added to the anguish of a heart already overwhelmed in grief! They had small pretensions indeed to explicitness; but they sufficiently told, that the case admitted not of remedy.

Mary was incapable of sustaining her equanimity in this pressing emergency. "Love, dear, delusive love!" as she expressed herself to a friend some time afterwards, "rigorous reason had forced her to resign; and now her rational prospects were blasted, just as she had learned to be contented with rational enjoyments."[1] Thus situated, life became an intolerable burthen. While she was absent from Mr. Imlay, she could talk of purposes of separation and independence. But, now that they were in the same house, she could not withhold herself from endeavours to revive their mutual cordiality; and unsuccessful endeavours continually added fuel to the fire that destroyed her. She formed a desperate purpose to die.

This part of the story of Mary is involved in considerable obscurity. I only know, that Mr. Imlay became acquainted with her purpose, at a moment when he was uncertain whether or no it were already executed, and that his feelings were roused by the intelligence. It was perhaps owing to his activity and representations, that her life was, at this time, saved. She determined to continue to exist. Actuated by this purpose, she took a resolution, worthy both of the strength and affectionateness of her mind. Mr. Imlay was involved in a question of considerable difficulty, respecting a mercantile adventure in Norway.[2] It

---

1 The "friend" was probably Godwin himself.

2 Wollstonecraft was authorized by Imlay to intervene in a lawsuit against a Norwegian shipmaster, Peder Ellefsen, begun by Backman on Imlay's behalf. Ellefsen had been hired by Imlay to sail the *Maria and Margaretha*, a French cargo ship, which Imlay had bought and re-registered as a neutral vessel in Ellefsen's name, from Le

seemed to require the presence of some very judicious agent, to conduct the business to its desired termination. Mary determined to make the voyage, and take the business into her own hands. Such a voyage seemed the most desireable thing to recruit her health, and, if possible, her spirits, in the present crisis. It was also gratifying to her feelings, to be employed in promoting the interest of a man, from whom she had experienced such severe unkindness, but to whom she ardently desired to be reconciled. The moment of desperation I have mentioned, occurred in the close of May, and, in about a week after, she set out upon this new expedition.

The narrative of this voyage is before the world,[1] and perhaps a book of travels that so irresistibly seizes on the heart, never, in any other instance, found its way from the press. The occasional harshness and ruggedness of character, that diversify her Vindication of the Rights of Woman, here totally disappear. If ever there was a book calculated to make a man in love with its author, this appears to me to be the book. She speaks of her sorrows, in a way that fills us with melancholy, and dissolves us in tenderness, at the same time that she displays a genius which commands all our admiration. Affliction had tempered her heart to a softness almost more than human; and the gentleness of her spirit seems precisely to accord with all the romance of unbounded attachment.

Thus softened and improved, thus fraught with imagination and sensibility, with all, and more than all, "that youthful poets fancy, when they love,"[2] she returned to England, and, if he had so pleased, to the arms of her former lover. Her return was hastened by the ambiguity, to her apprehension, of Mr. Imlay's conduct. He had promised to meet her upon her return from Norway, probably at Hamburgh; and they were then to pass some time in Switzerland. The style however of his letters to

---

Havre to Gothenburg, a Swedish port, carrying a large quantity of silver bars. However, on the journey both the ship and the silver disappeared. Wollstonecraft's task was to ascertain the fate of the silver and to try and mediate a settlement with Ellefsen. (Nyström 22-26.)

1   In *Letters from Norway*.
2   Rowe, *The Fair Penitent*, III. i. 256 (adapted).

her during her tour, was not such as to inspire confidence; and she wrote to him very urgently, to explain himself, relative to the footing upon which they were hereafter to stand to each other. In his answer, which reached her at Hamburgh, he treated her questions as "extraordinary and unnecessary," and desired her to be at the pains to decide for herself. Feeling herself unable to accept this as an explanation, she instantly determined to sail for London by the very first opportunity, that she might thus bring to a termination the suspense that preyed upon her soul.

It was not long after her arrival in London in the commencement of October, that she attained the certainty she sought. Mr. Imlay procured her a lodging. But the neglect she experienced from him after she entered it, flashed conviction upon her, in spite of his asseverations. She made further enquiries, and at length was informed by a servant, of the real state of the case. Under the immediate shock which the painful certainty gave her, her first impulse was to repair to him at the ready-furnished house he had provided for his new mistress. What was the particular nature of their conference I am unable to relate. It is sufficient to say that the wretchedness of the night which succeeded this fatal discovery, impressed her with the feeling, that she would sooner suffer a thousand deaths, than pass another of equal misery.

The agony of her mind determined her; and that determination gave her a sort of desperate serenity. She resolved to plunge herself in the Thames; and, not being satisfied with any spot nearer to London, she took a boat, and rowed to Putney. Her first thought had led her to Battersea-bridge, but she found it too public. It was night when she arrived at Putney, and by that time had begun to rain with great violence. The rain suggested to her the idea of walking up and down the bridge, till her clothes were thoroughly drenched and heavy with the wet, which she did for half an hour without meeting a human being. She then leaped from the top of the bridge, but still seemed to find a difficulty in sinking, which she endeavoured to counteract by pressing her clothes closely round her. After some time she became insensible; but she always spoke of the pain she underwent as such, that, though she could afterwards have determined upon almost any other species of voluntary death, it would have been impossible for her to resolve upon encountering the same sensations again. I am doubtful, whether this is to be ascribed to the mere nature of suffocation, or was not rather owing to the preternatural action of a desperate spirit.

After having been for a considerable time insensible, she was recovered by the exertions of those by whom the body was found. She had sought, with cool and deliberate firmness, to put a period to her existence, and yet she lived to have every prospect of a long possession of enjoyment and happiness. It is perhaps not an unfrequent case with suicides, that we find reason to suppose, if they had survived their gloomy purpose, that they would, at a subsequent period, have been considerably happy.[1] It arises indeed, in some measure, out of the very nature of a spirit of self-destruction; which implies a degree of anguish, that the constitution of the human mind will not suffer to remain long undiminished. This is a serious reflection. Probably no man would destroy himself from an impatience of present pain, if he felt a moral certainty that there were years of enjoyment still in reserve for him. It is perhaps a futile attempt, to think of reasoning with a man in that state of mind which precedes suicide. Moral reasoning is nothing but the awakening of certain feelings; and the feeling by which he is actuated, is too strong to leave us much chance of impressing him with other feelings, that should have force enough to counterbalance it. But, if the prospect of future tranquillity and pleasure cannot be expected to have much weight with a man under an immediate purpose of suicide, it is so much the more to be wished, that men would impress their minds, in their sober moments, with a conception, which, being rendered habitual, seems to promise to act as a successful antidote in a paroxysm of desperation.

The present situation of Mary, of necessity produced some further intercourse between her and Mr. Imlay. He sent a

---

1   For Godwin's earlier views on suicide, see Appendix B.1.i.

physician to her; and Mrs. Christie, at his desire, prevailed on her to remove to her house in Finsbury-square. In the mean time Mr. Imlay assured her that his present was merely a casual, sensual connection; and, of course, fostered in her mind the idea that it would be once more in her choice to live with him. With whatever intention the idea was suggested, it was certainly calculated to increase the agitation of her mind. In one respect however it produced an effect unlike that which might most obviously have been looked for. It roused within her the characteristic energy of mind, which she seemed partially to have forgotten. She saw the necessity of bringing the affair to a point, and not suffering months and years to roll on in uncertainty and suspence. This idea inspired her with an extraordinary resolution. The language she employed, was, in effect, as follows: "If we are ever to live together again, it must be now. We meet now, or we part for ever. You say, You cannot abruptly break off the connection you have formed. It is unworthy of my courage and character, to wait the uncertain issue of that connection. I am determined to come to a decision. I consent then, for the present, to live with you, and the woman to whom you have associated yourself. I think it important that you should learn habitually to feel for your child the affection of a father. But, if you reject this proposal, here we end. You are now free. We will correspond no more. We will have no intercourse of any kind. I will be to you as a person that is dead."[1]

The proposal she made, extraordinary and injudicious as it was, was at first accepted; and Mr. Imlay took her accordingly, to look at a house he was upon the point of hiring, that she might judge whether it was calculated to please her. Upon second thoughts however he retracted his concession.

In the following month, Mr. Imlay, and the woman with whom he was at present connected, went to Paris, where they remained three months. Mary had, previously to this, fixed herself in a lodging in Finsbury-place, where, for some time, she saw scarcely any one but Mrs. Christie, for the sake of whose neighbourhood she had chosen this situation; "existing," as she

---

1 Probably a paraphrase of Wollstonecraft's conversation.

expressed it, "in a living tomb, and her life but an exercise of fortitude, continually on the stretch."[1]

Thus circumstanced, it was unavoidable for her thoughts to brood upon a passion, which all that she had suffered had not yet been able to extinguish. Accordingly, as soon as Mr. Imlay returned to England, she could not restrain herself from making another effort, and desiring to see him once more. "During his absence, affection had led her to make numberless excuses for his conduct," and she probably wished to believe that his present connection was, as he represented it, purely of a casual nature. To this application, she observes, that "he returned no other answer, except declaring, with unjustifiable passion, that he would not see her."[2]

This answer, though, at the moment, highly irritating to Mary, was not the ultimate close of the affair. Mr. Christie was connected in business with Mr. Imlay,[3] at the same time that the house of Mr. Christie was the only one at which Mary habitually visited. The consequence of this was, that, when Mr. Imlay had been already more than a fortnight in town, Mary called at Mr. Christie's one evening, at a time when Mr. Imlay was in the parlour. The room was full of company. Mrs. Christie heard Mary's voice in the passage, and hastened to her, to intreat her not to make her appearance. Mary however was not to be controlled. She thought, as she afterwards told me, that it was not consistent with conscious rectitude, that she should shrink, as if abashed, from the presence of one by whom she deemed herself injured. Her child was with her. She entered; and, in a firm manner, immediately led up the child, now near two years of age, to the knees of its father. He retired with Mary into another apartment, and promised to dine with her at her lodging, I believe, the next day.

In the interview which took place in consequence of this appointment, he expressed himself to her in friendly terms, and in a manner calculated to sooth her despair. Though he could

---

1 "Letters to Imlay," LXXV (27 November [1795]), *WMW* 6: 434 (adapted).
2 Probably a paraphrase of Wollstonecraft's conversation.
3 Christie was the Paris agent of the London firm of Turnbull, Forbes & Co., with whom Imlay had an agreement for the delivery of corn to Paris.

conduct himself, when absent from her, in a way which she censured as unfeeling; this species of sternness constantly expired when he came into her presence. Mary was prepared at this moment to catch at every phantom of happiness; and the gentleness of his carriage, was to her as a sun-beam, awakening the hope of returning day. For an instant she gave herself up to delusive visions; and, even after the period of delirium expired, she still dwelt, with an aching eye, upon the air-built and unsubstantial prospect of a reconciliation.

At his particular request, she retained the name of Imlay, which, a short time before, he had seemed to dispute with her. "It was not," as she expresses herself in a letter to a friend, "for the world that she did so—not in the least—but she was unwilling to cut the Gordian knot, or tear herself away in appearance, when she could not in reality."[1]

The day after this interview, she set out upon a visit to the country, where she spent nearly the whole of the month of March. It was, I believe, while she was upon this visit, that some epistolary communication with Mr. Imlay, induced her resolutely to expel from her mind, all remaining doubt as to the issue of the affair.

Mary was now aware that every demand of forbearance towards him, of duty to her child, and even of indulgence to her own deep-rooted predilection, was discharged. She determined to rouse herself, and cast off for ever an attachment, which to her had been a spring of inexhaustible bitterness. Her present residence among the scenes of nature, was favourable to this purpose. She was at the house of an old and intimate friend, a lady of the name of Cotton, whose partiality for her was strong and sincere. Mrs. Cotton's nearest neighbour was Sir William East, baronet;[2] and, from the joint effect of the kindness of her friend, and the hospitable and distinguishing attentions of this respectable family, she derived considerable benefit. She had been amused and interested in her journey to Norway; but with this difference, that, at that time, her mind perpetually

---

1   Not further identified.
2   Sir William East (1737-1819, first baronet from 1766) lived at Hall Place, Buckinghamshire.

returned with trembling anxiety to conjectures respecting Mr. Imlay's future conduct, whereas now, with a lofty and undaunted spirit, she threw aside every thought that recurred to him, while she felt herself called upon to make one more effort for life and happiness.

Once after this, to my knowledge, she saw Mr. Imlay; probably, not long after her return to town. They met by accident upon the New Road;[1] he alighted from his horse, and walked with her for some time; and the rencounter passed, as she assured me, without producing in her any oppressive emotion.

Be it observed, by the way, and I may be supposed best to have known the real state of the case, she never spoke of Mr. Imlay with acrimony, and was displeased when any person, in her hearing, expressed contempt of him. She was characterised by a strong sense of indignation; but her emotions of this sort were short-lived, and in no long time subsided into a dignified sereneness and equanimity.

The question of her connection with Mr. Imlay, as we have seen, was not complete dismissed, till March 1796. But it is worthy to be observed, that she did not, like ordinary persons under extreme anguish of mind, suffer her understanding, in the mean time, to sink into listlessness and debility. The most inapprehensive reader may conceive what was the mental torture she endured, when he considers, that she was twice, with an interval of four months, from the end of May to the beginning of October, prompted by it to purposes of suicide. Yet in this period she wrote her Letters from Norway. Shortly after its expiration she prepared them for the press, and they were published in the close of that year. In January 1796, she finished the sketch of a comedy, which turns, in the serious scenes, upon the incidents of her own story. It was offered to both the winter-managers,[2] and remained among her papers at the

---

1   Now part of the Euston Road, running between King's Cross and Marylebone.
2   The managers of Covent Garden and Drury Lane, the two London theatres which held the sole patents for the performance of legitimate drama. In the winter of 1796 Thomas Harris (d. 1820) was proprietor-manager of Covent Garden, and John Philip Kemble (1757-1823) was manager at Drury Lane, though the proprietor Richard Brinsley Sheridan (1751-1816) retained overall control and may also have read Wollstonecraft's play.

period of her decease; but it appeared to me to be in so crude and imperfect a state, that I judged it most respectful to her memory to commit it to the flames. To understand this extraordinary degree of activity, we must recollect however the entire solitude, in which most of her hours were at that time consumed.

CHAP. IX.

1796, 1797.

I AM now led, by the progress of the story, to the last branch of her history, the connection between Mary and myself. And this I shall relate with the same simplicity that has pervaded every other part of my narrative. If there ever were any motives of prudence or delicacy, that could impose a qualification upon the story, they are now over. They could have no relation but to factitious rules of decorum. There are no circumstances of her life, that, in the judgment of honour and reason, could brand her with disgrace. Never did there exist a human being, that needed, with less fear, expose all their actions, and call upon the universe to judge them. An event of the most deplorable sort, has awfully imposed silence upon the gabble of frivolity.

We renewed our acquaintance in January 1796,[1] but with no particular effect, except so far as sympathy in her anguish, added in my mind to the respect I had always entertained for her talents. It was in the close of that month that I read her Letters from Norway; and the impression that book produced upon me has been already related.

It was on the fourteenth of April that I first saw her after her excursion into Berkshire. On that day she called upon me in Somers Town,[2] she having, since her return, taken a lodging in Cumming-street, Pentonville, at no great distance from the place of my habitation. From that time our intimacy increased, by regular, but almost imperceptible degrees.

The partiality we conceived for each other, was in that

1 Godwin and Wollstonecraft met again on 8 January 1796 for tea at the lodgings of their mutual friend, the author Mary Hays (1760-1843); the other guest was Godwin's closest friend, the novelist, playwright and translator Thomas Holcroft (1745-1809) (Godwin's diary, Abinger MSS, Dep. e. 202).

2 Godwin lodged at 25 Chalton Street, Somers Town (now King's Cross).

mode, which I have always regarded as the purest and most refined style of love. It grew with equal advances in the mind of each. It would have been impossible for the most minute observer to have said who was before, and who was after. One sex did not take the priority which long-established custom has awarded it, nor the other overstep that delicacy which is so severely imposed. I am not conscious that either party can assume to have been the agent or the patient, the toil-spreader or the prey, in the affair. When, in the course of things, the disclosure came, there was nothing, in a manner, for either party to disclose to the other.

In July 1796 I made an excursion into the county of Norfolk, which occupied nearly the whole of that month. During this period Mary removed, from Cumming-street, Pentonville, to Judd place West, which may be considered as the extremity of Somers Town. In the former situation, she had occupied a furnished lodging. She had meditated a tour to Italy or Switzerland, and knew not how soon she should set out with that view. Now however she felt herself reconciled to a longer abode in England, probably without exactly knowing why this change had taken place in her mind. She had a quantity of furniture locked up at a broker's ever since her residence in Store-street, and she now found it adviseable to bring it into use. This circumstance occasioned her present removal.

The temporary separation attendant on my little journey, had its effect on the mind of both parties. It gave a space for the maturing of inclination. I believe that, during this interval, each furnished to the other the principal topic of solitary and daily contemplation. Absence bestows a refined and aërial delicacy upon affection, which it with difficulty acquires in any other way. It seems to resemble the communication of spirits, without the medium, or the impediment, of this earthly frame.

When we met again, we met with new pleasure, and, I may add, with a more decisive preference for each other. It was however three weeks longer, before the sentiment which trembled upon the tongue, burst from the lips of either. There was, as I have already said, no period of throes and resolute explanation attendant on the tale. It was friendship melting into love.

Previously to our mutual declaration, each felt half-assured, yet each felt a certain trembling anxiety to have assurance complete.

Mary rested her head upon the shoulder of her lover, hoping to find a heart with which she might safely treasure her world of affection; fearing to commit a mistake, yet, in spite of her melancholy experience, fraught with that generous confidence, which, in a great soul, is never extinguished. I had never loved till now; or, at least, had never nourished a passion to the same growth, or met with an object so consummately worthy.

We did not marry.[1] It is difficult to recommend any thing to indiscriminate adoption, contrary to the established rules and prejudices of mankind; but certainly nothing can be so ridiculous upon the face of it, or so contrary to the genuine march of sentiment, as to require the overflowing of the soul to wait upon a ceremony, and that which, wherever delicacy and imagination exist, is of all things most sacredly private, to blow a trumpet before it, and to record the moment when it has arrived at its climax.

There were however other reasons why we did not immediately marry. Mary felt an entire conviction of the propriety of her conduct. It would be absurd to suppose that, with a heart withered by desertion, she was not right to give way to the emotions of kindness which our intimacy produced, and to seek for that support in friendship and affection, which could alone give pleasure to her heart, and peace to her meditations. It was only about six months since she had resolutely banished every thought of Mr. Imlay; but it was at least eighteen that he ought to have been banished, and would have been banished, had it not been for her scrupulous pertinacity in determining to leave no measure untried to regain him. Add to this, that the laws of etiquette ordinarily laid down in these cases, are essentially absurd, and that the sentiments of the heart cannot submit to be directed by the rule and the square. But Mary had an extreme aversion to be made the topic of vulgar discussion; and, if there be any weakness in this, the dreadful trials through

---

1   For Godwin's early criticism of the institution of marriage, see Appendix B.1.ii; for his revised position, see Appendix E.

which she had recently passed, may well plead in its excuse. She felt that she had been too much, and too rudely spoken of, in the former instance; and she could not resolve to do any thing that should immediately revive that painful topic.

For myself, it is certain that I had for many years regarded marriage with so well-grounded an apprehension, that, notwithstanding the partiality for Mary that had taken possession of my soul, I should have felt it very difficult, at least in the present stage of our intercourse, to have resolved on such a measure. Thus, partly from similar, and partly from different motives, we felt alike in this, as we did perhaps in every other circumstance that related to our intercourse.

I have nothing further that I find it necessary to record, till the commencement of April 1797. We then judged it proper to declare our marriage, which had taken place a little before.[1] The principal motive for complying with this ceremony, was the circumstance of Mary's being in a state of pregnancy. She was unwilling, and perhaps with reason, to incur that exclusion from the society of many valuable and excellent individuals, which custom awards in cases of this sort. I should have felt an extreme repugnance to the having caused her such an inconvenience. And, after the experiment of seven months of as intimate an intercourse as our respective modes of living would admit, there was certainly less hazard to either, in the subjecting ourselves to those consequences which the laws of England annex to the relations of husband and wife. On the sixth of April we entered into possession of a house,[2] which had been taken by us in concert.

In this place I have a very curious circumstance to notice, which I am happy to have occasion to mention, as it tends to expose certain regulations of polished society, of which the absurdity vies with the odiousness. Mary had long possessed the advantage of an acquaintance with many persons of genius, and with others whom the effects of an intercourse with elegant society, combined with a certain portion of information and good sense, sufficed to render amusing companions. She

---

1 On 29 March 1797.
2 No. 29, Polygon Buildings, at the corner of Phoenix and Chalton Streets.

had lately extended the circle of her acquaintance in this respect; and her mind, trembling between the opposite impressions of past anguish and renovating tranquillity, found ease in this species of recreation. Wherever Mary appeared, admiration attended upon her. She had always displayed talents for conversation; but maturity of understanding, her travels, her long residence in France, the discipline of affliction, and the smiling, new-born peace which awaked a corresponding smile in her animated countenance, inexpressibly increased them. The way in which the story of Mr. Imlay was treated in these polite circles, was probably the result of the partiality she excited. These elegant personages were divided between their cautious adherence to forms, and the desire to seek their own gratification. Mary made no secret of the nature of her connection with Mr. Imlay; and in one instance, I well know, she put herself to the trouble of explaining it to a person totally indifferent to her, because he never failed to publish every thing he knew, and, she was sure, would repeat her explanation to his numerous acquaintance. She was of too proud and generous a spirit to stoop to hypocrisy. These persons however, in spite of all that could be said, persisted in shutting their eyes, and pretending they took her for a married woman.

Observe the consequence of this! While she was, and constantly professed to be, an unmarried mother; she was fit society for the squeamish and the formal. The moment she acknowledged herself a wife, and that by a marriage perhaps unexceptionable, the case was altered. Mary and myself, ignorant as we were of these elevated refinements, supposed that our marriage would place her upon a surer footing in the calendar of polished society, than ever. But it forced these people to see the truth, and to confess their belief of what they had carefully been told; and this they could not forgive. Be it remarked, that the date of our marriage had nothing to do with this, that question being never once mentioned during this period. Mary indeed had, till now, retained the name of Imlay which had first been assumed from necessity in France; but its being retained thus long, was purely from the aukwardness that attends the introduction of a change, and not from an apprehension of consequences of this sort. Her scrupulous explicitness as to the nature of her situation, surely sufficed to make the name she bore perfectly immaterial.

It is impossible to relate the particulars of such a story, but in the language of contempt and ridicule. A serious reflection however upon the whole, ought to awaken emotions of a different sort. Mary retained the most numerous portion of her acquaintance, and the majority of those whom she principally valued. It was only the supporters and the subjects of the unprincipled manners of a court, that she lost. This however is immaterial. The tendency of the proceeding, strictly considered, and uniformly acted upon, would have been to proscribe her from all valuable society. And who was the person proscribed? The firmest champion, and, as I strongly suspect, the greatest ornament her sex ever had to boast! A woman, with sentiments as pure, as refined, and as delicate, as ever inhabited a human heart! It is fit that such persons should stand by, that we may have room enough for the dull and insolent dictators, the gamblers and demireps of polished society!

Two of the persons, the loss of whose acquaintance Mary principally regretted upon this occasion, were Mrs. Inchbald and Mrs. Siddons.[1] Their acquaintance, it is perhaps fair to observe, is to be ranked among her recent acquisitions. Mrs. Siddons, I am sure, regretted the necessity, which she conceived to be imposed on her by the peculiarity of her situation, to conform to the rules I have described. She is endowed with that rich and generous sensibility, which should best enable its possessor completely to feel the merits of her deceased friend. She very truly observes, in a letter now before me, that the Travels in Norway were read by no one, who was in possession of "more reciprocity of feeling, or more deeply impressed with admiration of the writer's extraordinary powers."[2]

---

1 Elizabeth Inchbald, *née* Simpson (1753-1821), the former actress, novelist, and playwright, met Godwin in late 1792 and became a close friend and literary colleague until his intimacy with Wollstonecraft began in the spring of 1796. Sarah Siddons, *née* Kemble (1755-1831), the great tragic actress, had known Godwin since 1795.

2 Not further identified.

Mary felt a transitory pang, when the conviction reached her of so unexpected a circumstance, that was rather exquisite. But she disdained to sink under the injustice (as this ultimately was) of the supercilious and the foolish, and presently shook off the impression of the first surprize. That once subsided, I well know that the event was thought of, with no emotions, but those of superiority to the injustice she sustained; and was not of force enough, to diminish a happiness, which seemed hourly to become more vigorous and firm.

I think I may venture to say, that no two persons ever found in each other's society, a satisfaction more pure and refined. What it was in itself, can now only be known, in its full extent, to the survivor. But, I believe, the serenity of her countenance, the increasing sweetness of her manners, and that consciousness of enjoyment that seemed ambitious that every one she saw should be happy as well as herself, were matters of general observation to all her acquaintance. She had always possessed, in an unparalleled degree, the art of communicating happiness, and she was now in the constant and unlimited exercise of it. She seemed to have attained that situation, which her disposition and character imperiously demanded, but which she had never before attained; and her understanding and her heart felt the benefit of it.

While we lived as near neighbours only, and before our last removal, her mind had attained considerable tranquillity, and was visited but seldom with those emotions of anguish, which had been but too familiar to her. But the improvement in this respect, which accrued upon our removal and establishment, was extremely obvious. She was a worshipper of domestic life. She loved to observe the growth and affection between me and her daughter, then three years of age, as well as my anxiety respecting the child not yet born. Pregnancy itself, unequal as the decree of nature seems to be in this respect, is the source of a thousand endearments. No one knew better than Mary how to extract sentiments of exquisite delight, from trifles, which a suspicious and formal wisdom would scarcely deign to remark. A little ride into the country with myself and the child, has sometimes produced a sort of opening of the heart, a general expression of confidence and affectionate soul, a sort of infantine, yet dignified endearment, which those who have felt may understand, but which I should in vain attempt to pourtray.

In addition to our domestic pleasures, I was fortunate enough to introduce her to some of my acquaintance of both sexes, to whom she attached herself with all the ardour of approbation and friendship.

Ours was not an idle happiness, a paradise of selfish and transitory pleasures. It is perhaps scarcely necessary to mention, that, influenced by the ideas I had long entertained upon the subject of cohabitation, I engaged an apartment,[1] about twenty doors from our house in the Polygon, Somers Town, which I designed for the purpose of my study and literary occupations. Trifles however will be interesting to some readers, when they relate to the last period of the life of such a person as Mary. I will add therefore, that we were both of us of opinion, that it was possible for two persons to be too uniformly in each other's society. Influenced by that opinion, it was my practice to repair to the apartment I have mentioned as soon as I rose, and frequently not to make my appearance in the Polygon, till the hour of dinner. We agreed in condemning the notion, prevalent in many situations in life, that a man and his wife cannot visit in mixed society, but in company with each other; and we rather sought occasions of deviating from, than of complying with, this rule. By these means, though, for the most part, we spent the latter half of each day in one another's society, yet we were in no danger of satiety. We seemed to combine, in a considerable degree, the novelty and lively sensation of a visit, with the more delicious and heart-felt pleasures of domestic life.

Whatever may be thought, in other respects, of the plan we laid down to ourselves, we probably derived a real advantage from it, as to the constancy and uninterruptedness of our literary pursuits. Mary had a variety of projects of this sort, for the exercise of her talents, and the benefit of society; and, if she had lived, I believe the world would have had very little reason to

---

1 At No. 17, Evesham Buildings, in Chalton Street.

complain of any remission of her industry. One of her projects, which has been already mentioned, was of a series of Letters on the Management of Infants. Though she had been for some time digesting her ideas on this subject with a view to the press, I have found comparatively nothing that she had committed to paper respecting it. Another project, of longer standing, was of a series of books for the instruction of children. A fragment she left in execution of this project, is inserted in her Posthumous Works.[1]

But the principal work, in which she was engaged for more than twelve months before her decease, was a novel, entitled, The Wrongs of Woman. I shall not stop here to explain the nature of the work, as so much of it as was already written, is now given to the public. I shall only observe that, impressed, as she could not fail to be, with the consciousness of her talents, she was desirous, in this instance, that they should effect what they were capable of effecting. She was sensible how arduous a task it is to produce a truly excellent novel; and she roused her faculties to grapple with it. All her other works were produced with a rapidity, that did not give her powers time fully to expand. But this was written slowly and with mature consideration. She began it in several forms, which she successively rejected, after they were considerably advanced. She wrote many parts of the work again and again, and, when she had finished what she intended for the first part, she felt herself more urgently stimulated to revise and improve what she had written, than to proceed, with constancy of application, in the parts that were to follow.

---

1   "Lessons," *PW* 2: 171-96, *WMW* 4: 467-74.

CHAP. X.

I AM now led, by the course of my narrative, to the last fatal scene of her life. She was taken in labour on Wednesday, the thirtieth of August. She had been somewhat indisposed on the preceding Friday, the consequence, I believe, of a sudden alarm. But from that time she was in perfect health. She was so far from being under any apprehension as to the difficulties of child-birth, as frequently to ridicule the fashion of ladies in England, who keep their chamber for one full month after delivery. For herself, she proposed coming down to dinner on the day immediately following. She had already had some experience on the subject in the case of Fanny;[1] and I cheerfully submitted in every point to her judgment and her wisdom. She hired no nurse. Influenced by ideas of decorum, which certainly ought to have no place, at least in cases of danger, she determined to have a woman to attend her in the capacity of midwife. She was sensible that the proper business of a midwife, in the instance of a natural labour, is to sit by and wait for the operations of nature, which seldom, in these affairs, demand the interposition of art.

At five o'clock in the morning of the day of delivery, she felt what she conceived to be some notices of the approaching labour. Mrs. Blenkinsop,[2] matron and midwife to the Westminster Lying in Hospital, who had seen Mary several times previous to her delivery, was soon after sent for, and arrived about nine. During the whole day Mary was perfectly cheerful. Her pains came on slowly; and, in the morning, she wrote several notes, three addressed to me,[3] who had gone, as usual, to my apartments, for the purpose of study. About two o'clock in the afternoon, she went up to her chamber,—never more to descend.

---

1   See Wollstonecraft to Everina Wollstonecraft, 20 September 1792, *LMW* 262.
2   Properly, Blenkensop. On the significance of Wollstonecraft's preference for a female midwife at a time when man-midwives were the norm, see Jones 193-203.
3   *G&M* 119-20 (see Appendix C.2.ix-xi).

The child[1] was born at twenty minutes after eleven at night. Mary had requested that I would not come into the chamber till all was over, and signified her intention of then performing the interesting office of presenting the new-born child to its father. I was sitting in a parlour; and it was not till after two o'clock on Thursday morning, that I received the alarming intelligence, that the placenta was not yet removed, and that the midwife dared not proceed any further, and gave her opinion for calling in a male practitioner. I accordingly went for Dr. Poignand,[2] physician and man-midwife to the same hospital, who arrived between three and four hours after the birth of the child. He immediately proceeded to the extraction of the placenta, which he brought away in pieces, till he was satisfied that the whole was removed. In that point however it afterwards appeared that he was mistaken.

The period from the birth of the child till about eight o'clock the next morning, was a period full of peril and alarm. The loss of blood was considerable, and produced an almost uninterrupted series of fainting fits. I went to the chamber soon after four in the morning, and found her in this state. She told me some time on Thursday, "that she should have died the preceding night, but that she was determined not to leave me." She added, with one of those smiles which so eminently illuminated her countenance, "that I should not be like Porson,"[3] alluding to the circumstance of that great man having lost his wife, after being only a few months married. Speaking of what she had already passed through, she declared, "that she had never known what bodily pain was before."

On Thursday morning Dr. Poignand repeated his visit. Mary had just before expressed some inclination to see Dr. George Fordyce, a man probably of more science than any other medical professor in England,[4] and between whom and

---

1 Mary Wollstonecraft Godwin (1797-1851), later Shelley, a prolific woman of letters.
2 Mr Louis Poignand, a French surgeon, attempted the standard emergency procedure for the manual removal of the placenta.
3 Richard Porson (1759-1808), regius professor of Greek at Cambridge, married in November 1796 Mrs Lunan, née Perry, who died early the following year.
4 Though a physician, Fordyce was not trained in midwifery.

herself there had long subsisted a mutual friendship. I mentioned this to Dr. Poignand, but he rather discountenanced the idea, observing that he saw no necessity for it, and that he supposed Dr. Fordyce was not particularly conversant with obstetrical cases; but that I would do as I pleased. After Dr. Poignand was gone, I determined to send for Dr. Fordyce. He accordingly saw the patient about three o'clock on Thursday afternoon. He however perceived no particular cause of alarm; and, on that or the next day, quoted, as I am told, Mary's case, in a mixed company, as a corroboration of a favourite idea of his, of the propriety of employing females in the capacity of midwives. Mary "had had a woman, and was doing extremely well."

What had passed however in the night between Wednesday and Thursday, had so far alarmed me, that I did not quit the house, and scarcely the chamber, during the following day. But my alarms wore off, as time advanced. Appearances were more favourable, than the exhausted state of the patient would almost have permitted me to expect. Friday morning therefore I devoted to a business of some urgency,[1] which called me to different parts of the town, and which, before dinner, I happily completed. On my return, and during the evening, I received the most pleasurable sensations from the promising state of the patient. I was now perfectly satisfied that every thing was safe, and that, if she did not take cold, or suffer from any external accident, her speedy recovery was certain.

Saturday was a day less auspicious than Friday, but not absolutely alarming.

Sunday, the third of September, I now regard as the day, that finally decided on the fate of the object dearest to my heart that the universe contained. Encouraged by what I considered as the progress of her recovery, I accompanied a friend in the morning in several calls,[2] one of them as far as Kensington, and

---

1   On Friday 1 September Godwin called on several close colleagues and friends: the publisher George Robinson (1737-1801), the scientific writer William Nicholson (1754-1815), Carlisle, and Mary Hays (Godwin's diary, Abinger MSS, Dep. e. 203).

2   The friend was Basil Montagu (1770-1851), one of Godwin's closest associates in the 1790s and later a distinguished barrister and writer on legal matters. On Sun-

did not return till dinner-time. On my return I found a degree of anxiety in every face, and was told that she had had a sort of shivering fit, and had expressed some anxiety at the length of my absence. My sister and a friend of hers,[1] had been engaged to dine below stairs, but a message was sent to put them off, and Mary ordered that the cloth should not be laid, as usual, in the room immediately under her on the first floor, but in the ground-floor parlour. I felt a pang at having been so long and so unseasonably absent, and determined that I would not repeat the fault.

In the evening she had a second shivering fit, the symptoms of which were in the highest degree alarming. Every muscle of the body trembled, the teeth chattered, and the bed shook under her. This continued probably for five minutes. She told me, after it was over, that it had been a struggle between life and death, and that she had been more than once, in the course of it, at the point of expiring. I now apprehend these to have been the symptoms of a decided mortification,[2] occasioned by the part of the placenta that remained in the womb. At the time however I was far from considering it in that light. When I went for Dr. Poignand, between two and three o'clock on the morning of Thursday, despair was in my heart. The fact of the adhesion of the placenta was stated to me; and, ignorant as I was of obstetrical science, I felt as if the death of Mary was in a manner decided. But hope had re-visited my bosom; and her chearings were so delightful, that I hugged her obstinately to my heart. I was only mortified at what appeared to me a new delay in the recovery I so earnestly longed for. I immediately sent for Dr. Fordyce, who had been with her in the morning, as

day 3 September the two men called on two acquaintances with medical training— Dr John Wolcot (1738-1819), who practised medicine for ten years before turning to a literary career, and Dr Gilbert Thompson (1728-1803), who had been a teacher before practising medicine—but neither man was at home. They also visited the artists John Opie (1761-1807), who had painted Wollstonecraft's portrait in the summer of 1797, and Thomas Lawrence (1769-1830), who had produced a sketch and portrait of Godwin in 1794 and 1795 respectively.

1 Hannah Godwin (d. 1817) and her friend Louisa Jones, who later became Godwin's housekeeper.

2 Wollstonecraft's shivering fit marked the onset of septicaemia.

well as on the three preceding days. Dr. Poignand had also called this morning, but declined paying any further visits, as we had thought proper to call in Dr. Fordyce.

The progress of the disease was now uninterrupted. On Tuesday I found it necessary again to call in Dr. Fordyce in the afternoon, who brought with him Dr. Clarke of New Burlington-street,[1] under the idea that some operation might be necessary. I have already said, that I pertinaciously persisted in viewing the fair side of things; and therefore the interval between Sunday and Tuesday evening, did not pass without some mixture of cheerfulness. On Monday, Dr. Fordyce forbad the child's having the breast, and we therefore procured puppies to draw off the milk. This occasioned some pleasantry of Mary with me and the other attendants. Nothing could exceed the equanimity, the patience and affectionateness of the poor sufferer. I intreated her to recover; I dwelt with trembling fondness on every favourable circumstance; and, as far as it was possible in so dreadful a situation, she, by her smiles and kind speeches, rewarded my affection.

Wednesday was to me the day of greatest torture in the melancholy series. It was now decided that the only chance of supporting her through what she had to suffer, was by supplying her rather freely with wine. This task was devolved upon me. I began about four o'clock in the afternoon. But for me, totally ignorant of the nature of diseases and of the human frame, thus to play with a life that now seemed all that was dear to me in the universe, was too dreadful a task. I knew neither what was too much, nor what was too little. Having begun, I felt compelled, under every disadvantage, to go on. This lasted for three hours. Towards the end of that time, I happened foolishly to ask the servant who came out of the room, "What she thought of her mistress?" she replied, "that, in her judgment, she was going as fast as possible." There are moments, when any creature that lives, has power to drive one into madness. I

---

1 Dr John Clarke (1761–1815), distinguished surgeon and man-midwife of the General Lying-in Hospital in Store Street, Bedford Square, was the author of *Practical Essays on the Management of Pregnancy and Labour; and on the Inflammatory and Febrile Diseases of Lying-in Women* (1793), in which he criticized the use of female midwives because of their alleged lack of education.

seemed to know the absurdity of this reply; but that was of no consequence. It added to the measure of my distraction. A little after seven I intreated a friend to go for Mr. Carlisle, and bring him instantly wherever he was to be found. He had voluntarily called on the patient on the preceding Saturday, and two or three times since. He had seen her that morning, and had been earnest in recommending the wine-diet. That day he dined four miles out of town,[1] on the side of the metropolis, which was furthest from us. Notwithstanding this, my friend returned with him after three-quarters of an hour's absence. No one who knows my friend, will wonder either at his eagerness or success, when I name Mr. Basil Montagu. The sight of Mr. Carlisle thus unexpectedly, gave me a stronger alleviating sensation, than I thought it possible to experience.

Mr. Carlisle left us no more from Wednesday evening, to the hour of her death. It was impossible to exceed his kindness and affectionate attention. It excited in every spectator a sentiment like adoration. His conduct was uniformly tender and anxious, ever upon the watch, observing every symptom, and eager to improve every favourable appearance. If skill or attention could have saved her, Mary would still live. In addition to Mr. Carlisle's constant presence, she had Dr. Fordyce and Dr. Clarke every day. She had for nurses, or rather for friends, watching every occasion to serve her, Mrs. Fenwick, author of an excellent novel, entitled Secrecy, another very kind and judicious lady, and a favourite female servant.[2] I was scarcely ever out of the room. Four friends, Mr. Fenwick, Mr. Basil Montagu, Mr. Marshal, and Mr. Dyson,[3] sat up nearly the whole of

---

1   At Brixton, four miles south-east of London.

2   Eliza Fenwick (1776-1840), whose gothic novel *Secresy; or, The Ruin on the Rock* (1795) (misspelled by Godwin) examined critically the social conditions of women; the other "very kind and judicious lady" was Mary Hays (Kegan Paul 1: 282); the "favourite female servant" was probably "Mary," who is mentioned in letters between Wollstonecraft and Godwin.

3   John Fenwick (d. 1820), radical editor and Godwin's first biographer (see Appendix D.2.iv); James Marshall (d. 1832), translator and index-maker, who met Godwin at Hoxton Dissenting Academy and became a lifelong friend; George Dyson (d. 1822), painter and translator, was subsequently included in Godwin's list of the "four principal oral instructors to whom I feel my mind indebted for improvement" (Kegan Paul 1: 17).

the last week of her existence in the house, to be dispatched, on any errand, to any part of the metropolis, at a moment's warning.

Mr. Carlisle being in the chamber, I retired to bed for a few hours on Wednesday night. Towards morning he came into my room with an account that the patient was surprisingly better. I went instantly into the chamber. But I now sought to suppress every idea of hope. The greatest anguish I have any conception of, consists in that crushing of a new-born hope which I had already two or three times experienced. If Mary recovered, it was well, and I should see it time enough. But it was too mighty a thought to bear being trifled with, and turned out and admitted in this abrupt way.

I had reason to rejoice in the firmness of my gloomy thoughts, when, about ten o'clock on Thursday evening, Mr. Carlisle told us to prepare ourselves, for we had reason to expect the fatal event every moment. To my thinking, she did not appear to be in that state of total exhaustion, which I supposed to precede death; but it is probable that death does not always take place by that gradual process I had pictured to myself; a sudden pang may accelerate his arrival. She did not die on Thursday night.

Till now it does not appear that she had any serious thoughts of dying; but on Friday and Saturday, the two last days of her life, she occasionally spoke as if she expected it. This was however only at intervals; the thought did not seem to dwell upon her mind. Mr. Carlisle rejoiced in this. He observed, and there is great force in the suggestion, that there is no more pitiable object, than a sick man, that knows he is dying. The thought must be expected to destroy his courage, to co-operate with the disease, and to counteract every favourable effort of nature.

On these two days her faculties were in too decayed a state, to be able to follow any train of ideas with force or any accuracy of connection. Her religion, as I have already shown, was not calculated to be the torment of a sick bed; and, in fact, during her whole illness, not one word of a religious cast fell from her lips.

She was affectionate and compliant to the last. I observed on Friday and Saturday nights, that, whenever her attendants recommended to her to sleep, she discovered her willingness to yield, by breathing, perhaps for the space of a minute, in the manner of a person that sleeps, though the effort, from the state of her disorder, usually proved ineffectual.

She was not tormented by useless contradiction. One night the servant, from an error in judgment, teazed her with idle expostulations, but she complained of it grievously, and it was corrected. "Pray, pray, do not let her reason with me," was her expression. Death itself is scarcely so dreadful to the enfeebled frame, as the monotonous importunity of nurses everlastingly repeated.

Seeing that every hope was extinct, I was very desirous of obtaining from her any directions, that she might wish to have followed after her decease. Accordingly, on Saturday morning, I talked to her for a good while of the two children. In conformity to Mr. Carlisle's maxim of not impressing the idea of death, I was obliged to manage my expressions. I therefore affected to proceed wholly upon the ground of her having been very ill, and that it would be some time before she could expect to be well; wishing her to tell me any thing that she would choose to have done respecting the children, as they would now be principally under my care. After having repeated this idea to her in a great variety of forms, she at length said, with a significant tone of voice, "I know what you are thinking of," but added, that she had nothing to communicate to me upon the subject.

The shivering fits had ceased entirely for the two last days. Mr. Carlisle observed that her continuance was almost miraculous, and he was on the watch for favourable appearances, believing it highly improper to give up all hope, and remarking, that perhaps one in a million, of persons in her state might possibly recover. I conceive that not one in a million, unites so good a constitution of body and of mind.

These were the amusements of persons in the very gulph of despair. At six o'clock on Sunday morning, September the tenth, Mr. Carlisle called me from my bed to which I had retired at one, in conformity to my request, that I might not be left to receive all at once the intelligence that she was no more. She expired at twenty minutes before eight.

Her remains were deposited, on the fifteenth of September, at ten o'clock in the morning, in the church-yard of the parish church of St. Pancras, Middlesex.[1] A few of the persons she most esteemed, attended the ceremony;[2] and a plain monument is now erecting on the spot, by some of her friends, with the following inscription:

MARY WOLLSTONECRAFT GODWIN,

AUTHOR OF

A VINDICATION

OF THE RIGHTS OF WOMAN.

BORN, XXVII APRIL MDCCLIX.

DIED, X SEPTEMBER MDCCXCVII.

The loss of the world in this admirable woman, I leave to other men to collect; my own I well know, nor can it be improper to describe it. I do not here allude to the personal pleasures I enjoyed in her conversation: these increased every day, in proportion as we knew each other better, and as our mutual confidence increased. They can be measured only by the treasures of her mind, and the virtues of her heart. But this is a subject

----

1   The church of St Pancras, then a village a mile to the north of London and a short walk across the fields from the Polygon, was the same one in which the pair had been married. On his death in 1836 Godwin was buried there alongside Mary Wollstonecraft, but when Mary Shelley died in 1851, her son Sir Percy Florence Shelley (1819-89) had their remains exhumed and reburied in a common grave with their daughter's, according to her wish, in St Peter's Churchyard, Bournemouth.

2   Godwin himself did not attend the funeral but spent the day at Marshall's lodgings, where he wrote a letter to Carlisle (see Appendix C.3.i).

for meditation, not for words. What I purposed alluding to, was the improvement that I have for ever lost.

We had cultivated our powers (if I may venture to use this sort of language) in different directions; I chiefly an attempt at logical and metaphysical distinction, she a taste for the picturesque. One of the leading passions of my mind has been an anxious desire not to be deceived. This has led me to view the topics of my reflection on all sides; and to examine and re-examine without end, the questions that interest me.

But it was not merely (to judge at least from all the reports of my memory in this respect) the difference of propensities, that made the difference in our intellectual habits. I have been stimulated, as long as I can remember, by an ambition for intellectual distinction; but, as long as I can remember, I have been discouraged, when I have endeavoured to cast the sum of my intellectual value, by finding that I did not possess, in the degree of some other men, an intuitive perception of intellectual beauty. I have perhaps a strong and lively sense of the pleasures of the imagination; but I have seldom been right in assigning to them their proportionate value, but by dint of persevering examination, and the change and correction of my first opinions.

What I wanted in this respect, Mary possessed, in a degree superior to any other person I ever knew. The strength of her mind lay in intuition. She was often right, by this means only, in matters of mere speculation. Her religion, her philosophy, (in both of which the errors were comparatively few, and the strain dignified and generous) were, as I have already said, the pure result of feeling and taste. She adopted one opinion, and rejected another, spontaneously, by a sort of tact, and the force of a cultivated imagination; and yet, though perhaps, in the strict sense of the term, she reasoned little, it is surprising what a degree of soundness is to be found in her determinations. But, if this quality was of use to her in topics that seem the proper province of reasoning, it was much more so in matters directly appealing to the intellectual taste. In a robust and unwavering judgment of this sort, there is a kind of witchcraft; when it decides justly, it produces a responsive vibration in every ingenuous mind. In this sense, my oscillation and scepticism were fixed by her boldness. When a true opinion emanated in this way from another mind, the conviction produced in my own assumed a similar character, instantaneous and firm. This species of intellect probably differs from the other, chiefly in the relation of earlier and later. What the one perceives instantaneously (circumstances having produced in it, either a premature attention to objects of this sort, or a greater boldness of decision) the other receives only by degrees. What it wants, seems to be nothing more than a minute attention to first impressions, and a just appreciation of them; habits that are never so effectually generated, as by the daily recurrence of a striking example.

This light was lent to me for a very short period, and is now extinguished for ever!

While I have described the improvement I was in the act of receiving, I believe I have put down the leading traits of her intellectual character.

THE END.

Appendix A: Biographical Models

1. Jean-Jacques Rousseau, *The Confessions* (1782-9), trans. J. M. Cohen (Harmondsworth: Penguin Books, 1953) 21, 169-70.

i.

I had one brother seven years older than myself, who was learning my father's trade. The extraordinary affection lavished upon me led to his being somewhat neglected, which I consider very wrong. Moreover his education had suffered by this neglect, and he was acquiring low habits even before he arrived at an age at which he could in fact indulge them. He was apprenticed to another master, with whom he took the same liberties as he had taken at home. I hardly ever saw him. Indeed, I can hardly say that I ever knew him, but I did not cease to love him dearly, and he loved me as well as a scoundrel can love. I remember once when my father was correcting him severely and angrily, throwing myself impetuously between them, and clasping my arms tightly around him. Thus I covered him with my body, and received the blows intended for him. So obstinately did I maintain my hold that, either as a result of my tearful cries or so as not to hurt me more than him, my father let him off his punishment. In the end my brother became so bad that he ran away and completely disappeared. We heard some time later that he was in Germany. But he did not write at all, and we had no more news of him after that. So it was that I became an only son.

ii.

These long details of my early youth may well seem extremely childish, and I am sorry for it. Although in certain respects I have been a man since birth, I was for a long time, and still am, a child in many others. I never promised to present the public with a great personage. I promised to depict myself as I am; and to know me in my latter years it is necessary to have known me well in my youth. As objects generally make less impression on me than does the memory of them, and as all my ideas take pictorial form, the first features to engrave themselves on my mind have remained there, and such as have subsequently imprinted themselves have combined with these rather than obliterated them. There is a certain sequence of impressions and ideas which modify those that follow them, and it is necessary to know the original set before passing any judgements. I endeavour in all cases to explain the prime causes, in order to convey the interrelation of results. I should like in some way to make my soul transparent to the reader's eye, and for that purpose I am trying to present it from all points of view, to show it in all lights, and to contrive that none of its movements shall escape his notice, so that he may judge for himself of the principle which has produced them.

If I made myself responsible for the result and said to him, "Such is my character", he might suppose, if not that I am deceiving him, at least that I am deceiving myself. But by relating to him in simple detail all that has happened to me, all that I have done, all that I have felt, I cannot lead him into error, unless wilfully; and even if I wish to, I shall not easily succeed by this method. His task is to assemble these elements and to assess the being who is made up of them. The summing-up must be his, and if he comes to wrong conclusions, the fault will be of his own making. But, with this in view, it is not enough for my story to be truthful, it must be detailed as well. It is not for me to judge of the relative importance of events; I must relate them all, and leave the selection to him. That is the task to which I have devoted myself up to this point with all my courage, and I shall not relax in the sequel. But memories of middle age are always less sharp than those of early youth. So I have begun by making the best possible use of the former. If the latter come back to me in the same strength, impatient readers will perhaps be bored, but I shall not be displeased with my labours. I have only one thing to fear in this enterprise; not that I may say too much or tell untruths, but that I may not tell everything and may conceal the truth.

2. James Boswell, *Life of Johnson* (1791), ed. G.B. Hill, rev'd. L.F. Powell, 6 vols. (Oxford: Oxford University Press, 1934-50) 1: 25-26, 29-33.

To write the Life of him who excelled all mankind in writing the lives of others, and who, whether we consider his extraordinary endowments, or his various works, has been equalled by few in any age, is an arduous, and may be reckoned in me a presumptuous task.

Had Dr. Johnson written his own life, in conformity with the opinion which he has given,[1] that every man's life may be best written by himself; had he employed in the preservation of his own history, that clearness of narration and elegance of language in which he has embalmed so many eminent persons, the world would probably have had the most perfect example of biography that was ever exhibited. But although he at different times, in a desultory manner, committed to writing many particulars of the progress of his mind and fortunes, he never had persevering diligence enough to form them into a regular composition. Of these memorials a few have been preserved; but the greater part was consigned by him to the flames, a few days before his death.

As I had the honour and happiness of enjoying his friendship for upwards of twenty years; as I had the scheme of writing his life constantly in view; as he was well apprised of this circumstance, and from time to time obligingly satisfied my inquiries, by communicating to me the incidents of his early years; as I acquired a facility in recollecting, and was very assiduous in recording, his conversation, of which the extraordinary vigour and vivacity constituted one of the first features of his character; and as I have spared no pains in obtaining materials concerning him, from every quarter where I could discover that they were to be found, and have been favoured with the most liberal communications by his friends; I flatter myself that few biographers have entered upon such a work as this, with more advantages; independent of literary abilities, in which I

---

1 *Idler*, No. 84. BOSWELL.

am not vain enough to compare myself with some great names who have gone before me in this kind of writing ...

If authority be required, let us appeal to Plutarch, the prince of ancient biographers. Οὔτε ταῖς ἐπιφανεστάταις πράξεσι πάντως ἔνεστι δήλωσις ἀρετῆς ἢ κακίας, ἀλλὰ πρᾶγμα βραχὺ πολλάκις, καὶ ῥῆμα, καὶ παιδιά τις ἔμφασιν ἤθους ἐπίησεν μᾶλλον ἢ ἡάχαι ἡυριόνεκροι, <καὶ> παρατάξεις αἱ μέγισται, καὶ πολιορκία πόλεων. "Nor is it always in the most distinguished atchievements that men's virtues or vices may be best discerned; but very often an action of small note, a short saying, or a jest, shall distinguish a person's real character more than the greatest sieges, or the most important battles."[1]

To this may be added the sentiments of the very man whose life I am about to exhibit.

> The business of the biographer is often to pass slightly over those performances and incidents which produce vulgar greatness, to lead the thoughts into domestick privacies, and display the minute details of daily life, where exteriour appendages are cast aside, and men excel each other only by prudence and by virtue. The account of Thuanus is with great propriety said by its authour to have been written, that it might lay open to posterity the private and familiar character of that man, *cujus ingenium et candorem ex ipsius scriptis sunt olim semper miraturi*, whose candour and genius will to the end of time be by his writings preserved in admiration.
>
> There are many invisible circumstances, which whether we read as enquirers after natural or moral knowledge, whether we intend to enlarge our science, or increase our virtue, are more important than publick occurrences. Thus Sallust, the great master of nature, has not forgot in his account of Catiline to remark, that his walk was now quick, and again slow, as an indication of a mind revolving with violent commotion. Thus the story

---

1   Plutarch's Life of Alexander (cap. i.) Langhorne's Translation. BOSWELL.

of Melancthon affords a striking lecture on the value of time, by informing us, that when he had made an appointment, he expected not only the hour, but the minute to be fixed, that the day might not run out in the idleness of suspence; and all the plans and enterprises of De Wit are now of less importance to the world than that part of his personal character, which represents him as careful of his health, and negligent of his life.

But biography has often been allotted to writers, who seem very little acquainted with the nature of their task, or very negligent about the performance. They rarely afford any other account than might be collected from publick papers, but imagine themselves writing a life, when they exhibit a chronological series of actions or preferments; and have so little regard to the manners or behaviour of their heroes, that more knowledge may be gained of a man's real character, by a short conversation with one of his servants, than from a formal and studied narrative, begun with his pedigree, and ended with his funeral.

There are, indeed, some natural reasons why these narratives are often written by such as were not likely to give much instruction or delight, and why most accounts of particular persons are barren and useless. If a life be delayed till interest and envy are at an end, we may hope for impartiality, but must expect little intelligence; for the incidents which give excellence to biography are of a volatile and evanescent kind, such as soon escape the memory, and are transmitted by tradition. We know how few can pourtray a living acquaintance, except by his most prominent and observable particularities, and the grosser features of his mind; and it may be easily imagined how much of this little knowledge may be lost in imparting it, and how soon a succession of copies will lose all resemblance of the original.[1]

---

1   Rambler, No. 60. BOSWELL.

I am fully aware of the objections which may be made to the minuteness on some occasions of my detail of Johnson's conversation, and how happily it is adapted for the petty exercise of ridicule, by men of superficial understanding and ludicrous fancy; but I remain firm and confident in my opinion, that minute particulars are frequently characteristick, and always amusing, when they relate to a distinguished man. I am therefore exceedingly unwilling that any thing, however slight, which my illustrious friend thought it worth his while to express, with any degree of point, should perish.

3. Madame Roland, *An Appeal to Impartial Posterity, by Citizenness Roland, Wife of the Minister of the Home Department; or, A Collection of Pieces Written by her during her Confinement in the Prisons of the Abbey, and St Pélagie. Translated from the French*, 2 vols. (London: J. Johnson, 1795) 1: i-viii, 143-46.

i. Advertisement from the Editor

Citizenness Roland, the wife of a man of science, was persuaded, that the celebrity of a woman ought to be confined to the esteem arising from the practice of domestic virtues. On this account she always refused to publish writings, which would have procured her literary fame. It was even necessary to be intimately acquainted with her, and enjoy her confidence, to be enabled to form a just estimate of her native merit, her acquired talents, and the strength of her character.

Citizenness Roland, the wife of a minister, retained the same principles. She assisted her husband in his political labours, as she had before assisted him in his scientific pursuits, without suffering her name to appear. But her situation was changed. Before she was confined within a narrow circle of friends: now, become the centre of a numerous group, the enthusiastic admiration of her friends, and the invidious malevolence of her enemies, soon combined to give her that renown, which she was still far from seeking.

Imprisoned, calumniated on all sides, having nought but the scaffold before her, citizenness Roland could not avoid seeking the esteem of posterity, to console her for the injustice of her contemporaries, and future glory, as an indemnification for premature death.

Then alone she appeared to separate her reputation from that of her husband: then alone she assumed the pen, to make herself known as an individual, and to furnish materials for history in her own name. It will be seen, however, that the sole desire of her own reputation, and her own fame, determined not her resolution: every page will show, that she was particularly animated with the duty of repelling the calumnious charges accumulated against her husband, and revenging the memory of Roland, if he should not have it in his power, to write or publish his last justification.

The public, already prejudiced in her favour, will judge from a perusal of her writings, whether she were really deserving of the commendations bestowed on her by her friends, and whether she did not deserve the hatred of the villains, who finally condemned her to the block.

Malevolence, assuming the mask of criticism, will endeavour, no doubt, to depreciate this monument erected by a woman to the glory of her sex; but the impartial reader will discover her traits. I will only say, as an excuse for some superfluous relations, and some negligences of style, that citizenness Roland composed the part entitled Historical Memoirs, two thirds of which, and those the most interesting, are lost, in the space of one month, and all the rest in two and twenty days, in the midst of vexations and disquietudes of every kind; and that the manuscript had very few corrections ...

It was my intention, to have given the public the whole of the work at once; but the delays of the press at the present moment, and the observations of some good citizens, have determined me to publish it in parts. There will be four; which will follow each other, as speedily as circumstances will permit. The second will be filled with several detached pieces, respecting the events of the revolution, and the papers that relate to her death, or immediately preceded it. The third and fourth will contain her private life, written precisely after the manner, and with the intentions, of the Confessions of Rousseau: to which will be added some familiar letters, which I have found amongst my papers. I much lament, that I have not a more complete series of her correspondence to publish:[1] it is in the effusions of friendship, that the mind displays itself fully, and our opinions, inclinations, and acquirements, exhibit themselves unveiled. Hence I consider these letters, though at first view they appear to concern only our friendship, tastes, and studies, as necessary supplements to her private memoirs. In them will be seen how ardent a republican she was from the first: and certainly, on the 28th of august, 1792, she could not possibly foresee, that France would become a republic; still less that she was destined, to act a part in it.

Citizenness Roland was very fond of exercising her pen in epistolary writing. She employed it on all subjects with incredible facility, and much grace. As a letter writer she was superiour, in my opinion, to a Sevigné or a Maintenon: because she was far better informed than either of those two celebrated women, and her correspondence consisted of things, not words.

I wish to collect all her letters, that may have been preserved; which I here request them, who are in possession of them, to send me, in the original, free of expense as far as possible; and I propose to publish them at the end of several literary productions of citizenness Roland, which are known to me, and which I think worthy of seeing the light.

Roland, during his retreat, had also composed some historical memoirs; but they were consigned to the flames, the moment the courageous woman, who concealed him, was taken into custody. At the conclusion of his first ministry, he published a collection of pieces, calculated to make known to posterity his conduct in office; and I intend to continue it, by collecting such as relate to his second ministry.

But that I may be enabled to accomplish this object, as well as the preceding one, it is requisite, that the national conven-

---

1 This correspondence was very active for several years, frequently diurnal during her abode at Amiens. My memory retraces imperfectly some very interesting letters. I cannot now find them: possibly they are with several others in the hands of Lanthenas, to whom this correspondence was frequently common. He then considered it, and with reason, as of great importance; but now!—

tion, either by general law, solicited by all the friends of justice, or a private decree, desired by every true friend of liberty, restore to the daughter of Roland the property, to which she has a just claim. I must have liberty to search amongst the papers still under seal at Villefranche, as well as those taken from the house at Paris, after the sale of the furniture by the agents of the national domains. It is the part of all sincere republicans, victims of tyranny, persecuted for their virtues or talents, as Roland and his wife, to favour my wishes with their influence, and promote the restoration of my engaging ward to all her rights.

Let me be permitted to conclude with a single observation, perhaps not unnecessary. This work is, at least at present, the sole fortune of Eudora, the beloved daughter, the only child of Roland. Woe be to the villain who dares to pirate it! For certainly he would not be able to sell one copy of it, yet I would not fail to call down upon him all the vengeance of the law.

The portrait of citizenness Roland, engraved by the worthy Pasquier, the countryman of Roland, and the friend of them both, ought to have been placed at the beginning of the first part; but it cannot be gotten ready for delivery, till the publication of the last.

BOSC.

Paris, germinal 20, in the year of the republic 3 [april 9, 1795]

ii. Madame Roland's execution

Such was the sentence that sent to the scaffold, at thirty-nine years of age, a woman, whose energetic disposition, feeling heart, and cultivated mind, rendered her the delight and admiration of all who knew her. Her death reflects equal glory upon her sex, and disgrace upon her executioners.

It does not belong to me to draw her character: her writings speak; her conduct bears witness in her favour; and history will some day or other revenge the injustice of her contemporaries.

This sentence was preceded, for form's sake, and according to the custom of that horrible tribunal, by a mock trial (*débats*), in which citizenness Roland was not allowed to speak, and in which hired ruffians vomited forth the most palpable calumnies before other ruffians, the execrable tools of Robespierre, so unworthily honoured with the title of judges and jurors. I have not been able to procure the proceedings, which, as every body knows, must not be taken down in writing: but I know that only one person paid a tribute to truth, and that he was some time after sent on that account to the scaffold. I mean the worthy Lecocq, who for eight months only had lived with Roland as a servant, and whose excellent qualities rendered him worthy of a better fate.

Citizenness Roland did not deceive the expectation of her friends. She went to the scaffold with all the calmness of a great mind, superior to the idea of death, and possessing sufficient powers to overcome our natural horror of dissolution. To exhibit a picture of her last moments, I cannot do better than borrow the elegant and impressive pen of Roiusse. The following is the account he gives of them in his work, intituled the *Memoires d'un détenu, pour servir á l'histoire de la tyrannie de Robespierre*; a work which will furnish history with more than one trait, and which will never be read without emotion.

"The blood of the *twenty-two* was still warm when citizenness Roland was brought to the *Conciergerie*. Well aware of the fate that awaited her, her peace of mind continued undisturbed. Though past the prime of life, she was still a charming woman: she was tall and of elegant make; and her countenance was expressive; but her misfortune and a long confinement had left traces of melancholy upon her face, which tempered its natural vivacity. She had the soul of a republican in a body made up of graces, and fashioned by a certain courtly style of politeness. Something more than is generally found in the eyes of women beamed from hers, which were large, black, and full of softness and expression. She often spoke to me at the grate with the freedom and energy of a great man. This republican language, from the mouth of a pretty French woman, for whom the scaffold was getting ready, was one of the miracles of the revolution to which we were not yet accustomed. We all stood listening round her, in a kind of admiration and astonishment. Her conversation was serious without being frigid; and she expressed herself with a choice of words, a harmony, and a cadence, that made of her language a kind of music with which the ear was never satisfied. She always spoke of the members, who had just been put to death, with respect; but she spoke of them at the same time without feminine pity, and even reproached them with not having adopted measures sufficiently energetic. She generally styled them *our friends*, and often sent for Clavieres to converse with him. Sometimes her sex would recover the ascendancy; and it was easy to see, that the recollection of her daughter and her husband had drawn tears from her eyes. This mixture of natural softness, and of fortitude, rendered her only the more interesting. The woman, who waited upon her, said to me one day, '*Before* YOU *she calls up all her courage; but in her own room she sometimes stands for three hours, leaning against her window, and weeping.*' The day she was sent for to be examined, we saw her pass with her usual firmness; but when she returned the tears were glistening in her eyes: she had been treated with so much harshness, and questions so injurious to her honour had been asked her, that her tears and her indignation had burst forth together. A mercenary pedant coldly insulted this woman, celebrated for the excellence of her understanding, and who, at the bar of the National Convention, had reduced her enemies to silence, and forced them to admire the easy graces of her eloquence. She remained eight days at the *Conciergerie*; and in that short time rendered herself dear to all the prisoners, who sincerely deplored her fate.

The day when she was condemned, she was neatly dressed in white; and her long black hair flowed loosely to her waist. She would have moved the most savage heart, but those monsters had no heart at all. Her dress, however, was not meant to excite pity; but was chosen as a symbol of the purity of her mind. After her condemnation, she passed through the wicket with a quick step, bespeaking something like joy; and indicated, by an expressive gesture, that she was condemned to die. She had, for the companion of her misfortune, a man whose fortitude was not equal to her own, but whom she found means to inspire with gaiety, so cheering and so real, that it several times brought a smile upon his face.

At the place of execution, she bowed down before the statue of Liberty, and pronounced these memorable words, *O Liberty, how many crimes are committed in thy name!*

She often said, that her husband would not survive her; and soon after we learned in our dungeons, that the virtuous Roland had killed himself upon the highway, thereby indicating his wish to die irreproachable in regard to courageous hospitality.

My heart, though suffering so many cruel torments in that horrible abode, felt no pang more severely than the one occasioned by the death of this celebrated woman.—The remembrance of her murder, added to that of my unfortunate friends, will make my mind a prey to inconsolable sorrow to the last period of my existence.["]

Appendix B: Works by Godwin

1. From William Godwin, *An Enquiry concerning Political Justice, and its Influence on General Virtue and Happiness* (1793), *Political and Philosophical Writings of William Godwin*, gen. ed. Mark Philp, 7 vols. (London: Pickering and Chatto, 1993) 3: 55-56 (Book 2, Chapter 2); 453-54 (Book 8, Chapter 6).

i. APPENDIX I

OF SUICIDE

Motives of suicide: 1. Escape from pain.—2. Benevolence.—Martyrdom considered.

This reasoning will explain to us the long disputed case of suicide. "Have I a right under any circumstances to destroy myself in order to escape from pain or disgrace?" Probably not. It is perhaps impossible to imagine a situation, that shall exclude the possibility of future life, vigour, and usefulness. The motive assigned for escape is eminently trivial, to avoid pain, which is a small inconvenience; or disgrace, which is an imaginary evil. The example of fortitude in enduring them, if there were no other consideration, would probably afford a better motive for continuing to live.

"Is there then no case in which suicide is a virtue?" What shall we think of the reasoning of Lycurgus, who, when he determined upon a voluntary death, remarked, "that all the faculties a rational being possessed were capable of a moral use, and that, after having spent his life in the service of his country, a man ought, if possible, to render his death a source of additional benefit?" This was the motive of the suicide of Codrus, Leonidas, and Decius. If the same motive prevailed in the much admired suicide of Cato, if he were instigated by reasons purely benevolent, it is impossible not to applaud his intention, even if he were mistaken in the application.

The difficulty is to decide in any instance whether the recourse to a voluntary death can overbalance the usefulness I may exert in twenty or thirty years of additional life. But surely it would be precipitate to decide that there is no such instance. There is a proverb which affirms, "that the blood of the martyrs is the seed of the church." It is commonly supposed that Junius Brutus did right in putting his sons to death in the first year of the Roman republic, and that this action contributed more than any other cause, to generate that energy and virtue for which his country was afterwards so eminently distinguished. The death of Cato produced an effect somewhat similar to this. It was dwelt on with admiration by all the lovers of virtue under the subsequent tyrants of Rome. It seemed to be the lamp from which they caught the sacred flame. Who can tell how much it has contributed to revive that flame in after ages, when it seemed to have been so long extinct?

Let it be observed that all martyrs [μαρῖυρες] are suicides by the very signification of the term. They die for a testimony [μαρῖυριο]; that is, they have a motive for dying. But motives respect only our own voluntary acts, not the violence put upon us by another.

ii. On cohabitation and marriage

This subject of cohabitation is particularly interesting, as it includes in it the subject of marriage. It will therefore be proper to extend our enquiries somewhat further upon this head. Cohabitation is not only an evil as it checks the independent progress of mind; it is also inconsistent with the imperfections and propensities of man. It is absurd to expect that the inclinations of two human beings should coincide through any long period of time. To oblige them to act and live together, is to subject them to some inevitable portion of thwarting, bickering and unhappiness. This cannot be otherwise, so long as man has failed to reach the standard of absolute perfection. The supposition that I must have a companion for life, is the result of a complication of vices. It is the dictate of cowardice, and not of fortitude. It flows from the desire of being loved and esteemed for something that is not desert.

But the evil of marriage as it is practised in European countries lies deeper than this. The habit is, for a thoughtless and romantic youth of each sex to come together, to see each other for a few times and under circumstances full of delusion, and then to vow to each other eternal attachment. What is the consequence of this? In almost every instance they find themselves deceived. They are reduced to make the best of an irretrievable mistake. They are presented with the strongest imaginable temptation to become the dupes of falshood. They are led to conceive it their wisest policy to shut their eyes upon realities, happy if by any perversion of intellect they can persuade themselves that they were right in their first crude opinion of their companion. The institution of marriage is a system of fraud; and men who carefully mislead their judgments in the daily affair of their life, must always have a crippled judgment in every other concern. We ought to dismiss our mistake as soon as it is detected; but we are taught to cherish it. We ought to be incessant in our search after virtue and worth; but we are taught to check our enquiry, and shut our eyes upon the most attractive and admirable objects. Marriage is law, and the worst of all laws. Whatever our understandings may tell us of the person from whose connexion we should derive the greatest improvement, of the worth of one woman and the demerits of another, we are obliged to consider what is law, and not what is justice.

Add to this, that marriage is an affair of property, and the worst of all properties. So long as two human beings are forbidden by positive institution to follow the dictates of their own mind, prejudice is alive and vigorous. So long as I seek to engross one woman to myself, and to prohibit my neighbour from proving his superior desert and reaping the fruits of it, I am guilty of the most odious of all monopolies. Over this imaginary prize men watch with perpetual jealousy, and one man will find his desires and his capacity to circumvent as much excited, as the other is excited to traverse his projects and frustrate his hopes. As long as this state of society continues, philanthropy will be crossed and checked in a thousand ways, and the still augmenting stream of abuse will continue to flow.

The abolition of marriage will be attended with no evils. We are apt to represent it to ourselves as the harbinger of brutal lust and depravity. But it really happens in this as in other cases, that the positive laws which are made to restrain our vices, irritate and multiply them. Not to say, that the same sentiments of justice and happiness which in a state of equal property would destroy the relish for luxury, would decrease our inordinate appetites of every kind, and lead us universally to prefer the pleasures of intellect to the pleasures of sense.

The intercourse of the sexes will in such a state fall under the same system as any other species of friendship. Exclusively of all groundless and obstinate attachments, it will be impossible for me to live in the world without finding one man of a worth superior to that of any other whom I have an opportunity of observing. To this man I shall feel a kindness in exact proportion to my apprehension of his worth. The case will be precisely the same with respect to the female sex. I shall assiduously cultivate the intercourse of that woman whose accomplishments shall strike me in the most powerful manner. "But it may happen that other men will feel for her the same preference that I do." This will create no difficulty. We may all enjoy her conversation; and we shall all be wise enough to consider the sensual intercourse as a very trivial object. This, like every other affair in which two persons are concerned, must be regulated in each successive instance by the unforced consent of either party. It is a mark of the extreme depravity of our present habits, that we are inclined to suppose the sensual intercourse any wise material to the advantages arising from the purest affection. Reasonable men now eat and drink, not from the love of pleasure, but because eating and drinking are essential to our healthful existence. Reasonable men then will propagate their species, not because a certain sensible pleasure is annexed to this action, but because it is right the species should be propagated; and the manner in which they exercise this function will be regulated by the dictates of reason and duty.

2. From William Godwin, *The Enquirer: Reflections on Education, Manners, and Literature. In a Series of Essays* (1797), *Political and Philosophical Writings of William Godwin*, gen. ed. Mark Philp, 7 vols. (London: Pickering and Chatto, 1993) 5: 118-21 (Part 1).

ESSAY X

OF COHABITATION

No subject is of more importance in the morality of private life than that of cohabitation.

Every man has his ill humours, his fits of peevishness and exacerbation. Is it better that he should spend these upon his fellow beings, or suffer them to subside of themselves?

It seems to be one of the most important of the arts of life, that men should not come too near each other, or touch in too many points. Excessive familiarity is the bane of social happiness.

There is no practice to which the human mind adapts itself with greater facility, than that of apologising to itself for its miscarriages, and giving to its errors the outside and appearance of virtues.

The passionate man, who feels himself continually prompted to knock every one down that seems to him pertinacious and perverse, never fails to expatiate upon the efficacy of this mode of correcting error, and to satirise with great vehemence the Utopian absurdity of him who would set them right by ways of mildness and expostulation.

The dogmatist, who, satisfied of the truth of his own opinions, treats all other modes of thinking as absurd, and can practise no forbearance for the prejudices of his neighbours, can readily inform you of the benefit which the mind receives from a rude shock, and the unceasing duration of errors which are only encountered with kindness and reason.

The man who lives in a state of continual waspishness and bickering, easily alleges in his favour the salutary effects which arise from giving pain, and that men are not to be cured of

their follies but by making them severely feel the ill consequences that attend on them.

The only method therefore of accurately trying a maxim of
private morality, is to put out of the question all personal retro-
spect, and every inducement to the apologising for our own
habits, and to examine the subject purely upon its general merits.

In the education of youth no resource is more frequent than
to a harsh tone and a peremptory manner. This child does
amiss, and he is rebuked. If he overlook this treatment, and
make overtures of kindness, the answer is, No, indeed, I shall
take no notice of you, for you have done wrong.

All this is the excess of familiarity.

The tyrant governor practises this, and applauds himself for
his virtue. He reviews his conduct with self-complacence; he
sees in fancy the admirable consequences that will result from
it; and, if it fails, he congratulates himself at least that he has
proceeded with the most exemplary virtue.

He does not know that, through the whole scene, he has
been only indulging the most shameful vices. He had merely
been accumulating a certain portion of black bile, and in this
proceeding he has found a vent for it. There was no atom of
virtue or benevolence in his conduct. He was exercising his
despotism in security, because its object was unable to resist. He
was giving scope to the overflowings of his spite, and the child,
who was placed under his direction, was the unfortunate victim.

There is a reverence that we owe to every thing in human
shape. I do not say that a child is the image of God. But I do
affirm that he is an individual being, with powers of reasoning,
with sensations of pleasure and pain, and with principles of
morality; and that in this description is contained abundant
cause for the exercise of reverence and forbearance. By the system of nature he is placed by himself; he has a claim upon his
little sphere of empire and discretion; and he is entitled to his
appropriate portion of independence.

Violate not thy own image in the person of thy offspring.
That image is sacred. He that does violence to it, is the genuine

blasphemer. The most fundamental of all the principles of morality is the consideration and deference that man owes to man; nor is the helplessness of childhood by any means unentitled to the benefit of this principle. The neglect of it among mankind at large, is the principal source of all the injustice, the revenge, the bloodshed and the wars, that have so long stained the face of nature. It is hostile to every generous and expansive sentiment of our dignity; it is incompatible with the delicious transports of self-complacence.

The object of the harshness thus employed, is to bring the delinquent to a sense of his error. It has no such tendency. It simply proves to him, that he has something else to encounter, beside the genuine consequences of his mistake; and that there are men, who, when they cannot convince by reason, will not hesitate to overbear by force. Pertinacious and persuaded as he was before in the proceeding he adopted, he is confirmed in his persuasion, by the tacit confession which he ascribes to your conduct, of the weakness of your cause. He finds nothing so conspicuous in your behaviour as anger and ill humour, and anger and ill humour have very little tendency to impress upon a prejudiced spectator an opinion of the justice of your cause. The direct result of your proceeding, is to fill him with indignation against your despotism, to inspire him with a deep sense of the indignity to which he is subjected, and to perpetuate in his mind a detestation of the lesson that occasioned his pain.

If we would ascertain the true means of conviction, we have only to substitute in our minds, instead of this child placed under our care, a child with whom we have slight acquaintance, and no vicious habits of familiarity. I will suppose that we have no prejudices against this child, but every disposition to benefit him. I would then ask any man of urbane manners and a kind temper, whether he would endeavour to correct the error of this stranger child, by forbidding looks, harsh tones and severe language?

No; he would treat the child in this respect as he would an adult of either sex. He would know that to inspire hatred to himself and distaste to his lessons, was not the most promising road to instruction. He would endeavour to do justice to his views of the subject in discussion; he would communicate his ideas with all practicable perspicuity; but he would communicate them with every mark of conciliation and friendly attention. He would not mix them with tones of acrimony, and airs of lofty command. He would perceive that such a proceeding had a direct tendency to defeat his purpose. He would deliver them as hints for consideration, not as so many unappealable decisions from a chair of infallibility. But we treat adults of either sex, when upon a footing of undue familiarity, our wife or our comrade, in a great degree as we do children. We lay aside the arts of ingenuous persuasion; we forsake the mildness of expostulation; and we expect them to bow to the despotism of command or the impatience of anger. No sooner have we adopted this conduct, than in this case, as in the case of education, we are perfectly ready to prove that it has every feature of wisdom, profound judgment and liberal virtue.

The ill humour which is so prevalent through all the different walks of life, is the result of familiarity, and consequently of cohabitation. If we did not see each other too frequently, we should accustom ourselves to act reasonably and with urbanity. But, according to a well known maxim, familiarity breeds contempt. The first and most fundamental principle in the intercourse of man with man, is reverence; but we soon cease to reverence what is always before our eyes. Reverence is a certain collectedness of the mind, a pause during which we involuntarily impress ourselves with the importance of circumstances and the dignity of persons. In order that we may properly exercise this sentiment, the occasions for calling it forth towards any particular individual, should be economised and rare. It is true, that genuine virtue requires of us a certain frankness and unreserve. But it is not less true, that it requires of us a quality in some degree contrasted with this, that we set a guard upon the door of our lips, that we carefully watch over our passions, that we never forget what we owe to ourselves, and that we maintain a vigilant consciousness strictly animadverting and commenting upon the whole series of our actions.

These remarks are dictated with all the licence of a sceptical philosophy. Nothing, it will be retorted, is more easy than to raise objections. All that is most ancient and universal among men is liable to attack. It is a vulgar task to destroy; the difficulty is to build.

With this vulgar and humble office however let us rest contented upon the present occasion. Though nothing further should result than hints for other men to pursue, our time perhaps will not have been misemployed.

Every thing human has its advantages and disadvantages. This, which is true as a general maxim, is probably true of cohabitation.

There are two different uses that may flow from these hints. Grant that they prove cohabitation fundamentally an erroneous system. It is then reasonable that they should excite the inquisitive to contemplate and unfold a mode of society, in which it should be superseded. Suppose for a moment that cohabitation is indispensible, or that its benefits outweigh those of an opposite principle. Yet the developing its fundamental evil, is perhaps of all modes of proceeding best calculated to excite us to the reduction and abridgment of this evil, if we cannot annihilate it.

3. From William Godwin, "Essay of History and Romance" (1797), *Political and Philosophical Writings of William Godwin*, gen. ed. Mark Philp, 7 vols. (London: Pickering and Chatto, 1993) 5: 292–95.

The study of individual man can never fail to be an object of the highest importance. It is only by comparison that we come to know any thing of mind or of ourselves. We go forth into the world; we see what man is; we enquire what he was; and when we return home and engage in the solemn act of self-investigation, our most useful employment is to produce the materials we have collected abroad, and, by a sort of magnetism, cause those particulars to start out to view in ourselves, which might otherwise have lain for ever undetected.

But the study of individual history has a higher use than merely as it conduces to the elucidation of science. It is the most fruitful source of activity and motive. If a man were condemned to perfect solitude, he would probably sink into the deepest and most invariable lethargy of soul. If he only associate, as most individuals are destined to do, with ordinary men, he will be in danger of becoming such as they are. It is the contemplation of illustrious men, such as we find scattered through the long succession of ages, that kindles into a flame the hidden fire within us. The excellence indeed of sages, of patriots and poets, as we find it exhibited at the period of their maturity, is too apt to overwhelm and discourage us with its lustre. But history takes away the cause of our depression. It enables us to view minutely and in detail what to the uninstructed eye was too powerful to be gazed at; and, by tracing the progress of the virtuous and the wise from its first dawn to its meridian lustre, shows us that they were composed of materials merely human. It was the sight of the trophies of Mithrades, that recurred to break the infant slumbers of his more illustrious successor. While we admire the poet and the hero, and sympathise with his generous ambition or his ardent exertions, we insensibly imbibe the same spirit, and burn with kindred fires.

But let us suppose that the genuine purpose of history, was to enable us to understand the machine of society, and to direct it to its best purposes. Even here individual history will perhaps be found in point of importance to take the lead of general. General history will furnish us with precedents in abundance, will show us how that which happened in one country has been repeated in another, and may perhaps even instruct us how that which has occurred in the annals of mankind, may under similar circumstances be produced again. But, if the energy of our minds should lead us to aspire to something more animated and noble than dull repetition, if we love the happiness of mankind enough to feel ourselves impelled to explore new and untrodden paths, we must then not rest contented with considering society in a mass, but must analyse the materials of which it is composed. It will be necessary for us to scrutinise the nature of man, before we can pronounce what it is of which social man is capable. Laying aside the generalities of historical abstraction, we must mark the operation of human passions; must observe the empire of motives whether groveling or elevated; and must note the influence that one human being exercises over another, and the ascendancy of the daring and the wise over the vulgar multitude. It is thus, and thus only, that we shall be enabled to add, to the knowledge of the past, a sagacity that can penetrate into the depths of futurity. We shall not only understand those events as they arise, which are no better than old incidents under new names, but shall judge truly of such conjunctures and combinations, their sources and effects, as, though they have never yet occurred, are within the capacities of our nature. He that would prove the liberal and spirited benefactor of his species, must connect the two branches of history together, and regard the knowledge of the individual, as that which can alone give energy and utility to the records of our social existence.

From these considerations one inference may be deduced, which constitutes perhaps the most important rule that can be laid down respecting the study of history. This is, the wisdom of studying it in detail, and not in abridgment. The prolixity of dullness is indeed contemptible. But the copiousness of wisdom and genius is treasure inestimable. To read a history which, expanding itself through several volumes, treats only of a short period, is true economy. To read historical abridgments, in which each point of the subject is touched upon only, and immediately dismissed, is a wanton prodigality of time worthy only of folly or of madness.

The figures which present themselves in such a history, are like the groupes that we sometimes see placed in the distance of a landscape, that are just sufficiently marked to distinguish the man from the brute, or the male dress from the female, but are totally unsusceptible of discrimination of form or expression of sentiment. The men I would study upon the canvas of history, are men worth the becoming intimately acquainted with.

It is in history, as it is in life. Superficial acquaintance is nothing. A scene incessantly floating, cannot instruct us; it can scarcely become a source of amusement to a cultivated mind. I would stop the flying figures, that I may mark them more nearly. There must be an exchange of real sentiments, or an investigation of subtle peculiarities, before improvement can be the result. There is a magnetical virtue in man; but there must be friction and heat, before the virtue will operate.

Pretenders indeed to universal science, who examine nothing, but imagine they understand every thing, are ready from the slightest glance to decypher the whole character. Not so the genuine scholar. His curiosity is never satiated. He is ever upon the watch for further, and still further particulars. Trembling for his own fallibility and frailty, he employs every precaution to guard himself against them.

There are characters in history that may almost be said to be worth an eternal study. They are epitomes of the world, of its best and most exalted features, purified from their grossness. I am not contented to observe such a man upon the public stage, I would follow him into his closet. I would see the friend and the father of a family, as well as the patriot. I would read his works and his letters, if any remain to us. I would observe the turn of his thoughts and the character of his phraseology. I would study his public orations. I would collate his behaviour in prosperity with his behaviour in adversity. I should be glad to know the course of his studies, and the arrangement of his time. I should rejoice to have, or to be enabled to make, if that were possible, a journal of his ordinary and minutest actions. I believe I should be better employed in thus studying one man, than in perusing the abridgment of Universal History in sixty volumes. I would rather be acquainted with a few trivial particulars of the actions and dispositions of Virgil and Horace, than with the lives of many men, and the history of many nations.

Appendix C: Letters

1. From Mary Wollstonecraft, *Letters to Imlay, The Works of Mary Wollstonecraft*, ed. Janet Todd and Marilyn Butler, 7 vols. (London: Pickering and Chatto, 1989) 6: 382, 401–02, 408–10, 430–31, 437–38.

i. Letter XVI [Paris, 14 January 1794]

Tuesday Morning.

I seize this opportunity to inform you, that I am to set out on Thursday with Mr ————, and hope to tell you soon (on your lips) how glad I shall be to see you. I have just got my passport, so I do not foresee any impediment to my reaching H————, to bid you good-night next Friday in my new apartment—where I am to meet you and love, in spite of care, to smile me to sleep—for I have not caught much rest since we parted.

You have, by your tenderness and worth, twisted yourself more artfully round my heart, than I supposed possible.—Let me indulge the thought, that I have thrown out some tendrils to cling to the elm by which I wish to be supported.—This is talking a new language for me!—But, knowing that I am not a parasite-plant, I am willing to receive the proofs of affection, that every pulse replies to, when I think of being once more in the same house with you.—God bless you!

Yours truly
★★★★

ii. Letter XXXVI [Paris, 1795]

Feb. 10.

You talk of "permanent views and future comfort"—not for me, for I am dead to hope. The inquietudes of the last winter have finished the business, and my heart is not only broken, but my constitution destroyed. I conceive myself in a galloping consumption, and the continual anxiety I feel at the thought of leaving my child, feeds the fever that nightly devours me. It is on her account that I again write to you, to conjure you, by all that you hold sacred, to leave her here with the German lady you may have heard me mention! She has a child of the same age, and they may be brought up together, as I wish her to be brought up. I shall write more fully on the subject. To facilitate this, I shall give up my present lodgings, and go into the same house. I can live much cheaper there, which is now become an object. I have had 3000 livres from ————, and I shall take one more, to pay my servant's wages, etc. and then I shall endeavour to procure what I want by my own exertions. I shall entirely give up the acquaintance of the Americans.

———— and I have not been on good terms a long time. Yesterday he very unmanlily exulted over me, on account of your determination to stay. I had provoked it, it is true, by some asperities against commerce, which have dropped from me, when we have argued about the propriety of your remaining where you are; and it is no matter, I have drunk too deep of the bitter cup to care about trifles.

When you first entered into these plans, you bounded your views to the gaining of a thousand pounds. It was sufficient to have procured a farm in America, which would have been an independence. You find now that you did not know yourself, and that a certain situation in life is more necessary to you than you imagined—more necessary than an uncorrupted heart— For a year or two, you may procure yourself what you call pleasure; eating, drinking, and women; but, in the solitude of declining life, I shall be remembered with regret—I was going to say with remorse, but checked my pen.

As I have never concealed the nature of my connection with you, your reputation will not suffer. I shall never have a confident: I am content with the approbation of my own mind; and, if there be a searcher of hearts, mine will not be despised. Reading what you have written relative to the desertion of women, I have often wondered how theory and practice could be so different, till I recollected, that the sentiments of passion, and the resolves of reason, are very distinct. As to my sisters, as you are so continually hurried with business, you need not write to them—I shall, when my mind is calmer. God bless you! Adieu!

****

This has been such a period of barbarity and misery, I ought not to complain of having my share. I wish one moment that I had never heard of the cruelties that have been practised here, and the next envy the mothers who have been killed with their children. Surely I had suffered enough in life, not to be cursed with a fondness, that burns up the vital stream I am imparting. You will think me mad: I would I were so, that I could forget my misery—so that my head or heart would be still.—

iii. Letter XLIV [Hull, 1795]

Friday, June 12.

I have just received yours dated the 9th, which I suppose was a mistake, for it could scarcely have loitered so long on the road. The general observations which apply to the state of your own mind, appear to me just, as far as they go; and I shall always consider it as one of the most serious misfortunes of my life, that I did not meet you, before satiety had rendered your senses so fastidious, as almost to close up every tender avenue of senti- ment and affection that leads to your sympathetic heart. You have a heart, my friend, yet, hurried away by the impetuosity of inferior feelings, you have sought in vulgar excesses, for that gratification which only the heart can bestow.

The common run of men, I know, with strong health and gross appetites, must have variety to banish *ennui*, because the imagination never lends its magic wand, to convert appetite into love, cemented by according reason.—Ah! my friend, you know not the ineffable delight, the exquisite pleasure, which arises from a unison of affection and desire, when the whole soul and senses are abandoned to a lively imagination, that renders every emotion delicate and rapturous. Yes; these are emotions, over which satiety has no power, and the recollection of which, even disappointment cannot disenchant; but they do not exist without self-denial. These emotions, more or less strong, appear to me to be the distinctive characteristic of genius, the foundation of taste, and of that exquisite relish for the beauties of nature, of which the common herd of eaters and drinkers and *child-begeters*, certainly have no idea. You will smile at an observation that has just occurred to me:—I consider those minds as the most strong and original, whose imagination acts as the stimulus to their senses.

Well! you will ask, what is the result of all this reasoning? Why I cannot help thinking that it is possible for you, having great strength of mind, to return to nature, and regain a sanity of constitution, and purity of feeling—which would open your heart to me.—I would fain rest there!

Yet, convinced more than ever of the sincerity and tenderness of my attachment to you, the involuntary hopes, which a determination to live has revived, are not sufficiently strong to dissipate the cloud, that despair has spread over futurity. I have looked at the sea, and at my child, hardly daring to own to myself the secret wish, that it might become our tomb; and that the heart, still so alive to anguish, might there be quieted by death. At this moment ten thousand complicated sentiments press for utterance, weigh on my heart, and obscure my sight.

Are we ever to meet again? and will you endeavour to render that meeting happier than the last? Will you endeavour to restrain your caprices, in order to give vigour to affection, and to give play to the checked sentiments that nature intended should expand your heart? I cannot indeed, without agony, think of your bosom's being continually contaminated; and bitter are the tears which exhaust my eyes, when I recollect why my child and I are forced to stray from the asylum, in which, after so many storms, I had hoped to rest, smiling at angry fate.—These are not common sorrows; nor can you perhaps conceive, how much active fortitude it requires to labour perpetually to blunt the shafts of disappointment.

Examine now yourself, and ascertain whether you can live in something-like a settled stile. Let our confidence in future be unbounded; consider whether you find it necessary to sacrifice me to what you term "the zest of life;" and, when you have once a clear view of your own motives, of your own incentive to action, do not deceive me!

The train of thoughts which the writing of this epistle awoke, makes me so wretched, that I must take a walk, to rouse and calm my mind. But first, let me tell you, that, if you really wish to promote my happiness, you will endeavour to give me as much as you can of yourself. You have great mental energy; and your judgment seems to me so just, that it is only the dupe of your inclination in discussing one subject.

The post does not go out to-day. To-morrow I may write more tranquilly. I cannot yet say when the vessel will sail in which I have determined to depart.

Saturday Morning.

Your second letter reached me about an hour ago. You were certainly wrong, in supposing that I did not mention you with respect; though, without my being conscious of it, some sparks of resentment may have animated the gloom of despair—Yes; with less affection, I should have been more respectful. However the regard which I have for you, is so unequivocal to myself, I imagine that it must be sufficiently obvious to every body else. Besides, the only letter I intended for the public eye was to —————, and that I destroyed from delicacy before you saw them, because it was only written (of course warmly in your praise) to prevent any odium being thrown on you.

I am harrassed by your embarrassments, and shall certainly use all my efforts, to make the business terminate to your satisfaction in which I am engaged.

My friend—my dearest friend—I feel my fate united to yours by the most sacred principles of my soul, and the yearns of—yes, I will say it—a true, unsophisticated heart.

Yours most truly

★★★★

If the wind be fair, the captain talks of sailing on Monday; but I am afraid I shall be detained some days longer. At any rate, continue to write, (I want this support) till you are sure I am where I cannot expect a letter; and, if any should arrive after my departure, a gentleman (not Mr. —————'s friend, I promise you) from whom I have received great civilities, will send them after me.

Do write by every occasion! I am anxious to hear how your affairs go on; and, still more, to be convinced that you are not separating yourself from us. For my little darling is calling papa, and adding her parrot word—Come, Come! And will you not come, and let us exert ourselves?—I shall recover all my energy, when I am convinced that my exertions will draw us more closely together. One more adieu!

iv. Letter LXIX [London, c. 10 October 1795]

I write to you now on my knees; imploring you to send my child and the maid with —————, to Paris, to be consigned to the care of Madame —————, rue —————, section de ————. Should they be removed, ————— can give their direction.

Let the maid have all my clothes, without distinction.

Pray pay the cook her wages, and do not mention the confession which I forced from her—a little sooner or later is of no consequence. Nothing but my extreme stupidity could have rendered me blind so long. Yet, whilst you assured me that you had no attachment, I thought we might still have lived together.

I shall make no comments on your conduct; or any appeal to the world. Let my wrongs sleep with me! Soon, very soon shall I be at peace. When you receive this, my burning head will be cold.

I would encounter a thousand deaths, rather than a night like the last. Your treatment has thrown my mind into a state of chaos; yet I am serene. I go to find comfort, and my only fear is, that my poor body will be insulted by an endeavour to recal my hated existence. But I shall plunge into the Thames where there is the least chance of my being snatched from the death I seek.

God bless you! May you never know by experience what you have made me endure. Should your sensibility ever awake, remorse will find its way to your heart; and, in the midst of business and sensual pleasure, I shall appear before you, the victim of your deviation from rectitude.

★★★★

v. Letter LXXVIII [London, c. December 1795]

You must do as you please with respect to the child.—I could wish that it might be done soon, that my name may be no more mentioned to you. It is now finished.—Convinced that you have neither regard nor friendship, I disdain to utter a reproach, though I have had reason to think, that the "forbearance" talked of, has not been very delicate.—It is however of no consequence.—I am glad you are satisfied with your own conduct.

I now solemnly assure you, that this is an eternal farewel.—Yet I flinch not from the duties which tie me to life.

That there is "sophistry" on one side or other, is certain; but now it matters not on which. On my part it has not been a question of words. Yet your understanding or mine must be strangely warped—for what you term "delicacy," appears to me to be exactly the contrary. I have no criterion for morality, and have thought in vain, if the sensations which lead you to follow an ancle or step, be the sacred foundation of principle and affection. Mine has been of a very different nature, or it would not have stood the brunt of your sarcasms.

The sentiment in me is still sacred. If there be any part of me that will survive the sense of my misfortunes, it is the purity of my affections. The impetuosity of your senses, may have led you to term mere animal desire, the source of principle; and it may give zest to some years to come.—Whether you will always think so, I shall never know.

It is strange that, in spite of all you do, something like conviction forces me to believe, that you are not what you appear to be.

I part with you in peace.

2. From *Godwin & Mary: Letters of William Godwin and Mary Wollstonecraft*, ed. Ralph M. Wardle (Lincoln and London: University of Nebraska Press, 1967) 14-16, 16-17, 18-19, 19-20, 24-25, 27-29, 35, 119-20.

i. Mary to Godwin [17 August 1796]

I have not lately passed so painful a night as the last. I feel that I cannot speak clearly on the subject to you, let me then briefly explain myself now I am alone. Yet, struggling as I have been a long time to attain peace of mind (or apathy) I am afraid to trace emotions to their source, which border on agony.

Is it not sufficient to tell you that I am thoroughly out of humour with myself? Mortified and humbled, I scarcely know why—still, despising false delicacy I almost fear that I have lost sight of the true. Could a wish have transported me to France or Italy, last night, I should have caught up my Fanny and been off in a twinkle, though convinced that it is my mind, not the place, which requires changing. My imagination is for ever betraying me into fresh misery, and I perceive that I shall be a child to the end of the chapter. You talk of the roses which grow profusely in every path of life—I catch at them; but only encounter the thorns.—

I would not be unjust for the world—I can only say that you appear to me to have acted injudiciously; and that full of your own feelings, little as I comprehend them, you forgot mine—or do not understand my character. It is my turn to have a fever to day—I am not well—I am hurt—But I mean not to hurt you. Consider what has passed as a fever of your imagination; one of the slight mortal shakes to which you are liable—and I—will become again a *Solitary Walker*. Adieu! I was going to add God bless you!—

Wednesday Morning

ii. Godwin to Mary [17 August 1796]

How shall I answer you? In one point we sympathize; I had rather at this moment talk to you on paper than in any other mode. I should feel ashamed in seeing you.

You do not know how honest I am. I swear to you that I told you nothing but the strict & literal truth, when I described to you the manner in which you set my imagination on fire on Saturday. For six & thirty hours I could think of nothing else. I longed inexpressibly to have you in my arms. Why did not I come to you? I am a fool. I feared still that I might be deceiving myself as to your feelings, & that I was feeding my mind with groundless presumptions. I determined to suffer the point to arrive at its own denouement. I was not aware that the fervour of my imagination was exhausting itself. Yet this, I believe, is no uncommon case.

Like any other man, I can speak only of what I know. But this I can boldly affirm, that nothing that I have seen in you would in the slightest degree authorise the opinion, that, *in despising the false delicacy, you have lost sight of the true.* I see nothing in you but what I respect & adore.

I know the acuteness of your feelings, & there is perhaps nothing upon earth that would give me so pungent a remorse, as to add to your unhappiness.

Do not hate me. Indeed I do not deserve it. Do not cast me off. Do not become again a *solitary walker.* Be just to me, & then, though you will discover in me much that is foolish and censurable, yet a woman of your understanding will still regard me with some partiality.

Upon consideration I find in you one fault, & but one. You have the feelings of nature, & you have the honesty to avow them. In all this you do well. I am sure you do. But do not let them tyrannise over you. Estimate every thing at its just value. It is best that we should be friends in every sense of the word; but in the mean time let us be friends.

Suffer me to see you. Let us leave every thing else to its own course. My imagination is not dead, I suppose, though it sleeps. But, be it as it will, I will torment you no more. I will be your friend, the friend of your mind, the admirer of your excellencies. All else I commit to the disposition of futurity, glad, if completely happy; passive & silent in this respect, while I am not so.

Be happy. Resolve to be happy. You deserve to be so. Every

thing that interferes with it, is weakness & wandering; & a woman, like you, can, must, shall, shake it off. Afford, for instance, no food for the morbid madness, & no triumph to the misanthropical gloom, of your afternoon visitor.[1] Call up, with firmness, the energies, which, I am sure, you so eminently possess.

Send me word that I may call on you in a day or two. Do you not see, while I exhort you to be a philosopher, how painfully acute are my own feelings? I need some soothing, though I cannot ask it from you.

Wednesday

iii. Mary to Godwin [17 August 1796]

I like your last—may I call it *love* letter? better than the first—and can I give you a higher proof of my esteem than to tell you, the style of my letter will whether I will or no, that it has calmed my mind—a mind that had been painfully active all the morning, haunted by old sorrows that seemed to come forward with new force to sharpen the present anguish—Well! well—it is almost gone—I mean all my unreasonable fears—and a whole train of tormentors, which you have routed—I can scarcely describe to you their ugly shapes so quickly do they vanish—and let them go, we will not bring them back by talking of them. You may see me when you please. I shall take this letter, just before dinner time, to ask you to come and dine with me, and Fanny, whom I have shut out to day. Should you be engaged come in the evening. Miss H—— seldom stays late, never to supper—or to morrow—as you wish—I shall be content—You say you want soothing—will it sooth you to tell you the truth? I cannot hate you—I do not think you deserve it. Nay, more I cannot withhold my friendship from you, and will try to merit yours, that *necessity* may bind you to me.

One word of my ONLY fault—our imaginations have been rather differently employed—I am more of a painter than you—I like to tell the truth, my taste for the picturesque has

---

1   Mary Hays.

been more cultivated—I delight to view the grand scenes of nature and the various changes of the human countenance— Beautiful as they are animated by intelligence or sympathy— My affections have been more exercised than yours, I believe, and my senses are quick, without the aid of fancy—yet tenderness always prevails, which inclines me to be angry with myself, when I do not animate and please those I [love?].

Now will you not be a good boy, and smile upon me, I dine at half past four—you ought to come and give me an appetite for my dinner, as you deprived me of one for my breakfast.

Mary

Two O'Clock

iv. Godwin to Mary [17 August 1796]

I left a letter for you at one o'clock. It was not till two hours later, that I suddenly became awake, & perceived the mistake I had made. Intent upon an idea I had formed in my own mind of furtive pleasure, I was altogether stupid & without intelligence as to your plan of staying, which it was morally impossible should not have given life to the dead.

Perhaps you will not believe that I could have been so destitute of understanding. It seems indeed incredible. I think however you will admit, that it is no proof of indifference to a subject, when a man's thoughts are so obstinately occupied by one view of it, that, though you were to blow a trumpet in his ear, you would not succeed in giving him an apprehension of any other.

I have now only left to apologise for my absurdity, which I do even with self-abhorrence. The mistake being detected, it is for you to decide whether it is too late to repair it. For my own part, I have not the presumption to offer even a word to implore your forgiveness.

Wednesday

I had written the above before you called. I hesitate now whether to deliver it. You say you are calmed, & I would not for the world change that state of mind for a state of anguish. My disposition however to utter all I think decides me. Take no notice of it for the present.

v. Mary to Godwin [26 August 1796]

I seem to want encouragement—I therefore send you my M.S. though not all I have written. Say when—or where, I am to see you Godwin.

Friday

vi. Mary to Godwin [27 August 1796]

The wind whistles through my trees.
    What do you say to our walk?
    Should the weather continue uncertain *suppose* you were to bring your tragedy here—and we shall be so snug—yet, you are such a kind creature, that I am afraid to express a preference, lest you should think of pleasing me rather than yourself—and is it not the same thing?—for I am never so well pleased with myself, as when I please you—I am not sure that please is the exact word to explain my sentiments—May I trust you to search in your own heart for the proper one?

                                                                    Mary

Saturday Morning

vii. Mary to Godwin [4 September 1796]

Labouring all the morning, in vain, to overcome an oppression of spirits, which some things you uttered yesterday, produced; I will try if I can shake it off by describing to you the nature of the feelings you excited.
    I allude to what you remarked, relative to my manner of writing—that there was a radical defect in it— a worm in the bud—&c What is to be done, I must either disregard your opinion, think it unjust, or throw down my pen in despair; and that would be tantamount to resigning existence; for at fifteen I

resolved never to marry for interested motives, or to endure a life of dependence. You know not how painfully my sensibility, call it false if you will, has been wounded by some of the steps I have been obliged to take for others. I have even now plans at heart, which depend on my exertions; and my entire confidence in Mr. Imlay plunged me into some difficulties, since we parted, that I could scarcely away with. I know that many of my cares have been the natural consequence of what, nine out of ten would [have] termed folly—yet I cannot coincide in the opinion, without feeling a contempt for mankind. In short, I must reckon on doing some good, and getting the money I want, by my writings, or go to sleep for ever. I shall not be content merely to keep body and soul together—By what I have already written Johnson, I am sure, has been a gainer. And, for I would wish you to see my heart and mind just as it appears to myself, without drawing any veil of affected humility over it, though this whole letter is a proof of painful diffidence, I am compelled to think that there is some thing in my writings more valuable, than in the productions of some people on whom you bestow warm elogiums—I mean more mind— denominate it as you will—more of the observations of my own senses, more of the combining of my own imagination— the effusions of my own feelings and passions than the cold workings of the brain on the materials procured by the senses and imagination of other writers—

I am more out of patience with myself than you can form any idea of, when I tell you that I have scarcely written a line to please myself (and very little with respect to quantity) since you saw my M.S. I have been endeavouring all this morning; and with such dissatisfied sensations I am almost afraid to go into company—But these are idle complaints to which I ought not to give utterance, even to you—I must then have done—

Mary

Sunday Morning

viii. Mary to Godwin [15 September 1796]

The virulence of my poor Fanny's distemper begins to abate, and with it my anxiety—yet this is not, I believe, a day sufficiently to be depended on, to tempt us to set out in search of rural felicity. We must then woo philosophy *chez vous* ce soir, nest-ce pas; for I do not like to lose my Philosopher even in the lover.

You are to give me a lesson this evening—And, a word in your ear, I shall not be very angry if you sweeten grammatical disquisitions after the Miltonic mode—Fancy, at this moment, has turned a conjunction into a kiss; and the sensation steals o'er my senses. N'oublierez pas, I pray thee, the graceful pauses, I am alluding to; nay, anticipating—yet now you have led me to discover that I write worse, than I thought I did, there is no stopping short—I must improve, or be dissatisfied with myself—

I felt hurt, I can scarcely trace why, last night, at your wishing time to roll back. The observation wounded the delicacy of my affection, as well as my tenderness—Call me not fastidious; I want to have such a firm *throne* in your heart, that even your imagination shall not be able to hurl me from it, be it ever so active.

Mary

ix. Mary to Godwin [30 August 1797]

I have no doubt of seeing the animal to day; but must wait for Mrs Blenkinsop to guess at the hour—I have sent for her—Pray send me the news paper—I wish I had a novel, or some book of sheer amusement, to excite curiosity, and while away the time—Have you any thing of the kind?

x. Mary to Godwin [30 August 1797]

Mrs. Blenkensop tells me that Every thing is in a fair way, and that there is no fear of the event being put off till another day—

Still, *at present*, she thinks, I shall not immediately be freed from my load—I am very well—Call before dinner time, unless you receive another message from me—

xi. Mary to Godwin [30 August 1797]

Mrs. Blenkinsop tells me that I am in the most natural state, and can promise me a safe delivery—But that I must have a little patience

3. Letters Transcribed from the Abinger Manuscripts

i. Godwin to Anthony Carlisle, unsigned, 15 September 1797, Abinger MSS, Dep. b. 215/2.

My dear Carlisle,

I am here sitting alone in Mr Marshal's lodgings during my wife's funeral. My mind is extremely sunk & languid. But I husband my thoughts, & shall do very well. I have been but once since you saw me, in a train of thought that gave me alarm. One of my wife's books now lies near me, but I avoid opening it. I took up a book on the education of children, but that impressed me too forcibly with my forlorn & disabled state with respect to the two poor animals left under my protection, & I threw it aside.

Nothing could be more soothing to my mind than to dwell in a long letter upon her virtues & accomplishments, & our mutual happiness past & in prospect. But the attractions of this subject are delusive, & I dare not trust myself with it.

I may dwell however with perfect safety upon your merits & kindness, & the indelible impression they have left on my mind. Your generous & unintermitted attendance upon the dear deceased, constituted the greatest consolation it was possible for me to receive, at that dreadful period when I most needed consolation. I may say to you on paper what I observed to you in our last interview, that I never, in the whole course of my life, met with the union of so clear & capacious an understanding, with so much goodness of heart & sweetness of manners.

It is pleasing to be loved by those we feel ourselves impelled to love. It is inexpressibly gratifying, where we find those qualities that most call forth our affections, to be regarded by that person with some degree of a correspondent feeling. If you have any of that kind of consolation in store for me, be at the pains to bestow it. But, above all, be severely sincere. I ought to be acquainted with my own defects, & to trace their nature in the effects they produce.

Yours, with fervent admiration & regard,

Sep. 15, 1797

ii. [Joseph Johnson], "A Few Facts," n.d., Abinger MSS, Dep. b. 210/3.

Mary came from Ireland in 1787 (Aug^t) & resided with me having determined to try to live by literary exertions & be independent.

She entered upon her house in George St. at Michaelmas following & continued there till Michaelmas 1791.

Here she wrote the Rights of Woman, Mary, Original Stories, a translation from ye dutch of young Grandison was put into her hands which she almost rewrote, translated Necker on religious opinions, compiled the Female Reader, introducing some original pieces, & prefixed a preface to it. Begun a novel under the title of the Cave of Fancy, what she wrote of this must be with her papers. Wrote many articles in the Anal^l Review. Answer to Burke. Elements of Morality from the German which she first studied here, and a translation of Lavater's Physiognomy from the french. This last has not been pub^d.

Her brothers & sisters were occasionally with her, when they were unsettled it was their home, & she took every method to improve & prepare them for respectable situations. She consulted with Mr Barlow[1] on ye probability of getting a farm in America for Charles, which was determined upon & he was placed with a farmer here for instructions, he left England the latter end of 1792. James who had been at sea was sent to Woolwich for a few months to be under Mr Bonnycastle & afterwards on board Ld Hood's fleet as a midshipman, where he was presently made a lieutenant. Much of the instructions which all of them obtained were obtained under her own roof, & most if not all the situations which her sisters had were procured by her own exertions. In the beginning of 1788 she sent Everina to Paris for improvement in ye fr. language.

During her stay in George Street she spent many of her afternoons & most of her evenings with me, she was incapable of disguise, whatever was the state of her mind it appeared when she entered, & the turn of conversation might easily be guessed; when harrassed, which was very often ye case, she was relieved by unbosoming herself & generally returned home calm, frequently in spirits. F.[2] was frequently with us.

In a part of this period, which certainly was the most active of her life, she had the care of her father's estate, which was attended with no little trouble to both of us. She could not during this time I think expend less than £200 upon her brothers & sisters.

At Michaelmas 1791 she went to Store Street & continued till Decr 1792, here her exertions seem to have been palsied, you know the cause. I saw her often but no[t] so frequently from ye distance.

In Decr she went to Paris.

---

1 Joel Barlow (1754-1812), American poet and political writer of republican views, went to Europe in 1788 as the agent for a land company, and visited London in 1791.
2 Fuseli.

iii. Eliza Fenwick to Everina Wollstonecraft, 12 September 1797, Abinger MSS, Dep. b. 215/2.

Sept. 12th 1797

I am a stranger to you, Miss Wolstoncraft & at present greatly enfeebled both in mind and body: but when Mr Godwin desired that I would inform you of the death of his most beloved & most excellent wife I was willing to undertake the task because it is some consolation to render him the slightest service & because my thoughts perpetually dwell upon her virtues & her loss. Mr Godwin himself cannot upon this occasion write to you.

Mrs Godwin died on Sunday Sept. 10th about eight in the morning. I was with her at the time of her delivery & with very little intermission untill the moment of her death. Every skilful effort that medical knowledge of the highest class could make was exerted to save her. It is not possible to describe the unremitting & devoted attentions of her Husband. Nor is it easy to give you an adequate idea of the affectionate zeal of many of her friends who were on the watch night & day to seize upon an opportunity of contributing towards her recovery or to lessen her sufferings.

No woman was ever more happy in marriage than Mrs Godwin—Who ever endured more anguish than Mr Godwin endures?—Her description of him in the very last moments of her recollection was, "He is the kindest best man in the world."

I know of no consolation for myself but in remembering how happy she had lately been & how much she was admired & almost idolized by some of the most eminent & best of human beings.

The Children are both well—the Infant in particular. It is the finest baby I ever saw.

Wishing you peace & prosperity
I remain your hum^{ble} Servant
Eliz. Fenwick

Mr Godwin requests you will make Mrs Bishop acquainted with the particulars of this afflicting event. He tells me that Mrs Godwin entertained a sincere & earnest affection for Mrs Bishop.

iv. I.B. Johnson to Godwin, 13 November 1797, Abinger MSS, Dep. b. 214/3.

Derby, Nov. 13th 1797

Sir

A Tour I was making in the Country when your Letter arrived, has prevented me from receiving & answering it sooner.

Those who had the pleasure to know Mrs Godwin, I am sure will gladly contribute any thing in their power that may tend to impress upon posterity her rare merit & amiable virtues— She had been several months in Paris previous to my acquaintance with her, which commenced in April 1793 & I left France the Septr following. During this period, a great part of her time was occupied in writing an account of the french Revolution. At her leisure hours the family she most frequented was that of my unfortunate friend Mr Thomas Christie,[1] where I used to meet her several times in the week, particularly in the Evening. The society besides his family, generally consisted of Mr George Forster[2] (the friend of Captn Cook), sometimes Mr Imlay who had been lately introduced to her & appeared to pay her more than common attention; Mr Paine likewise often made one of the party. I have occasionally seen some of the Deputies of the convention present such as Isnard, Roederer & even Barère previous to his Apostacy.[3] They were

---

1 Christie is described as "unfortunate" because of his death of fever on a business trip to Surinam in 1796.

2 The naturalist Johann Georg Adam Forster, FRS (1754-94), born in Germany but brought to England by his father in 1766, accompanied the British navigator Captain James Cook (1728-79) on his second voyage to the South Seas.

3 Maximin Isnard (1751-1825), a prominent Girondin, became president of the French National Convention from 16 to 30 May 1793. He and his more moderate colleague, Pierre Louis Roederer (1754-1835), went into hiding when the

well acquainted & visited Miss Wolstonecraft. When the avowed attachment between her & Mr Imlay took place, I cannot inform you. The most proper person to apply to on that subject is Miss Christie,[1] as well as for the names of the Hotels she resided in, which last has totally escaped my memory, & I am certain she will give you every information in her power. Miss Christie has since been married & has consequently changed her name, I can however procure her address, if you think it necessary. About the time the Jacobin party had attained the summit of their power, we used to pass our Evenings together very frequently either in conversation or any amusement [which] might tend to dissipate those gloomy impressions, the state of affairs naturally produced. Miss Wollstonecraft was always particularly anxious for the success of the Revolut^n & the hideous aspect of the then political horizon hurt her exceedingly. She always thought, however, it would finally succeed. Sometimes we met at Mr Paines or formed dining parties in which Baron Trenck, Madem^lle Theroigne &c joined us.[2]—She likewise visited Mad^e Rolande[3] whose misfortunes she greatly lamented.—Such are the principal heads of what I can recollect respecting Miss Wolstonecraft in whose society I have spent many pleasing hours & whose premature death I sincerely regret.

Girondins were proscribed in June 1793 (see above, 90, note 1), but reappeared in later years. Bertrand de Barère or Barère de Vieuzac (1755-1841), originally a moderate, voted for the death of the King in January 1793, after which he became increasingly identified with the left-wing deputies (Montagnards), and served on the Committee of Public Safety during the Terror.

1   Jane Christie, sister of Thomas, who lived in Paris with her brother and his wife.

2   Frédéric, Baron von der Trenck (1726-94), the celebrated German adventurer, settled in Paris during the early years of the Revolution and was later arrested as a Prussian spy, imprisoned, and guillotined. "Théroigne de Méricourt" (soubriquet of Anne-Joseph Terwagne) (1762-1817), originally a courtesan, became a supporter of the Revolution in 1789 and was involved in the popular demonstrations of 1792, but her main sympathies lay with the Girondins. (In May 1793 she was publicly stoned by radical women, from which she never recovered, and died insane.)

3   Marie-Jeanne (Manon) Roland, née Philipon (1754-93), wife of Jean-Marie Roland de la Platière (1734-93, minister of the interior from 1792 to 1793), used her salon as a centre for the Girondin faction. She was arrested following the proscription of the Girondins in June 1793 and became celebrated for the courage with which she faced the guillotine in November of that year. (See Appendix A.3.ii.)

It is my intention the next spring to pass a few weeks in London, I will then do myself the pleasure to call upon you. I am

Sir with great respect
I.B. Johnson

v. Hannah Godwin to Godwin, unsigned, date-stamped 5 February [1798], Abinger MSS, Dep. c. 811/1.

Sunday Morning

When Louisa told me you had sent the memoirs to my mother I was at first alarmed for the shock her prejudices will receive in reading some parts of them though the virtue and excellence the disinterested and ever amiable conduct which cannot fail to create her admiration esteem and love are sufficient to overturn all her prejudices. Be that as it may I have since thought it is better that you sent her a copy.

I thank you for my copy of the whole & the letters—my dear brother—they break my heart. What must they have done yours? Such an angel! to have been haunted by a fate so cruel! to have suffered in such various ways and so long before she met with the happiness she deserved! I should not repeat *to you* the reflections which naturally occur when I think of her past life—the wounds her sensibility was so long exposed to—and then her connection with you so untimely terminated. [B]ut great as must be your regret in having lost her so soon my dear brother, I know it must afford you a delightful though melancholly pleasure when you think how she loved you and inexpressible satisfaction that though for a short time you did restore to her life and happiness and healed the wounds which were worse to her than death.

I am sorry the engraving is not a better likeness, for when I have contemplated the interesting picture of her mind and soul, so exalted, and so amiable, till my heart is wholly melted with sympathy and affection I look up at it expecting it should bring more clearly to my recollection the person of her whom I feel inclined to fall down and worship, and when I do so I cannot but turn away disappointed. Yet I would not be without it either—for it certainly has a good deal of resemblance though not enough to satisfy one.

If I am mistaken my dear brother in supposing that your grief must have been aleviated by a mixture of reflections more than satisfactory—forgive me.

[F]or myself one great source of regret is that I did not see her oftener—that I trusted to a leisure time for making myself more acquainted with her and think I should be happy if I had contributed in the slightest degree to her happiness.

I anticipate with delight the pleasures you will have in Fanny and I am impatient for Mary to shew that she will be as like her poor Mamma as Fanny promises to be—or else as like papa. When I think of her I wish time would go on faster.

[M]ost earnestly do I wish that you may be blessed in them as you deserve to be, that your tender cares may be crowned with success and satisfaction. I will not envy Louisa for with humility I must own she assists you better than I could do.

Appendix D: Critical Reaction

1. Contemporary Reviews

i. From the *Analytical Review* 27 (Mar. 1798): 238-40.

Such is the narrative here offered to the public of the life of this very extraordinary woman. We feel ourselves impelled to make some observations both on these memoirs, and on the character of Mrs. G.

The narrative is easy, and we believe very faithful and true, so far it is entitled to praise. But it is obvious, that Mrs. G. entertained singular opinions, and reduced them into practice. This circumstance will invite many severely to criticise, and some to censure her character. As this is the case, we think it was due to Mrs. G., to have stated *how* those opinions were formed, and the *reasons* by which she supported them.

It is indeed a bald narrative of the life of a woman, very eventful and touching. We think it entitled to very limited praise. In another respect it is deficient. It gives us no correct history of the formation of Mrs. G.'s mind. We are neither informed of her favourite books, her hours of study, nor her attainments in languages and philosophy. She contemplated nature with rapture we are told, and enjoyed much of it's inspiration. Of this there can be no doubt; but as the chief use of biography is to teach us to attain to eminence in virtue and knowledge, we think too little is told us concerning the subjects of Mrs. G.'s study, and her manner of studying: but, perhaps, instead of censuring, we ought to lament the paucity of the means of information.

We conceive exceptions will be taken to her conduct in three respects; and we think too little attention is given to such probable exceptions in the narrative.

1st, Mrs. G.'s notions and practice respecting marriage will meet violent objection.

Without offering to vindicate her in these respects, we must be allowed to observe, that we think them questions of prudence rather than morality. He, who is not bewildered and lost in the mists of superstition, must be obliged to acknowledge, that there is something more necessary to render the sexual connection between man and woman pure, than the public ceremony of marriage; and that it is very easy for the vilest prostitution to exist under the sanction of this ceremony.

The sexual intercourse is common to all animals, and man in this respect differs from others only by connecting with that intercourse sentiments of affection and attachment to an individual subject. This mental approbation sublimes and purifies the appetite of nature and, *without this*, whatever ceremony may have taken place, the intercourse is brutal, and the offence of prostitution remains. Mrs. G. had the offer of marriage with a respectable man, whom she did not regard with this mental affection, as appears from her letters, but she rejected him under this conviction.

And if the ceremony of marriage cannot protect from the just charge of prostitution, in any case where a mental attachment has not preceded the sexual intercourse, neither can the neglect of the ceremony of marriage make that intercourse immoral, when that neglect has flowed from motives of benevolence, or the convictions of immoral imposition. The ceremony of marriage performed or neglected alters not the morality of the thing, but it is essentially and solely a question of prudence, as it is the legal tie by which the laws of men compel to certain attentions and responsibilities. When, therefore, we consider the present very corrupt state of men, we are inclined to conclude Mrs. G.'s confidence too great, and her conduct imprudent and hazardous. That marriage ought to be an *indissoluble union*, where the parties prove wholly incompatible, we do not believe; and we think, notwithstanding the powerful reasoning of Hume on this subject, that Milton was right, and that divorces should be allowed in many cases, where they cannot in this country be obtained.

Superficial minds will be apt to say, that the experience of Mrs. G. is the best refutation of her theory: but we dare not say this, as long as we see, which we daily do, thousands married, whose union is as *unhappy* as the union of this lady and Mr. Imlay.

If any think, that, without accusing Mrs. G. of *immorality*, a charge of *indelicacy* will fix, on account of her neglect of the established rules of the community; we have only to observe, that Mrs. G. was an original thinker, differed from the vulgar in most things, had long reflected on this subject and drawn decisive conclusions, and entered upon this connection with Mr. Imlay, *in France, and at a moment when the discussion of the subject of marriage agitated the national councils, and when a new system of thinking on that point almost universally obtained.* That, therefore, may appear to us in our circumstances indelicate, which *there* would not have appeared to be so.

We have however observed, that we think her conduct *imprudent*, while men continue as corrupt as they now are, and we are far from holding it up for imitation. Her nature was generous in the extreme, and inclined to place confidence, when it ought, perhaps, to have cherished suspicion.

2. The next charge we expect to hear advanced against the character of Mrs. G., is the versatility of her attachments. It will be said, to-day she loves Mr. Fuseli, to-morrow attaches herself to Mr. Imlay, and, the moment Imlay finally abandons her, we find her in the arms of Mr. Godwin.

But what is there in all this? Those, who feel powerfully one impression, are, no doubt, the most easily susceptible of another.

Rochefocault, in his maxims, the result of a profound study of mankind, asserts, that the heart, which is torn by a disappointed affection, is the best prepared to form a new one. *But did Mrs. G. ever renounce an attachment?* He who reads her letters will declare, that the possibility of such a conduct did not exist in her nature. Her love was more lasting than it's object.

Her attachment to Mr. Fuseli was conceived against her wishes and efforts. It grew into no connection. She travelled to banish his image, and no better expedient remains to her who would discard one recollection, than the assiduous cultivation of another. The only question in the case is, whether she abandoned Imlay too soon, who had abandoned her many months? Had he died, a thousand recollections might have played round her heart, and made her cherish his image. As it was, every thing conspired to convince her, that he ought to be banished from her mind. He who reads her letters will stand astonished at the fervour, strength, and duration of her affection for Imlay. At the bar of reason, in this respect, Mrs. G. is more than exculpated. It is of the nature of a second marriage, but there was less in this case to keep her affections from seeking a new object, or admitting one.

3. Her attempts to destroy herself, when she had a child deserted by it's father, will be thought worthy of censure. To this we can only say, that we possess not the scale of suffering by which to estimate what every one ought to endure before he seeks relief in death. We see Mrs. G. struggling with an overwhelming sorrow, and we have no power to throw an arrow at one so sadly pierced. We wish her character and conduct to be seriously and candidly examined, and we would protect it, if we could, from the freedom of licentious tongues. She appears to us another Heloise; and it is a reflection upon men, that Abelard should have possessed the first, and Imlay the second of these illustrious women.

A head of Mrs. G. is prefixed to these memoirs, which exhibits at once a striking likeness, and a very interesting figure. We think every one who reads these memoirs ought, in justice to Mrs. G., to read her letters; and we wish, indeed, that they had not been separately printed.

Imperfect as these memoirs are, we have no fellowship with him, who can read them without a tear.

ii. From the *Anti-Jacobin Review* 1 (July 1798): 94-99.

"There are (the author says) not many individuals with whose character the public welfare and improvement are more intimately connected, than the author of A Vindication of the Rights of Woman." Mr. Godwin, indeed, considers her as a model for imitation, and her life as *peculiarly* useful on account of the *precept and example* it affords. We coincide with him in his opinion of the *utility* of a life of Mrs. Wollstonecroft; though for a very different reason. Intended by him for a beacon, it serves for a buoy; if it does not shew what it is wise to pursue, it manifests what it is wise to avoid. It illustrates both the sentiments and conduct resulting from such principles as those of Mrs. Wollstonecroft and Mr. Godwin. It also in some degree accounts for the formation of such visionary theories and pernicious doctrines.

Mary Wollstonecroft was the eldest daughter of Edward John Wollstonecroft, who lived on Epping Forest. Mary was born the 27ᵗʰ of April, 1759. Her father, was a weak, foolish, and violent man. Mary, however, very early assumed towards him such a tone as KEPT HIM IN AWE. From this circumstance she passed in the family for a young woman of extraordinary strength of mind. Mr. Wollstonecroft's dissipation and inattention to his children prevented Mary from receiving a regular education. No pains were employed to season her youthful mind with sound principles of reasoning, morality, or religion. Thus her fancy, naturally lively, and her feelings ardent, wanted the regulation of judicious discipline. Her imagination and passions became her guides through life.

After she arrived at the age of womanhood, she formed an intimate friendship with a Miss Blood, who had received a tolerable education, and had made some proficiency in the usual studies and accomplishments of ladies. From her, Mary acquired some knowledge of grammar, and other elementary parts of literature. Miss Blood being a woman of ordinary talents, Mary, whose abilities were of a higher class, soon outstripped her in acquirements. Still, however, she had no instructor to assist her expanding mind, and to guard her from erroneous opinion. Being in very limited circumstances she was advised to set up a day-school; and in that occupation received much praise from her employers. Newington-Green was the scene of her instructions. There she became acquainted with several men of letters; and as her conversation bespoke her considerably superior to common female teachers, and her manners were engaging, she was much liked by those gentlemen. Finding herself superior to many of those ladies with whom she was acquainted, she fancied that she who was merely a woman of lively, but neither strong nor profound, genius, was a phœnomenon of nature, born to give a new direction to human opinions and conduct. Her literary career was begun in the Analytical Review; a performance in which, it seems, learning and sound reasoning were not then esteemed indispensibly necessary any more than they are at the present time. Such a mind as Mary's very naturally takes the direction of those with whom it is most conversant. From the writers in that work she probably derived the anti-hierarchical and anti-monarchical doctrines, which it has been the uniform object of that Review to disseminate. The French revolution afforded her, she thought, an opportunity of giving to the world, in a continuous work, those stores of wisdom which her mind contained. When Edmund Burke wrote his book, Mrs. Wollstonecroft, confident of her own ratiocinative powers, and of her thorough knowledge of human nature, of moral and political science, *undertook* to answer that wonderful production. Mary's Reply, as might be expected from a writer handling a subject and a work so much beyond her ability, was superficial and extravagant; where she was just, she was trite; where she tried to be ingenious or deep, she was visionary. Next succeeded her *Rights of Woman*, which the superficial fancied to be profound, and the profound knew to be superficial: it indeed had very little title to the character of ingenuity. Her doctrines are almost all obvious corollaries from the theorems of Paine. If we admit his principle, that all men have an equal right to be governors and statesmen, without any regard to their talents and virtues, there can be no reason for excluding women or even children. Such was the intellectual process by which Mary was led to her extravagant, absurd, and destructive theories. Mrs. W. having ardent sensibility, and a vigorous imagination, possessed no small excellence in description, but had neither materials nor habits of close reasoning and cautious investigation, and therefore ought to have avoided discussions in which these were necessary. Mr. Godwin himself allows that in her decisions respecting truth, she proceeded from taste and feeling, and not from logical disquisition. Speaking on this subject, he accuses himself of adhering too closely to logical precision. If that be a defect, candour obliges us to confess, that it is a defect with which he charges himself, with more modesty than truth. So far are his theories from manifesting logical precision, that they are generally the creatures of his own fancy, without any proof to support them, and with the experience of all mankind to demonstrate their absurdity. That argumentation which is wholly founded on assumptions, not only without evidence, but diametrically opposite to evidence, is very far from logical precision, in the usual acceptation; but is, however, the substance of the reasoning of jacobinical writers.

The substance of Mrs. Wollstonecraft's moral sentiments and history was briefly this—the creature of impulse, some of her propensities were benevolent, and frequently operated to the good of those who were placed within the sphere of her actions. Not directed, however, by sound principles, she considered herself as exempted from those restraints on inclination, which are necessary to the welfare of society. Prompted by the feeling of the time, she even in her friendly acts proceeded much farther than virtue, guided by reason, would dictate. Intent on one object only, she disregarded other relations, to which it was her duty to attend. She was evidently totally unused to that balance of affections in which the soundest philosophers and wisest men have placed the supreme good of mankind. From love to Miss Blood, Mary, when she was in bad health, left her engagements and duties at home to accompany her abroad: to her feeling (benevolent we allow) she sacrificed the good of the pupils who had been entrusted to her care, who were reaping more advantage from her than they could do in the same time from new teachers; the means of subsistence to her father and sisters who depended on her for support; and involved her own circumstances, and so lessened the sphere of her utility. Thus, though kind to her relations, and, indeed, disposed to benevolence to the utmost of her power, hurried on by her feelings, she was much less beneficent than if these had been under the controul of reason and sound principles. Her constitution, as the philosopher, her husband, bears testimony, was very amorous. Her passions were farther inflamed "by the state of celibacy and restraint in which she had hitherto lived, and to which the rules of polished society *condemn* an unmarried woman." The amorous lady fell in love with a Mr. Fuseli, a married man, and continued long to have a violent affection for him: to what length it was indulged has not appeared. At the close of the year 1792 she went over to France, then on the eve of war with her country, and continued for more than two years under that virtuous government which Robespiere administered. While this patriotic lady resided with the enemies of her country, her most intimate acquaintances were Helen Maria Williams, Mr. Thomas Christie, one of the most zealous advocates for the French principles, and Mr. Thomas Paine. "It is almost unnecessary (says Godwin) to mention that she was personally acquainted with the majority of the leaders of the French revolution." The author probably thinks, that the coincidence of opinion was sufficient to produce acquaintance between Mary and those worthies. But a still stronger motive than admiration of the political justice which France exhibited, prolonged her stay in that free and happy land. "She entered (says Godwin) into *that species of connection,* for which *her heart* secretly *panted,* and which had the effect of diffusing an immediate tranquillity and cheerfulness over her manners." The state to which he attributes such beneficial consequences, to the mind of her whom he afterwards made his wife, was *concubinage.* She became the concubine of Mr. Imlay, an American. The biographer does not mention many of her amours. Indeed it was unnecessary: two or three instances of action often decide a character as well as a thousand. Juvenal, by reciting the adventures of one night, makes us as thoroughly acquainted with the character of Messalina, as if he had enumerated all the amorous exploits of that FEELING lady. Besides such recitals are often very difficult—"*Promptius expediam quot amaverit Hippia mæchos*"—Here we must observe, that Mary's theory, that it is the right of women to indulge their inclinations with every man they like, is so far from being new, that it is as old as prostitution.

Among other advantages, which this just woman planned from her amour, was a trip to America, where she might have eluded her creditors. As the gallants of kept mistresses cannot have that confidence, which is one of the strongest motives to constancy, Mary was forsaken by her paramour. At first she imputed his absence to necessary business, and believed his letters to that purport. Imlay had gone to London. In his absence she derived *particular gratification* from Archibald Hamilton Rowan, whom she celebrates for *integrity of disposition and kindness of heart*. Whether her pleasure in the society of this *righteous and benevolent* person was chiefly owing to admiration of his virtues, approbation of his political principles and conduct, or any other cause, the biographer does not narrate. However that may be, she in pursuit of Imlay went to England, (although the author says) "*a country for which she expressed a repugnance that almost amounted to horror.*" Deserted by her gallant, she resolved to drown herself, and actually plunged into the Thames from Putney Bridge.—But, being restored to life, she transferred her love from an *absent* to a PRESENT man—from the adventurer Imlay, to the philosopher Godwin. Although they at last married, yet, as the *philosopher himself bears testimony, they lived for several months in a state of illicit commerce*. The biographer, in speaking of their intercourse, is much more particular than decency permits us to state. He, however, gives us his own virtuous and beneficial notions, as well as those of Mary, in terms which we shall venture to quote. "We did not marry. It is difficult to recommend any thing to indiscriminate adoption, contrary to the established rules and *prejudices* of mankind; but certainly nothing can be so ridiculous upon the face of it, or so contrary to the genuine march of sentiments, as to require the overflowing of the soul to wait upon a ceremony; and that which, wherever delicacy and imagination exist, is of all things most sacredly private, to blow a trumpet before it, and to record the moment when it arrived at its climax.

"There were, however, other reasons why we did not immediately marry. *Mary felt an entire conviction* OF THE PROPRIETY OF HER CONDUCT. It would be absurd to suppose that, with a heart withered by desertion, she was not right to give way to the emotions of kindness which our intimacy produced, and to seek for that support in friendship and affection, which could alone give pleasure to her heart, and peace to her meditations."

The reader is to observe, that the biographer afterwards married the lady. Soon after her death, *to do honour to the memory of his wife, and to himself in chusing such a wife*, he records her adventures. The moral sentiments and moral conduct of Mrs. Wollstonecroft, resulting from their principles and theories, exemplify and illustrate JACOBIN MORALITY.

The biographer affords us in the *religious* sentiments of Mrs. Wollstonecroft, one cause of a conduct so opposite to the established rules of female virtue. "She had received few lessons of religion in her youth, and her religion was almost entirely of her own creation.—*She could not recollect the time when she had believed the doctrine of future punishments.*" For some time, however, she frequented public worship, but as she advanced in the new lights "her attendance became less constant, and in no long time was wholly discontinued." This discontinuance draws from the philosopher the following observation, "*I believe it may be admitted as a maxim, that no person of a well furnished mind, that has shaken off the implicit subjection of youth, and is not the zealous partisan of a sect, can bring himself to conform to the public and regular routine of sermons and prayers.*" Were not the minds of Addison, Locke, and Sir Isaac Newton as well furnished as that of the philosopher Godwin? This indeed is one of the common-place superficial remarks by which the abettors of the new doctrines endeavour to shake the respect of mankind for those institutions by which religious sentiments are cherished. Let parents, anxious for the welfare of their children, statesmen for the happiness of the community in which they preside, say, if they would wish the members of their families and states to be such as Godwin has taught, and Mrs. Wollstonecroft taught and practised. Let philosophers consider whether such sentiments and conduct be conducive to the general good of mankind. We doubt not, that wise parents, enlightened statesmen, sound and comprehensive philosophers, must concur with us in reprobating such inculcations, whether by precept or example, as destructive of domestic, civil, and political society.

Vulgar tears fall and evaporate without leaving any trace behind them: but the tear of affection is often chrystalised by the power of genius, and converted into a permanent literary brilliant. Mr. Godwin, whose abilities are indisputable, endeavours thus to dignify and render illustrious his sorrows for the loss of his wife; we therefore regret the necessity of observing that not only the general reader, but the most judicious and reflecting part of mankind, will arraign the prudence and the utility of these memoirs, though he himself commences them with this sentence of high expectation:–"there are not many individuals with whose character the *public welfare* and *improvement* are more ultimately connected, than the author of A Vindication of the Rights of Woman."

After an exordium so splendid, we could not expect to find such a narrative;—a narrative which we must indeed read with pity and concern, but which we should have advised the author to bury in oblivion. Blushes would suffuse the cheeks of most husbands, if they were *forced* to relate those anecdotes of their wives which Mr. Godwin voluntarily proclaims to the world. The extreme excentricity of Mr. G.'s sentiments will account for his conduct. Virtue and vice are weighed by him in a balance of his own. He neither looks to marriage with respect, nor to suicide with horror. He relates with complacency of Mary Wollstonecraft, afterward his wife, that she cultivated a *platonic* affection for Mr. Fuseli the painter:—that she cohabited with Mr. Imlay as his wife, took his name, and had a child by him, without being married; and that she even lived with Mr. G. himself, and was pregnant by him; and that it was only her pregnancy which induced them to think of marriage; fearing that, otherwise, she might be excluded from society. He gravely records, also, (what was mentioned at the time in the Newspapers, and was considered by some persons as calumny,) her attempt to drown herself in the Thames, in consequence of the ill-treatment which she experienced from Mr. Imlay.

How the public welfare and improvement are connected with or can be advanced by the studied and uniform eulogium of such conduct will not be easily perceived; nor will any reader of discernment, who appreciates the merit of this unfortunate female, even on the evidence of her own husband, be able to say with him that "there are no circumstances in her life that, in the judgment of honour and reason, could brand her with disgrace." Peace to her manes! She was the child of genius, but of suffering: of talents, but of error!

Most of the incidents which composed her short life are neither very singular nor very striking. Where she was born her husband does not know. She commenced the career of fame, like Milton, Sir Richard Blackmore, Dr. Johnson, and others, by keeping a school;—and she then became a writer for a bookseller, and an occasional critic. She attracted notice by entering the lists against Mr. Burke, and particularly by her *Vindication of the Rights of Woman*; by the publication of which, in the opinion of her biographer, "she will perhaps be found to have performed more substantial service for the cause of her sex, than all the other writers, male or female, that ever felt themselves animated in the behalf of oppressed and injured beauty." Though this must be deemed exaggerated praise, it may be forgiven from a husband, who, no doubt, most sincerely mourns her loss; and our other female authors must not take it amiss that he should wish to have it believed, that "no female writer ever obtained so great a degree of celebrity throughout Europe."

Mr. and Mrs. Godwin possessed congenial minds, and perhaps no two people better suited each other; though, (as this memoir relates) at the first time of their meeting, they did not reciprocally excite any very prepossessing impressions. At last, however, a strong and mutual affection took place, and ripened into love.

"There was (Mr. G. says) no period of throes and resolute explanation attendant on the tale. It was friendship melting into love. Previously to our mutual declaration, each felt half-assured, yet each felt a certain trembling anxiety to have assurance complete."

"Mary rested her head upon the shoulder of her lover, hoping to find a heart with which she might safely treasure her world of affection, fearing to commit a mistake, yet in spite of her melancholy experience, fraught with that generous confidence, which, in a great soul, is never extinguished. I had never loved till now; or, at least, had never nourished a passion to the same growth, or met with an object so consummately worthy."

To this account of the sincerity and ardor of their mutual passion, it is concisely added–"*We did not marry;*" and then follows this attempt at a justification:

"It is difficult to recommend any thing to indiscriminate adoption, contrary to the established rules and prejudices of mankind; but certainly nothing can be so ridiculous upon the face of it, or so contrary to the general march of sentiment, as to require the overflowing of the soul to wait upon a ceremony, and that which, wherever delicacy and imagination exist, is of all things most sacredly private, to blow a trumpet before it, and to record the moment when it has arrived at its climax."

Apprehending that this very refined and sentimental logic would not be sufficient to convince the public of the propriety of their conduct in this respect, Mr. G. adds–"There were other reasons why we did not immediately marry. Mary felt an entire conviction of the propriety of her conduct."—We question this. Her experience, with Mr. Imlay, of the miserable consequences to which a woman exposes herself by an unmarried connection, *must* have taught her the *imprudence* at least of disregarding the law of society respecting marriage. No evil may result from recording the vow of love: but *many* evils *must* result from a contempt of marriage. It is one of the first institutions that are essential to social order.

iv. From the *New Annual Register for 1798* (1799): 271.

The "Memoirs of the Author of a Vindication of the Rights of Woman, by William Godwin," are a singular tribute of respect to the memory of a well beloved wife. The subject of them was a woman of undoubted talents and genius, and possessed of many excellent qualities. For the praise which he bestows upon the former, notwithstanding that it may be thought exaggerated, and for the sensibility with which he speaks of the latter, we find no difficulty in accounting. But she was one who, unhappily for herself, seems never to have had those good principles instilled into her mind, which would have enabled her to controul and govern her passions; and who, under the influence of a warm constitution, and warm imagination, formed to herself notions of female delicacy, and the intercourse between the sexes, in direct variance with those generally adopted by the world, and incompatible, in the opinion of all old fashioned moralists, with the order and well-being of society. Upon those notions she acted in life: and her husband has thought proper to present the public with a picture of her love adventures, and of some other extraordinary circumstances, which were whispered concerning her while living, but which the good natured part of mankind were willing to resolve into scandal and calumny. This appears to us to be a very extraordinary method of doing honour to her memory. And we should be sorry, could we suppose the moral taste of the world to be so vitiated as that these Memoirs would be much read, without exciting lively emotions of disgust and concern.

v. From the *Lady's Monitor* 1, No. 17 (12 Dec. 1801): 131.

She had strong passions, and a strong understanding. She was a great genius; but like most great geniuses, she was uncommon. Uncommon in her ideas of society, and those rules which, for the general good, must be borne with in particular instances. Business she hated; for, there was "nothing worth having to be purchased." She was as much at variance with your common maxims of prudence; and exclaimed, "there are arguments which convince the reason, whilst they carry death to the heart!" But indeed she was no modern philosopher.—

"Yet I am," says Mrs. G. to Imlay, "not angry with thee, my love, for I think that it is a peice of stupidity, and likewise of a milk-and-water affection, which comes to the same thing when the temper is governed by a square and compass.—There is nothing picturesque in this straight-lined equality, and the passions always give grace to the actions."

And, in all probability, had she been married well in early life, she had then been a happy woman, and universally respected.

We have seen her conduct toward Mr. Fuseli; her intimacy with Mr. Imlay; and her subsequent connection with Mr. Godwin; and we are as little disposed as any one can be, to palliate the essentially vicious; but is there nothing to be offered in extenuation of the subject of these memoirs? She had attained her thirtieth year before she became attached to Mr. Fuseli: it could not then have been altogether an affair of passion. His conversation delighted her; and she thought that she might listen to its charm without endangering the repose of her heart. In this she erred fatally—but it is an error too common with her sex: and to which women of sensibility and intellect are peculiarly liable. The determined manner with which she quitted this happiness, when it appeared hostile to the peace of her friend, has been related in an early stage of this sketch. To those who are acquainted with the heart, her love to Mr. Imlay will be no problem in the science of human passion. They know full well with what eagerness the sinking spirit, already thwarted and barbed by disappointment, clings for solace and relief to the first object that may engage its affection. She loved him— but he loved not her. He was leagued to her by desire—not love: he was detained to her by honour—not affection! This is the truth, and we must pity her.

That she ever loved Mr. Godwin, is at least improbable. It must at any rate have been but a *rational* love; for the heart does not admit of many real ones.

With this ample map of her life stretched out before us, where there is no corner of her soul undefined, nor even a zig-zag of her reason concealed, we cannot easily be mistaken in our estimate. She was a woman of high genius; and, as she felt the whole strength of her powers, she thought herself lifted, in a degree, above the ordinary trammels of civil communities. She enveighed bitterly against a code of regulations which she deemed derogatory to her sex; nor did she for an instant reflect, that unless women were equally qualified with herself, to act on the grand principles of all morality independent of tuition and restraint, the doctrines she inculcated, if received, must overturn the present basis of every civilized state. The mind must be *prepared* for wisdom, or wisdom will prove its greatest bane, and its ultimate destruction. We are aware of that squeamish kind of virtue, which looks more to the form than to essence of things. Much of it has been applied to Mrs. Godwin. The grand lines of her character have been confounded by persons of a narrow comprehension, or by prejudice, with the minuter inflexions of her soul. Her deviations from propriety, have been mistaken for her principles of action.

2. Other Responses

i. From Anna Seward, Letter to Humphrey Repton, 13 April 1798, *Letters of Anna Seward: Written Between the Years 1784 and 1807*, 6 vols. (Edinburgh: Constable, 1811) 5: 73-74.

You have seen this author's Memoirs of his wife—the famous authoress of the Rights of Woman. It is the fashion to abuse him for them violently. Bearing strong marks of impartial authenticity as to the character, sentiments, conduct, and destiny of a very extraordinary woman, they appear to be highly valuable. Since, on balancing her virtues and errors, the former greatly preponderate, it is no disgrace to any man to have united his destiny with hers. Nor can he be justly blamed as exposing the frailties of his wife, since, in her admired northern tour, she acknowledges herself a mother by Imlay, to whom she could not have been a legal wife, as he was known to be living when she married Godwin.

To reveal the motives on which she had acted;—to paint the strength of her basely betrayed attachment to that villain Imlay, was surely not injury but justice to the memory of a deceased wife.

I have but one fault to find with these Memoirs. It is, however, a great one—the needless display of his own infidelity as to revealed religion, and his seeking to involve her in the scepticism by implication, not by proof, since he allows she was habitually and fervently devout. Why then should he expose her to the censure of irreligion from the mass of mankind, who imagine God can be worshipped effectually in no way but their own?

ii. From [Richard Polwhele], *The Unsex'd Females: A Poem. Addressed to the Author of The Pursuits of Literature* (London: Cadell and Davies, 1798) 24–30.

> Alas! in every aspiration bold,
> I saw the creature of a mortal mould:
> Yes! not untrembling (tho' I half ador'd
> A mind by Genius fraught, by Science stor'd)
> I saw the Heroine mount the dazzling dome
> Where Shakespeare's spirit kindled, to illume
> His favourite FUSELI, and with magic might
> To earthly sense unlock'd a world of light!
>   Full soon, amid the high pictorial blaze,
> I saw a Sibyl-transport in her gaze:
> To the great Artist, from his wondrous Art,
> I saw transferr'd the whole enraptur'd Heart;
> Till, mingling soul with soul, in airy trance,
> Enlighten'd and inspir'd at every glance,
> And from the dross of appetite refin'd,*
> And, grasping at angelic food, all mind,
> Down from the empyreal heights she sunk, betray'd
> To poor Philosophy—a love-sick maid!†
> —But hark! lascivious murmurs melt around;
> And pleasure trembles in each dying sound.
> A myrtle bower, in fairest bloom array'd,

---

* "However gross, indeed, the food might be,
            … to taste
   Think not, she would be nice."…
            … for what redounds, transpires
   Thro' spirits with ease!" Paradise Lost, b. 5. l. 432.

† "Miss Wollstonecraft used often to meet Mr. Fuseli at the house of a common friend, where she was so charmed with his talents, and the tout ensemble, that she suffered herself to fall in love with him, though a married man." See Godwin's Memoirs.

To laughing Venus streams the silver shade:
Thrill'd with fine ardors *Collinsonias* glow,‡
And, bending, breathe their loose desires below.
Each gentle air a swelling anther heaves,
Wafts its full sweets, and shivers thro' the leaves.
     Bath'd in new bliss, the Fair-one greets the
         bower,
And ravishes a flame from every flower;
Low at her feet inhales the master's sighs,
And darts voluptuous poison from her eyes.
Yet, while each heart-pulse, in the Paphian grove,
Beats quick to IMLAY and licentious love,*
A sudden gloom the gathering tempest spreads;
The floral arch-work withers o'er their heads;
Whirlwinds the paramours asunder tear;
And wisdom falls, the victim of despair.†

---

‡   "The vegetable passion of love is agreeably seen in the flower of the Parnassia, in
which the males alternately approach and recede from the female, and in the flower
of Nigella, or Devil in the Bush, in which the tall females bend down to their dwarf
husbands. But I was, this morning, surprised to observe, among Sir Brooke Booth-
by's valuable collection of plants at Asbourn, the manifest adultery of several
females of the plant Collinsonia, who had bent themselves into contact with the
males of other flowers of the same plant, in their vicinity, neglectful of their own."
                           Botanic Garden, Part the First, p. 197—3d. Edit.

*   To smother in dissipation her passion for Fuseli, Miss W. had fled to France. There
she met with a paramour responsive to her sighs, a Mr. Imlay: with him she formed
a connexion, though not a matrimonial one; being always of opinion, with Eloisa,
that
        "Love, free as air, at sight of human ties,
         Spreads his light wings, and in a moment flies!"

†   Imlay soon left his lady to her "own imaginations." Thus abandoned, she returned
to London; and driven to desperation, attempted to put an end to her life, but was
recovered. She soon, however, made a second effort to plunge into eternity. In a
dark and tempestuous night, she repaired to Putney-bridge; where, determined to
throw herself into the river, she walked up and down, for half an hour, through the
rain, that her clothes, being thoroughly drenched and heavy, might facilitate her
descent into the water. She then leaped from the top of the bridge; but finding still
a difficulty in sinking, tried to press her clothes closely around her, and at last
became insensible; but at this moment she was discovered, and brought back to life.
See Godwin's Memoirs.

And dost thou rove, with no internal light,[†]
Poor maniac! thro' the stormy waste of night?
Hath thou no sense of guilt to be forgiv'n,
No comforter on earth, no hope in Heaven?
Stay, stay—thine impious arrogance restrain—
What tho' the flood may quench thy burning brain,
Rash woman! can its whelming wave bestow
Oblivion, to blot out eternal woe?

    "O come (a voice seraphic seems to say)
Fly that pale form—come sisters! come away.
Come, from those livid limbs withdraw your gaze,
Those limbs which Virtue views in mute amaze;
Nor deem, that Genius lends a veil, to hide
The dire apostate, the fell suicide.[*]—["]

[†]   "I do not think my sister so to seek,
    Or so unprincipled in Virtue's book,
    And the sweet peace that Goodness bosoms ever,
    As that the single want of light and noise
    Could stir the constant mood of her calm thoughts."
                See Milton's Comus, l. 570, &c. &c.

[*] I know nothing of Miss Wollstonecraft's character or conduct, but from the Memoirs of Godwin, with whom this lady was afterwards connected. "We did not marry," says, Godwin: but during her pregnancy by G. they married. She died in consequence of childbirth, in 1797. A woman who has broken through all religious restraints, will commonly be found ripe for every species of licentiousness. Miss W. had been bred to the established Church; but from her intimacy with the late Dr. Price, was induced, occasionally, to attend the sectarian worship. Thus "halting between two opinions," she at length regarded both, as the mere prejudices of education, and became equally averse from the church and the conventicle. And, accordingly, for the last ten years of her life, she frequented no place of public worship at all. How far a woman of such principles, was qualified to superintend the education of young ladies, is a point which I shall leave, to be discussed and determined by the circles of fashion and gallantry—intimating only, that Miss W. was a governess of the daughter of Lord Viscount Kingsborough.—Her meditated suicide, we shall contemplate with fresh horror, when we consider that, at the time of the desperate act, she was a mother, deserting a poor helpless offspring. But, burst the ties of religion; and the bands of nature will snap asunder! Sentiments of religion may, doubtless, exist in the heart, without the external profession of it: but, that this woman was neither a Christian, nor a Mahometan, nor even a Deist, is sufficiently evident from the triumphant report of Godwin. Godwin, then her husband, boasts that during her last illness (which continued ten days) not a word of a reli-

iii. From [Mary Hays], "Memoirs of Mary Wollstonecraft,"
Annual Necrology for 1797-8 (London: R. Phillips, 1800): 454-56.

The speculative opinions of Mr. Godwin rendered him adverse
to marriage; the pecuniary embarrassments of Mrs. Wollstonecraft, it can scarcely be supposed, were lessened; neither
can it be believed, that, on such a subject, a mind like hers
could be capable of reserve. Mr. Godwin, in consideration of
the inconveniences which had already been sustained, and to
which, from the habits of society, the woman he loved might
still be exposed, with a liberality which did him honour, waved
his own scruples, and gave to the union which took place
between them a legal sanction. Their marriage was not immediately declared, Mr. Godwin indulging the delicacy of his
wife, who shrunk from becoming again a subject of public discussion.

It was now that her exhausted heart began to find repose,
that at peace with herself, she diffused around her the tranquillity she enjoyed: her ideas of rational happiness had ever been
concentered in the circle of domestic affections; in seeking to
realize her plans, she had till this period been involved in unde-
served calumny and distress; to the calm satisfactions of nature
and social affection the best constituted minds are the most
exquisitely sensible. Had the sensibility of this extraordinary
woman early found its proper objects, softened by the sympathies, and occupied by the duties of a wife and mother, she had
serenely pursued her course. The placid stream, that gliding
through the meadows, fertilizes their banks, checked in its

---

gious tendency dropped from her lips.—I cannot but think, that the Hand of Prov-
idence is visible, in her life, her death, and in the Memoirs themselves. As she was
given up to her "heart's lusts," and let "to follow her own imaginations," that the
fallacy of her doctrines and the effects of an irreligious conduct, might be manifested to the world; and as she died a death that strongly marked the distinction of the
sexes, by pointing out the destiny of women, and the diseases to which they are
liable; so her husband was permitted, in writing her Memoirs, to labour under a
temporary infatuation, that every incident might be seen without a gloss—every
fact exposed without an apology.

course, becomes a destructive torrent: those strong passions, that, ravaging the mind, afflict and deform society, have their origin in opposition and constraint; if in this way talent is sometimes generated, it seems to be purchased too dear.

The laws of nature are paramount to the customs of society; its dictates will not be silenced by factitious precepts. Those who, without guilt or imprudence, find themselves excluded from the common solace of their species, will be led to consider the reasonableness of this privation, of which its injustice tends to aggravate its importance. From the expensive habits of society, and its consequent profligacy, a large proportion of women are destined to celibacy, while their importance, their establishment, their pleasures, and their respectability, are (with few exceptions) connected with marriage. Woe be to these victims of vice or superstition, if, too ingenuous for habitual hypocrisy, they cannot stifle in the bottom of their hearts those feelings which should constitute their happiness and their glory: that sensibility, which is the charm of their sex, in such situations becomes its bitterest curse; in submitting to their destiny they rarely escape insult; in overstepping the bounds prescribed to them, by a single error, they become involved in a labyrinth of perplexity and distress. In vain may reflection enable them to contemn distinctions, that, confounding truth and morals, poison virtue at its source: overwhelmed by a torrent of contumely and reproach, a host of foes encompass their path, exaggerate their weakness, distort their principles, misrepresent their actions, and, with deadly malice, or merciless zeal, seek to drive them from the haunts of civil life.

Of the truth of these remarks the vindicator of female rights had not been without an experience.

"Those who are bold enough (said she in a letter to a friend) to advance before the age they live in, and to throw off, by the force of their own minds, the prejudices which the maturing reason of the world will in time disavow, must learn to brave censure. We ought not to be too anxious respecting the opinion of others.—I am not fond of vindications.—Those who know me will suppose that I acted from principle.—Nay, as we in general give others credit for worth, in proportion as we possess it—I am easy with regard to the opinions of the *best* part of mankind—I *rest* on my own."

Her union with Mr. Godwin, though sanctioned by *forms* which the prudent will not lightly be induced to violate, did not wholly exempt her from reproach: some nice distinctions in the circle of her acquaintance which had at first excited her surprise, not unmingled with regret, were nevertheless quickly forgotten—a mind like hers justly rested on itself. More interesting hopes and sentiments now occupied her thoughts: surrounded by respectable and intelligent friends, who knew how to appreciate her fine qualities, happy in the bosom of domestic peace, her heart once more expanded itself, her genius resumed its tone and vigour. Literary avocations, domestic pleasures, and social engagements, occupied and diversified her time; while she anticipated with pleasure an approaching period, that, by adding to her maternal cares, would afford a new exercise to her affections.

iv. From [John Fenwick], "Mr. Godwin," *Public Characters of 1799-1800* (London: R. Phillips, 1801): 371-74.

The next publication of Mr. Godwin's pen that we have to notice, is connected with a story of peculiar interest. We allude to the Memoirs of Mrs. Godwin's Life. The story connected with that work deserves to be told at length, if it could come within our limits. It exhibited Mr. Godwin in that difficult moment for him when the lofty doctrines he had taught made heavy claims on his own practice. He had loudly proclaimed his objections to marriage, and his hatred of that state was indeed inveterate enough. The time came, when he was to subject the woman of his choice to unmerited obloquy, or comply with forms he could not approve. The situation was trying. But Mr. Godwin conceived the production of happiness to be the true criterion of morality; and he did not hesitate to choose, where unlimited mischiefs were to be incurred on one hand, and a definite and comparatively small evil endured on the other.

Mr. Godwin was married to Mrs. Wolstonecraft in 1797. He

had slightly known that most celebrated and most injured woman before her residence in France. After her return, accident brought him into her company. He learnt her sorrowful situation at that period; and with a zeal the vulgar are accustomed to call romantic, attached himself to the design of restoring a noble mind to itself and society. The elevated talents, and perhaps still more elevated temper, of Mrs. Wolstonecraft, were almost universally known in the world; and the sweetest of the feminine attractions were not less the qualities of this extraordinary woman than the grandeur of mind so generally acknowledged in her. She was one of those, that the powers of nature and the cultivation of society sometimes unite to form, for whom every sensible and polished mind almost loses its veneration in the excess of its love.

The manner in which Mr. and Mrs. Godwin lived together may be presented as a model for conjugal life. Mr. Godwin's former dislike of marriage was occasioned chiefly by the tyranny it almost always includes. It is not surprising, therefore, that his enlightened views of that intercourse should enable him to shun that rock. But it is not by the mere absence of prominent mischiefs that we can describe Mr. Godwin's roof while his wife lived. To all that is dignified in the delicate relation of married persons, we must add those innumerable requisites of domestic peace that are found in cheerfulness, good will, and mutual deference to the adverse opinions that, in two minds of great vigour, must almost necessarily exist. One of the passions that has the most powerful hold on Mr. Godwin's mind is, a fondness for conversation with persons of superior talents. He has always asserted it to be among the most fertile causes of intellectual improvement, when rich and congenial souls chance to meet. We shall not, therefore, be very much in danger of exaggerating, if we endeavour to form a picture of the perfection to which he now carried this favourite scheme of pleasure and improvement. So many accessary temptations as conversation offered him, in his intercourse with Mrs. Godwin, would not fail to bring its cultivation, in this instance, to a very unusual degree of excellence.

Mrs. Godwin died in September 1797. In the scenes that

belong to that afflicting period, Mr. Godwin was still to be exhibited in an unexpected light to those who were accustomed to regard him as a hard unfeeling theorist. He watched over the means attempted for her recovery with a fortitude and presence of mind, that recalled to his friends the recollection of the philosopher they had been used to contemplate in his writings; but, when hope was gone, he abandoned himself to sorrow that seemed to assimilate him with the weakest of mankind; and, when Mrs. Godwin was no more, he admitted of no consolation, in the first moments of his anguish, but that of paying a superstitious respect to her remains.

It was in January 1798 that Mr. Godwin published his Memoirs of the Life of Mrs. Godwin. In May of the same year a second edition of that work appeared. A painful choice seems to present itself to every ingenuous person who composes memoirs of himself or of any one so nearly connected with himself as in the present instance. He must either expose himself with disadvantage to the illiberal and malicious temper that exists in the world, or violate the honour and integrity of his feelings. Yet, that the heart should be known in all its windings, is an object of infinite importance to him who would benefit the human race. Mr. Godwin did not prefer a cowardly silence, nor treachery to the public, having chosen to write. Perhaps such works as the Memoirs of Mrs. Godwin's Life, and Rousseau's Confessions, will ever disgrace their writers with the meaner spirits of the world; but then it is to be remembered, that this herd neither confers nor can take away fame.

v. From [C. Kirkpatrick Sharpe], "The Vision of Liberty," *Anti-Jacobin Review* 9 (Aug. 1801): 518.

XV.

Then saw I mounted on a braying ass,
William and Mary, sooth, a couple jolly;
Who married, note ye how it came to pass,
Although each held that marriage was but folly?—
And she of curses would discharge a volley

If the ass stumbled, leaping pales or ditches:
Her husband, sans-culottes, was melancholy,
For Mary verily would wear the breeches—
God help poor silly men from such usurping b———s.

XVI.

Whilom this dame the Rights of Women writ,
That is the title to her book she places,
Exhorting bashful womankind to quit
All foolish modesty, and coy grimaces;
And name their backsides as it were their faces;
Such licence loose-tongued liberty adores,
Which adds to female speech exceeding graces;
Lucky the maid that on her volume pores,
A scripture, archly fram'd, for propagating w———s.

XVII.

William hath penn'd a waggon-load of stuff,
And Mary's life at last he needs must write,
Thinking her whoredoms were not known enough,
Till fairly printed off in black and white.—
With wondrous glee and pride, this simple wight
Her brothel feats of wantonness sets down,
Being her spouse, he tells, with huge delight,
How oft she cuckolded the silly clown,
And lent, O lovely piece! herself to half the town.

vi. Anon., "Ode to the Memory of Mary Wollstonecraft" (1804), signed "S. W.," transcribed from flyleaf of William Godwin, *Memoirs of the Author of a Vindication of the Rights of Woman*, 2nd edn., corrected (London: J. Johnson, 1798), Pierpont Morgan Library, PML 46004.

Ode to the Memory of Mary Wollstonecraft

Where Wollstonecraft's cold relics lie,
    May soft wing'd breezes, passing by
O'er death's low [?mansion] fling around perfume,
    May genius bend his honour'd head,
    Respectful, o'er her narrow bed,
And there the wild flower smile in constant bloom.

Vast was her energy of mind;
    And few there be of woman kind,
In power of intellect with her could vie:
    For her's was nature's Sterling ore,
    And fancy's fascinating lore,
And boundless thought, that proudly soar'd on high.

What boots it that her genius fir'd,
    Or that philosophy acquir'd
For her a seraph's praise, and wide renown?
    She climb'd up wisdom's summit high,
    But just to look around, and sigh,
And meet despair, and feel misfortune's frown.

Since then nor Skill nor genius give
    Their blest inheritor to live,
Screened from the shafts that wound the feeling soul,
    Thine be the virtuous maid sincere,
    Who blithely fills an humble sphere,
Though fame refuse her merits to enroll.

                                   S. W.
                                  1804

vii. From Amelia Opie, *Adeline Mowbray; or, The Mother and Daughter: A Tale*, 3 vols. (London: Longman, Hurst, Rees, and Orme, 1805) 2: 95-101.

"How strange and irrational," thought Adeline, "are the prejudices of society! Because an idle ceremony has not been muttered over me at the altar, I am liable to be thought a woman of vicious inclinations, and to be exposed to the most daring insults."

As these reflections occurred to her, she could scarcely help regretting that her principles would not allow her delicacy and virtue to be placed under the sacred shelter bestowed by that ceremony which she was pleased to call idle. And she was not long without experiencing still further hardships from the situation in which she had persisted so obstinately to remain. Their establishment consisted of a footman and a maid servant; but the latter had of late been so remiss in the performance of her duties, and so impertinent when reproved for her faults, that Adeline was obliged to give her warning.

"Warning, indeed!" replied the girl: "a mighty hardship, truly! I can promise you I did not mean to stay long; it is no such favour to live with a kept miss;—and if you come to that, I think I am as good as you."

Shocked, surprised, and unable to answer, Adeline took refuge in her room. Never before had she been accosted by her inferiors without respectful attention; and now, owing to her situation, even a servant-maid thought herself authorised to insult her, and to raise herself to her level!

"But surely," said Adeline mentally, "I ought to reason with her, and try to convince her that I am in reality as virtuous as if I were Glenmurray's wife, instead of his mistress."

Accordingly she went back into the kitchen: but her resolution failed her when she found the footman there, listening with a broad grin on his countenance to the relation which Mary was giving him of the "fine trimming" which she had given "madam."

Scarcely did the presence of Adeline interrupt or restrain

her; but at last she turned round and said, "And, pray, have you got any thing to say to me?"

"Nothing more now," meekly replied Adeline, "unless you will follow me to my chamber."

"With all my heart," cried the girl; and Adeline returned to her own room.

"I wish, Mary, to set you right," said Adeline, "with respect to my situation. You called me, I think, a kept miss, and seemed to think ill of me."

"Why, to be sure, ma'am," replied Mary, a little alarmed— "every body say you are a kept lady, and so I made no bones of saying so; but I am sure if so be you are not so, why I ax pardon."

"But what do you mean by the term kept lady?"

"Why, a lady who lives with a man without being married to him, I take it; and that I take to be your case, an't it, I pray?"

Adeline blushed and was silent:—it certainly was her case. However, she took courage and went on:

"But mistresses, or kept ladies in general, are women of bad character, and would live with any man; but I never loved, nor ever shall love, any man but Mr. Glenmurray. I look on myself as his wife in the sight of God; nor will I quit him till death shall separate us."

"Then if so be that you don't want to change, I think you might as well be married to him."

Adeline was again silent for a moment, but continued—

"Mr. Glenmurray would marry me to-morrow, if I chose."

"Indeed! Well, if master is inclined to make an honest woman of you, you had better take him at his word, I think."

"Gracious heaven!" cried Adeline, "what an expression! Why will you persist to confound me with those deluded women who are victims of their own weakness?"

"As to that," replied Mary, "you talk too fine for me; but a fact is a fact—are you or are you not my master's wife?"

"I am not."

"Why then you are his mistress, and a kept lady to all intents and purposes: so what signifies argufying the matter? I lived with a kept madam before; and she was as good as you, for aught I know."

Adeline, shocked and disappointed, told her she might leave the room.

"I am going," pertly answered Mary, "and to seek for a place: but I must beg that you will not own you are no better than you should be, when a lady comes to ask my character; for then perhaps I should not get any one to take me. I shall call you Mrs. Glenmurray."

"But I shall not call *myself* so," replied Adeline. "I will not say what is not true, on any account."

"There now, there's spite! and yet you pretend to call yourself a gentlewoman, and to be better than other kept ladies! Why, you are not worthy to tie the shoestrings of my last mistress—she did not mind telling a lie rather than lose a poor servant a place; and she called herself a married woman rather than hurt me."

"Neither she nor you, then," replied Adeline gravely, "were sensible of what great importance a strict adherence to veracity is, to the interests of society. I am;—and for the sake of mankind I will always tell the truth."

"You had better tell one innocent lie for mine," replied the girl pertly. "I dare to say the world will neither know nor care any thing about it: and I can tell you I shall expect you will."

So saying she shut the door with violence, leaving Adeline mournfully musing on the distresses attending on her situation, and even disposed to question the propriety of remaining in it.

viii. From Virginia Woolf, "Four Figures" (1929), in *The Common Reader*, 2nd Series (London: Hogarth Press, 1932) 161-63.

It was in this crisis that she again saw Godwin, the little man with the big head, whom she had met when the French Revolution was making the young men in Somers Town think that a new world was being born. She met him—but that is a euphemism, for in fact Mary Wollstonecraft actually visited him in his own house. Was it the effect of the French Revolution? Was it the blood she had seen spilt on the pavement and the cries of the furious crowd that had rung in her ears that made it seem a matter of no importance whether she put on her cloak and went to visit Godwin in Somers Town, or waited in Judd Street West for Godwin to come to her? And what strange upheaval of human life was it that inspired that curious man, who was so queer a mixture of meanness and magnanimity, of coldness and deep feeling—for the memoir of his wife could not have been written without unusual depth of heart— to hold the view that she did right—that he respected Mary for trampling upon the idiotic convention by which women's lives were tied down? He held the most extraordinary views on many subjects, and upon the relations of the sexes in particular. He thought that reason should influence even the love between men and women. He thought that there was something spiritual in their relationship. He had written that "marriage is a law, and the worst of all laws … marriage is an affair of property, and the worst of all properties". He held the belief that if two people of the opposite sex like each other, they should live together without any ceremony, or, for living together is apt to blunt love, twenty doors off, say, in the same street. And he went further; he said that if another man liked your wife "this will create no difficulty. We may all enjoy her conversation, and we shall all be wise enough to consider the sensual intercourse a very trivial object." True, when he wrote those words he had never been in love; now for the first time he was to experience that sensation. It came very quietly and naturally, growing "with equal advances in the mind of each" from those talks in Somers Town, from those discussions upon everything under the sun which they had held so improperly alone in his rooms. "It was friendship melting into love …", he wrote. "When, in the course of things, the disclosure came, there was nothing in a manner for either party to disclose to the other." Certainly they were in agreement upon the most essential points; they were both of opinion, for instance, that marriage was unnecessary. They would continue to live apart. Only when Nature again intervened, and Mary found herself with child, was it worth while to lose valued friends, she asked, for the sake of a theory?

She thought not, and they were married. And then that other theory—that it is best for husband and wife to live apart—was not that also incompatible with other feelings that were coming to birth in her? "A husband is a convenient part of the furniture of the house", she wrote. Indeed, she discovered that she was passionately domestic. Why not, then, revise that theory too, and share the same roof. Godwin should have a room some doors off to work in; and they should dine out separately if they liked—their work, their friends, should be separate. Thus they settled it, and the plan worked admirably. The arrangement combined "the novelty and lively sensation of a visit with the more delicious and heart-felt pleasures of domestic life". Mary admitted that she was happy; Godwin confessed that, after all one's philosophy, it was "extremely gratifying" to find that "there is someone who takes an interest in one's happiness". All sorts of powers and emotions were liberated in Mary by her new satisfaction. Trifles gave her an exquisite pleasure—the sight of Godwin and Imlay's child playing together; the thought of their own child who was to be born; a day's jaunt into the country. One day, meeting Imlay in the New Road, she greeted him without bitterness. But, as Godwin wrote, "Ours is not an idle happiness, a paradise of selfish and transitory pleasures". No, it too was an experiment, as Mary's life had been an experiment from the start, an attempt to make human conventions conform more closely to human needs. And their marriage was only a beginning; all sorts of things were to follow after. Mary was going to have a child. She was going to write a book to be called *The Wrongs of Women*. She was going to reform education. She was going to come down to dinner the day after her child was born. She was going to employ a midwife and not a doctor at her confinement—but that experiment was her last. She died in childbirth. She whose sense of her own existence was so intense, who had cried out even in her misery, "I cannot bear to think of being no more—of losing myself—nay, it appears to me impossible that I should cease to exist", died at the age of thirty-six. But she has her revenge. Many millions have died and been forgotten in the hundred and thirty years that have passed since she was buried; and yet as we read her letters and listen to her arguments and consider her experiments, above all, that most fruitful experiment, her relation with Godwin, and realise the high-handed and hot-blooded manner in which she cut her way to the quick of life, one form of immortality is hers undoubtedly: she is alive and active, she argues and experiments, we hear her voice and trace her influence even now among the living.

ix. John Whale, "Elegy: for Mary Wollstonecraft," *British Journal for Eighteenth-Century Studies* 20: 2 (Autumn 1997): 204-05.

It is twenty minutes before eight.
Downstairs, they lower their voices
and use two hands to open doors.
A plate chinks in the parlour.
A broom is sweeping the yard.
Fires flare silently into life
and the very air is muffled
with a clear understanding.
Objects in the grey room take on
the familiar shape of objects.
Outside, the cabs and carriages
on their way through the dust
rattle the cobbles with a sound
which is neither midsummer
nor the dead of winter.
In the room below, light
breaks like a stick of chalk
on a table set for two.

Room after room, door after door,
I search the house through
and come up with nothing.
Nothing touched it seems by her
as she went reeling through life.
And it took so many days to die.
I take her brave book of letters

which suits this frozen north
that grips the edges of my mind.
Her spirit melts happiness
to nothing less than true content.
Through my gloom of innumerable pines
a waterfall leaps the darkness
and its voice suddenly aches,
aches with a weight of water
flowing under Putney bridge.
I imagine her ghostly skirt
billowing in the cold Norwegian sea.

But she is striking out for life
alone on the wide ocean.
Before her floats a veil or gauze,
a cold transparent envelope
of water thickened into life
and marked for life with rings
like bloodstains in the snow.
It trails purple ribbons.
As my tears salt the sparkling waves
I begin to see through her bright I
as it meets the cold light of day.
Somewhere in the near distance,
a new-born baby starts to cry.
It is twenty minutes before eight.

Appendix E: Variants in the Second Edition

The following list gives substantive variants between the first and second editions of *Memoirs of the Author of a Vindication of the Rights of Woman*, published in January and August 1798 respectively. The reading preceding the square bracket is the one printed in this edition; the reading following the square bracket is the one printed in the second edition. Cuts to the first edition are indicated by the word *omitted*, and insertions are indicated by the word *added*. Page and line numbers refer to this edition, and passages are abbreviated by ellipsis when more than six words long.

43 CHAP. I. / 1759-1775.] *omitted*
43.5 thoughtless calumny, or malignant] malignant calumny, or thoughtless
43.10 due] *omitted*
43.14 them] *omitted*
43.21-22 an attachment to ... a sympathy in] a sympathy in their fate, and an attachment to
44.10 Mary] her whose story he now undertakes to record,
44.14 *added*: CHAP. I. / 1759-1775.
44.22-26 herself; he resides ... present in Ireland.] herself.
45.4 a very] an
45.9 five first] first five
45.10 some portion] the indications
45.13 whole course of her] course of her subsequent
45.14 but] *omitted*
45.18 quick, impetuous disposition,] quick and impetuous temper,
45.19 cruelty.] severity.
45.19 a despot,] absolute,
45.32 copying] tracing
46.5 despotism] rigidness
46.13 her] *omitted*
46.16 threaten similar violence towards] menace similar violence to

46.20-21 upon the landing-place near] at

46.24 held] pursued

46.25 of the same kind as that] similar to that which

46.28 very] *omitted*

46.30 In some instance of passion] Upon some occasion of severity

46.32 risen] arisen

47.5 most profoundly] eminently

47.5 sciences] science

47.9 persons die] persons actually die

47.10 period] stage

47.16 whom to name ... to honour,] a name eminently dear to genius and science,

47.17 out of numerous projects] of numerous purposes

47.24 amusements] toys

47.25 to female] to the amusement of female

47.30-31 habitation, and took ... Epping Forest,] habitation upon Epping Forest, and took a farm near the Whalebone,

48.6-9 Bamber Gascoyne resided ... family of Mary.] I mention this circumstance on account of its connection with the topography of the spot.

48.17 for] *omitted*

48.24 recollections] recollection

48.25 very] *omitted*

48.28 very] *omitted*

48.33-49.1 of some sort] *omitted*

49.7 at] *omitted*

49.8 is perhaps] might perhaps be

49.23 very] *omitted*

49.33 Mr. Clare.] *new paragraph added*: It is easy to perceive that this connection was of a character different from those to which she had hitherto been accustomed. It were to be desired that the biographer of persons of eminent talents, should possess the means of analysing the causes by which they were modified, and tracing methodically the progress of their minds. But though this can seldom be performed, he ought probably not to neglect to record the fragments of progress and cultivation that may have come down to him. A censurable fastidiousness only, could teach us to reject information, because that information is imperfect.

50.1 But a connection] A connection still

50.3 fervent,] warm,

50.7-8 original instrument ... friends acquainted,] person who introduced them to each other's acquaintance,

50.13 Mary] Fanny

50.13-15 bore a resemblance ... with Charlotte. She] was peculiarly adapted to conciliate a mind of simplicity and affection. Mary

50.16 peculiar] much

50.21 this spectacle] a scene, which so happily accorded with her two most cherished conceptions, the picturesque and the affectionate,

50.25 exquisite] uncommon

50.26 employment] exertion

51.1 exertions.] assiduity.

51.8 habitation] habitations

51.24-27 The principal acquaintance ... Josiah Wedgwood.] *omitted*

51.30-31 spirit of independence ... influence enough] ascendancy in some respects had now become considerable, was able

52.3 her] the

52.17 instigated] influenced

52.19-20 a widow lady ... already adult.] the widow of an opulent tradesman of the city of London.

52.25 respect,] article,

53.1-2 True to the calls of humanity,] *omitted*

53.6-7 that he now made it] to be now

53.7 being thought] it being consequently thought

53.9 property already in possession.] fortune.

53.28 in any degree] *omitted*

54.1 melancholy occasion,] critical circumstance,

55.4 and during the subsequent convalescence,] *omitted*

55.5 purposes of this sort.] plans for this purpose.

55.21 and folly.] *added*: Her mistakes in this respect were two: she engaged herself too minutely and too deeply in the care of their welfare; and she was too much impressed by any seeming want of ingenuous and honourable feeling on the part of those she benefited. In the mixed scene of human life, it is necessary that, while we take some care for others, we should leave scope for the display of their own prudence and reason; and that, when we have discharged our duty respecting them, we should be habituated to derive a principal consolation from the consciousness of having done so.

55.22 now] *omitted*

55.22-23 no other than] *omitted*

55.28 who] that

56.8 upon] *omitted*

56.22 creation.] creating.

56.23-25 attached to it, or ... future punishments.] attached to it.

56.29 future] *omitted*

56.31 sufficiently] *omitted*

57.13-16 Mary, whenever she ... this place, is] In the catalogue of friends acquired at this period, I may likewise include

57.16-17 now master of ... I shall have] a popular preacher in the established church, whom I shall have further

57.18 to mention hereafter.] *new paragraph added*: It was also during her residence at Newington Green, that she was introduced to the acquaintance of Dr. Johnson, who was at that time considered as in some sort the father of English literature. The doctor treated her with particular kindness and attention, had a long conversation with her, and desired her to repeat her visit often. This she firmly purposed to do; but the news of his last illness, and then of his death, intervened to prevent her seeing him a second time.

58.8 was accustomed] was for the most part accustomed

59.1-2 February 1785.] *added*: The advice of Mary in this instance, though dictated by the sincerest anxiety for her friend's welfare, is scarcely entitled to our approbation.

59.3-4 The change of climate ... life of Fanny] From change of climate and situation Fanny found but little benefit; and her life

59.10 in the utmost degree] *omitted*

59.20-23 imagine that she ... of their sentiments.] look into the minds of her acquaintance, and to approve or be displeased, in proportion as they manifested those sentiments, which the persons and the treatment they met with, ought, as she conceived, to excite.

59.31 were never exercised upon] entered not into her intercourse with

60.23-30 It was during ... a second visit.] *omitted*

63.27 courtship,] court,

66.8 has lately] has since lately

66.8 Ireland.] his country.

66.29-30 indeed be ... profoundest commiseration.] I believe, betray a total want of sensibility and taste.

67.15-17 At the same ... from the metropolis.] *omitted*

67.19-21 Bridge, which Mr. Johnson ... into the country.] Bridge.

67.23 period] part

68.16-17 of course,] *omitted*

69.17 mere] merely

69.20 within] in

70.1-2 Among effusions of ... interspersed some] Interspersed among occasional traits of an original mind, I find a portion

70.3 from] *omitted*

70.29 removed him;] effected a transfer of his indentures to another attorney,

70.31-2 basis she had provided,] preparation thus bestowed on him,

71.1 sort of] *omitted*

71.2-3 was, that her father ... his circumstances.] is to be traced to the embarrassed circumstances of her father.

71.3 having grown] having some time before grown

71.5-6 but Mary, not ... the business,] but, as they did not appear to benefit from the superintendence of their new manager, Mary about this time

71.10 which she supplied to] with which she supplied

72.3 the wreath of] *omitted*

72.13 fundamental] *omitted*

72.25 the lists of] *omitted*

73.7 was the] was nearly the

73.18-19 anecdote she told me concerning it,] circumstance

that occurred while it was under her hands,

73.20 the general] a frequent

73.21 a matter of importance,] important,

73.34 stimulus.] incentive.

73.34-5 not expected to ... Her friend's] expected reproach, rather than to be encouraged, in what she well knew to be unreasonable. Mr. Johnson's

74.25 "In every state ... slaves of men:"] "Through every state of life the slaves of man:"

75.17 true stamina of the writer's] writer's essential

75.19-20 *pro tempore*;] of the moment;

76.1-3 The contradiction ... when they considered] The pre-conceived ideas of the public were not less erroneous as to the person of the author, than those they had formed of

76.5-6 prompted to seek ... beholding] led to seek an opportunity of seeing

76.6-7 sturdy, muscular, raw-boned] rude, pedantic, dictatorial

76.11 undoubtedly] *omitted*

76.15 first class of human] class of finished

76.23-4 in the behalf ... injured beauty.] by the contemplation of their oppressed and injured fate.

76.29 six weeks.] *new paragraph added*: The remainder of the story I have to relate is less literary, than personal. For the rest of her life Mary was continually occupied by a train of circumstances, which roused all the prepossessions and passions of her mind.

76.31-33 Fuseli, which proved ... subsequent history.] Fuseli

76.33 republic] Union

77.4-5 produced solely upon the incitement] undertaken solely from the instigation

77.26-27 belles-lettres] miscellaneous

77.27 Of consequence,] When I say this, it is by no means intended to imply, that his intercourse with the writers of established fame is not considerable, or that he is not profoundly skilled in their beauties. One consequence however of his avocations from literature is, that

77.30-31 Milton, Shakespear ... his attention.] *omitted*

77.31-2 I believe,] *omitted*
78.3 abortiveness] futility
78.4 all our] our
78.10 amend.] mend.
78.25-79.23 What she experienced ... prescribed to herself.]
new paragraph: To understand this, we have only to recollect
how dear to persons of sensibility is the exercise of the affections. A sound morality requires that "nothing human should
be regarded by us with indifference;" but it is impossible that
we should not feel the strongest interest for those persons,
whom we know most intimately, and whose welfare and sympathies are united to our own. True wisdom will recommend
to us individual attachments; for with them our minds are more
thoroughly maintained in activity and life than they can be
under the privation of them, and it is better that man should be
a living being, than a stock or a stone. True virtue will sanction
this recommendation, since it is the object of virtue to produce
happiness, and since the man who lives in the midst of domestic relations, will have many opportunities of conferring pleasure, minute in the detail, yet not trivial in the amount, without
interfering with the purposes of general benevolence. Nay, by
kindling his sensibility, and harmonizing his soul, they may be
expected, if he is endowed with a liberal and manly spirit, to
render him more prompt in the service of strangers and of the
public.

But, in the catalogue of domestic charities, there are none so
capable of affording strong and permanent delight, as that of
two persons of opposite sexes who have conceived a preference
for each other. Human beings differ so much in their tempers
and views, that, except in cases of a tender attachment, cohabitation brings with it small prospect of harmony and of happiness. The connection between parents and children, between
grown persons and young, is of too unequal a nature; and is
bounded and restrained by a sense of responsibility on the one
side, and the inattention and heedlessness particularly incident
to the other. The charm of domestic life consists in a mutual
desire to study each other's gratification; and this can scarcely
subsist in sufficient force, but in this particular connection.

Mary had now lived for upwards of thirty years in a state of celibacy and seclusion. As her sensibilities were exquisitely acute, she had felt this sort of banishment from social charities, so frequent in a state of high civilisation and refinement, more painfully than persons in general are likely to feel it. Or rather, as I believe, she suffered occasional accesses of uneasiness, torpor and vacuity, without having clearly traced the sources and remedy of the evil. She was like what we are told of those lofty and aspiring geniuses, who, being formed for busy scenes and daring projects, find the activity of their temper, when debarred its proper field, corroding and preying upon itself. The sentiments which Mr. Fuseli excited in her mind, taught her the secret, to which she was so long in a manner a stranger. Let it not however be imagined, that this was any other than the dictate of a most refined sentiment, and the simple deduction of morality and reason. Never was there a woman on the face of the earth more alien to that mire and grossness, in which the sensual part of our species are delighted to wallow. Superior at the same time to the idleness of romance, and the pretence of an ideal philosophy, no one knew more perfectly how to assign the enjoyments of affection their respective rank, or to maintain in virgin and unsullied purity the chasteness of her mind.

It happened in the present case that Mr. Fuseli was already married; and, in visiting at his house, his wife became the acquaintance of Mary. Mary did not disguise from herself how desirable it would have been, that the man in whom she discovered qualities calling forth all the strength of her attachment, should have been equally free with herself. But she chearfully submitted to the empire of circumstances. She conceived it practicable to cultivate a distinguishing affection, and to foster it by the endearments of personal intercourse and a reciprocation of kindness, without departing from the consideration due to his previous engagements. She scorned to suppose, that she could feel a struggle, in conforming to the laws she should lay down to her conduct.

79.25 large and] *omitted*
79.33 (1791),] *omitted*

79.34-35 the person to whom it relates.] her who is the subject of it.

80.8 literary men are] men of leisure and reading are too

80.11 very] *omitted*

80.18-19 acquired, in a very blameable degree,] acquired

80.19 seeing every thing] looking

80.21 in any respect] perhaps only

80.25 ventilated] discussed

81.4 discussed] touched upon

81.7 touched upon] mentioned

81.8 upon any.] of any.

82.8 have had] *omitted*

83.2 limits] limit

83.16 gloominess] gloom

83.22 remarks] remarked

84.8 the French revolution.] *added*: Her country, combined with her known political sentiments, recommended her; and the celebrity of her writings had prepared the way for her personal reception.

84.12-13 acquaintance was more intimate] intercourse was greater

84.14-15 in December 1792] *omitted*

84.15-18 species of connection … over her manners.] connection, from which the tranquillity and the sorrows of the immediately succeeding years of her life were solely derived.

84.19 delicacy, to attempt] forbearance in this place

85.1 Mr. Imlay] this person

85.7 him, she] Mr. Imlay, Mary

85.10-11 that now … Mr. Imlay, that] which now occurred, that finally

85.14 inhabitants] inhabitant

85.20 obtain,] obtain of him,

85.23 which, as she observes, are] which she

86.1 The commencement … now formed,] In the commencement of the attachment she now formed, Mary

86.2-4 She always conceived … of the heart.] Delicacy, she thought, required the making an intercourse of this sort sacred and confidential.

86.18 sacred] inviolable

86.21 The decree however] Meanwhile the decree

86.24 connection,] connection (formed, on her part at least, with no capricious or fickle design),

86.30 was now] now thought herself

87.8 still more] *omitted*

87.28-30 rank, more from … their abstract nature.] rank less from their own nature, than from the temper of the mind that suffers them.

87.31 often] *omitted*

87.36 the same gaiety] gaiety

88.1 delicious] refined

88.2 fine] delicate

88.8 bosom] attachment

88.13-16 She was like … its happiest age.] *omitted*

88.26 individual] *omitted*

88.28-34 Her conception of … luxuriancies of affection.] *omitted*

88.34-89.1 entire; her love was unbounded.] entire.

89.2 of her nature.] *new paragraph added*: It might be considered as a trite remark, if I were to observe here, that the highest pleasures of human life are nearly connected with its bitterest sorrows, and that the being who restlessly aspires to superior gratifications, has some reason to fear, lest his refinement should be a precursor to anguish and repentance. Influenced by this anticipation, there are persons who resolutely circumscribe themselves within the sphere of a frigid and miserable separation from others, that they may be independent of their injustice or folly. But this is a sordid policy. The mistake of Mary in this instance is easy of detection. She did not give full play to her judgment in this most important choice of life. She was too much under the influence of the melancholy and disappointment which had driven her from her native land; and, gratified with the first gleam of promised relief, she ventured not to examine with too curious a research into the soundness of her expectation. The least that can be said of the connection that she now formed, is, that it was a very unequal one. In years the parties were a match for each other; in every other point they were ill fitted for so entire an intimacy.

89.3-4 I am now … new link, by] to which my narrative has

reached, the attachment of Mary gained a new link, by her

89.6-8 Their establishment … Imlay's entering into] The establishment she had formed at Paris, was however broken almost as soon as entered on, by the circumstance of Mr. Imlay's engaging in

89.10 in which he was engaged,] into which he entered,

90.27 represented as] represented by him as

90.28 once] *omitted*

91.19-20 an ill-starred, unhappy passion?] a passion, at once ill-assorted, and unpromising?

91.24 fixed all] placed

91.29-30 her rest. Mr. Imlay] her rest. Wounded affection, wounded pride, all those principles which hold most absolute empire in the purest and loftiest minds, urged her to still further experiments to recover her influence, and to a still more poignant desperation, long after reason would have directed her to desist, and resolutely call off her mind from thoughts of so hopeless and fatal a description. Mr. Imlay

92.3 from whose society … particular gratification,] whom Mary saw frequently about this time,

93.14 her penetrating glance.] her.

93.16 occurred to] pressed upon

93.24 for which] to which

94.4 in] *omitted*

94.11 of] a

94.26-27 or no it were] it was

94.30 exist.] live.

95.1 very] particularly

95.4 the most desireable thing] well calculated

95.21-24 Affliction had tempered … unbounded attachment.] *omitted*

95.25 softened] awakened

95.26-28 with all, and more … former lover.] she returned to England.

95.30-31 return from Norway,] journey home,

96.19 new mistress. What was] new mistress. The characteristic of her mind upon all trying occasions, was energy; but it was a concentrated energy, active in resolution, and not the unresisting slave of feeling; disdaining to waste itself in the empty war of words, and never hurried into any thing incompatible with the elevation of her character. What was

96.26 sort of] *omitted*

97.27-28 Thames; and, not ... to Putney.] Thames, and took a boat for that purpose.

96.30 public.] public, and accordingly proceeded further up the river.

96.31 time had] time it had

96.35 leaped] threw herself

97.6-7 a desperate spirit.] *new paragraph added*: How strange is the condition of our nature! The whole scene of human life may at last be pronounced a delusion! Speculation for ever deceives us, and is the appropriate office of castle-builders; but the active concerns of life cheat us still more! Mary was in the first instance mistaken in the object of her attachment, imputing to him qualities which, in the trial, proved to be imaginary. By insensible degrees she proceeded to stake her life upon the consequences of her error: and, for the disappointment of this choice, for a consideration so foreign to the true end of her powers and cultivation, she was willing to consign those powers and that cultivation, pregnant as they were with pleasure to herself and gratification to others, formed to adorn society, and give a relish the most delicate and unrivalled to domestic life, as well as, through the medium of the press, to delight, instruct, and reform mankind—she was willing, I say, to consign all these to premature destruction! How often is the sagacity of our moral judgment reserved for the hour of meditation, and how little does it sometimes bestead us in the time of our greatest need!

97.8 she] Mary

97.9-10 the body was found.] she was taken from the water.

99.18-19 Mr. Imlay] he

99.22 passage,] hall,

99.23 to intreat ... her appearance.] to prevent her from entering.

99.29 its father. He] its father. While she sought relief for the anguish of her mind, the mother was still uppermost in her gestures and manner; and the appeal her action appeared to make, or rather the sentence it inforced, would, one would have thought, have proved irresistible. Mr. Imlay

100.1 conduct himself,] act

100.16-17 the country,] Berkshire,

100.28-33 She was at the house … considerable benefit.] *omitted*

101.12-13 Mr. Imlay] this person

101.13 person] one

101.15 sort were] sort, however great might be the provocation that roused them, were

101.18 her connection with Mr. Imlay,] their connection,

101.30 sketch] draught

101.31-2 was offered to both the winter-managers, and] *omitted*

103.9 with disgrace. Never did] with disgrace. She had errors; but her errors, which were not those of a sordid mind, were connected and interwoven with the qualities most characteristic of her disposition and genius. Never did

103.18 that book] they

103.24-25 From that time … imperceptible degrees.] Her visit, it seems, is to be deemed a deviation from etiquette; but she had through life trampled on those rules which are built on the assumption of the imbecility of her sex; and had trusted to the clearness of her spirit for the direction of her conduct, and to the integrity of her views for the vindication of her character. Nor was she deceived in her trust. If, in the latter part of her life, she departed from the morality of vulgar minds too decidedly to be forgiven by its abettors, be it remembered that, till this offence was given, calumny itself had not dared to utter an insinuation against her.

104.9 prey, in the affair.] prey.

104.26 It] The sentiment produced, thus

105.2 trembling] *omitted*

105.3-4 Mary rested … hoping to find] The sort of connection of which I am here speaking, between persons with whom the intercourse of mind, and not sordid and casual gratification, is the object proposed, is certainly the most important choice in the departments of private life. Mary trusted to have found

105.8 great soul,] liberal spirit,

105.11-22 marry. It is difficult … of her conduct.] immediately marry. Ideas which I am now willing to denominate prejudices, made me by no means eager to conform to a ceremony as an individual, which, coupled with the conditions our laws annex to it, I should undoubtedly, as a citizen, be desirous to abolish. Fuller examination however has since taught me to rank this among those cases, where an accurate morality will direct us to comply with customs and institutions, which, if we had a voice in their introduction, it would have been incumbent on us to negative.

The motives of Mary, were not precisely those which influenced my judgment. She felt an entire conviction of the propriety of her conduct in forming this connection.

105.27-34 It was only about … square. But Mary] But she

106.1 in] omitted

106.5-12 For myself … to our intercourse.] omitted

107.5 upon] omitted

107.26-27 and that … perhaps unexceptionable,] omitted

109.3-4 (as this ultimately was)] (as this, when traced to its source, will be found to be)

109.19 and unlimited] omitted

109.26 with] by

109.38 sort of] omitted

110.36 very] omitted

111.25 finished] gone through

115.6 as usual,] as had been usual,

120.9 is now erecting] has been erected

120.15-16 XXVII APRIL … / … SEPTEMBER MDCCXCVII.] 27 April, 1759: / Died 10 September, 1797.

120.19 personal] omitted

121.3-22 We had cultivated … my first opinions.] A circumstance by which the two sexes are particularly distinguished from each other, is, that the one is accustomed more to the exercise of its reasoning powers, and the other of its feelings. Women have a frame of body more delicate and susceptible of impression than men, and, in proportion as they receive a less intellectual education, are more unreservedly under the empire of feeling. Feeling is liable to become a source of erroneous decisions, because a mind not accustomed to logical analysis, cannot be expected accurately to discriminate between the simple dictates of an ingenuous mind, and the factitious sentiments of a partial education. Habits of deduction enable us to correct this defect. But habits of deduction may generate habits of sophistry; and scepticism and discussion, while they undermine our prejudices, have sometimes a tendency to weaken or distort our feelings. Hence we may infer one of the advantages accruing from the association of persons of an opposite sex: they may be expected to counteract the principal mistake into which either is in danger to fall.

Mary and myself perhaps each carried farther than to its common extent the characteristic of the sexes to which we belonged. I have been stimulated, as long as I can remember, by the love of intellectual distinction; but, as long as I can remember, I have been discouraged, when casting the sum of my intellectual value, by finding that I did not possess, in the degree of some other persons, an intuitive sense of the pleasures of the imagination. Perhaps I feel them as vividly as most men; but it is often rather by an attentive consideration, than an instantaneous survey. They have been liable to fail of their effect in the first experiment; and my scepticism has often led me anxiously to call in the approved decisions of taste, as a guide to my judgment, or a countenance to my enthusiasm. One of the leading passions of my mind has been an anxious desire not to be deceived. This has led me to view the topics of my reflection on all sides, and to examine and re-examine without end the questions that interest me. Endless disquisition however is not always the parent of certainty.

121.24-122.15 The strength of … extinguished for ever!] Her feelings had a character of peculiar strength and decision; and the discovery of them, whether in matters of taste or of moral virtue, she found herself unable to control. She had viewed the objects of nature with a lively sense and an ardent admiration, and had developed their beauties. Her education had been fortunately free from the prejudices of system and bigotry, and her sensitive and generous spirit was left to the spontaneous exercise of its own decisions. The warmth of her heart defended her from artificial rules of judgment; and it is therefore surprising what a degree of soundness pervaded her sentiments. In the strict sense of the term, she had reasoned comparatively little; and she was therefore little subject to diffidence and scepticism. Yet a mind more candid in perceiving and retracting error, when it was pointed out to her, perhaps never existed. This arose naturally out of the directness of her sentiments, and her fearless and unstudied veracity.

A companion like this, excites and animates the mind. From such an one we imbibe, what perhaps I principally wanted, the habit of minutely attending to first impressions, and justly appreciating them. Her taste awakened mine; her sensibility determined me to a careful development of my feelings. She delighted to open her heart to the beauties of nature; and her propensity in this respect led me to a more intimate contemplation of them. My scepticism in judging, yielded to the coincidence of another's judgment; and especially when the judgment of the other was such, that the more I made experiment of it, the more was I convinced of its rectitude.

The improvement I had reason to promise myself, was however yet in its commencement, when a fatal event, hostile to the moral interests of mankind, ravished from me the light of my steps, and left to me nothing but the consciousness of what I had possessed, and must now possess no more!

122.18 character.] character from whom it flowed.

Select Bibliography

Manuscript Sources

Anon., "Ode to the Memory of Mary Wollstonecraft." Signed "S.W., 1804." On flyleaf of *Memoirs of the Author of a Vindication of the Rights of Woman*. By William Godwin. 2nd edn., corrected. London: J. Johnson, 1798. Pierpont Morgan Library, PML 46004.

Fenwick, Eliza. Letter to Everina Wollstonecraft, 12 September 1797. Abinger Manuscripts, Bodleian Library, Dep. b. 215/2.

Godwin, Hannah. Letter to William Godwin, 5 February [1798]. Abinger MSS, Dep. c. 811/1.

Godwin, William. Diary. Abinger Manuscripts, Dep. e.196-227.

——. Letter to Anthony Carlisle, 15 September 1797. Abinger MSS, Dep. b. 215/2.

Godwin, William, and Hays, Mary. Mary Hays Correspondence and Manuscripts. The Carl. H. Pforzheimer Collection of Shelley and His Circle, the New York Public Library, Astor, Lenox, and Tilden Foundations.

Hunt, Leigh. Annotations on flyleaf of his copy of *Memoirs of the Author of a Vindication of the Rights of Woman*. By William Godwin. 2nd edn., corrected. London: J. Johnson, 1798. Pierpont Morgan Library, PML 13040.

Johnson, I.B. Letter to William Godwin, 13 November 1797. Abinger MSS, Dep. b. 214/3.

[Johnson, Joseph.] "A few facts." n.d. Abinger MSS, Dep. b. 210/3.

Contemporary Reviews

Analytical Review 27 (Mar. 1798): 235-40.
Anti-Jacobin Review and Magazine 1 (July 1798): 94-102.
Lady's Monitor 1, Nos. 12-17 (7 Nov.-12 Dec. 1801): 91-131.
Monthly Review 27 (Nov. 1798): 321-24.
New Annual Register for 1798 (1799): 271.

Primary Texts

Boswell, James. *Life of Johnson*. Ed. G.B. Hill. Rev'd. L.F. Powell. 6 vols. Oxford: Oxford UP, 1934-50.

Brissot, Jacques-Pierre. *The Life of J.P. Brissot, Deputy from Eure and Loire, to the National Convention. Written by Himself. Translated from the French*. London: J. Debrett, 1794.

[Fenwick, John.] "Mr. Godwin." *Public Characters of 1799-1800*. London: R. Phillips, 1801. 358-75.

Godwin, William. "Analysis of Own Character, begun Sep. 26, 1798." Ed. Mark Philp. *Collected Novels and Memoirs of William Godwin*. Vol. 1. London: Pickering and Chatto, 1992.

——. *An Enquiry concerning Political Justice, and its Influence on General Virtue and Happiness*. Ed. Mark Philp. *Political and Philosophical Writings of William Godwin*. Vol. 3. London: Pickering and Chatto, 1993.

——. *The Enquirer: Reflections on Education, Manners, and Literature. In a Series of Essays*. Ed. Pamela Clemit. *Political and Philosophical Writings of William Godwin*. Vol. 5. London: Pickering and Chatto, 1993.

——. "Essay of History and Romance." Ed. Pamela Clemit. *Political and Philosophical Writings of William Godwin*. Vol. 5. London: Pickering and Chatto, 1993.

——. *Godwin & Mary: Letters of William Godwin and Mary Wollstonecraft*. Ed. Ralph M. Wardle. Lincoln and London: University of Nebraska P/London: Constable, 1967.

——. *Memoirs of the Author of a Vindication of the Rights of Woman*. London: J. Johnson/G.G. and J. Robinson, 1798.

——. *Memoirs of the Author of a Vindication of the Rights of Woman*. 2nd edn., corrected. London: J. Johnson, 1798.

——. Ed. *Posthumous Works of the Author of a Vindication of the Rights of Woman*. 4 vols. London: J. Johnson/G.G. and J. Robinson, 1798.

——. *St. Leon: A Tale of the Sixteenth Century*. Ed. Pamela Clemit. *Collected Novels and Memoirs of William Godwin*. Vol. 4. London: Pickering and Chatto, 1992.

———. *Thoughts: Occasioned by the Perusal of Dr Parr's Spital Sermon*. Ed. Mark Philp. *Political and Philosophical Writings of William Godwin*. Vol. 2. London: Pickering and Chatto, 1993.

[Hays, Mary.] Obituary of Mary Wollstonecraft. *Monthly Magazine*, 4 (September 1797): 231-33.

———. "Memoirs of Mary Wollstonecraft." *Annual Necrology for 1797-8*. London: R. Phillips, 1800. 411-60.

Johnson, Samuel. *The Rambler*. Ed. W.J. Bate and Albrecht B. Strauss. Yale Edition of the Works of Samuel Johnson. Vol. 3. New Haven and London: Yale UP, 1969.

Louvet de Couvray, Jean-Baptiste. *Narrative of the Dangers to which I have been Exposed, since the 31st of May, 1793. With Historical Memorandums. By John Baptiste Louvet, one of the Representatives proscribed in 1793*. London: J. Johnson, 1795.

Opie, Amelia, *Adeline Mowbray; or, The Mother and Daughter: A Tale*. 3 vols. London: Longman, Hurst, Rees, and Orme, 1805.

[Polwhele, Richard.] *The Unsex'd Females: A Poem. Addressed to the Author of The Pursuits of Literature*. London: Cadell and Davies, 1798.

Robberds, J.W., ed. *A Memoir of the Life and Writings of William Taylor of Norwich*. 2 vols. London: John Murray, 1824.

Roland, Madame Manon. *An Appeal to Impartial Posterity, by Citizenness Roland, Wife of the Minister of the Home Department; or, A Collection of Pieces Written by her during her Confinement in the Prisons of the Abbey, and St Pélagie. Translated from the French*. 2 vols. London: J. Johnson, 1795.

Rousseau, Jean-Jacques. *The Confessions*. Trans. J.M. Cohen. Harmondsworth: Penguin, 1953.

Seward, Anna. *Letters of Anna Seward: Written Between the Years 1784 and 1807*. 6 vols. Edinburgh: Constable, 1811.

[Sharpe, C. Kirkpatrick.] "The Vision of Liberty." *Anti-Jacobin Review* 9 (Aug. 1801): 515-20.

Whale, John. "Elegy: for Mary Wollstonecraft." *British Journal for Eighteenth-Century Studies* 20: 2 (Autumn 1997): 204-05.

Wollstonecraft, Mary. *Collected Letters of Mary Wollstonecraft*. Ed. Ralph M. Wardle. Ithaca: Cornell UP, 1979.

———. *Letters to Imlay*. Ed. Janet Todd and Marilyn Butler. *The Works of Mary Wollstonecraft*. Vol. 6. London: Pickering and Chatto, 1989.

———. *Letters Written during a Short Residence in Sweden, Norway, and Denmark*. Ed. Janet Todd and Marilyn Butler. *The Works of Mary Wollstonecraft*. Vol. 6. London: Pickering and Chatto, 1989.

———. *Vindication of the Rights of Woman*. Ed. Janet Todd and Marilyn Butler. *The Works of Mary Wollstonecraft*. Vol. 5. London: Pickering and Chatto, 1989.

Woolf, Virginia. "Four Figures." *The Common Reader*. 2nd Series. London: Hogarth P, 1932. 140-72.

Secondary Texts

Barker-Benfield, G.J. *The Culture of Sensibility: Sex and Society in Eighteenth-Century Britain*. Chicago and London: U of Chicago P, 1992.

Blum, Carol. *Rousseau and the Republic of Virtue: The Language of Politics in the French Revolution*. Ithaca and London: Cornell UP, 1986.

Brown, Nathaniel. *Sexuality and Feminism in Shelley*. Cambridge, MA: Harvard UP, 1979.

Browne, Alice O. *The Eighteenth-Century Feminist Mind*. Detroit: Wayne State UP, 1987.

Caine, Barbara. *English Feminism, 1780-1980*. Oxford: Oxford UP, 1997.

Clemit, Pamela. *The Godwinian Novel: The Rational Fictions of Godwin, Brockden Brown, Mary Shelley*. Oxford: Clarendon P, 1993.

Darnton, Robert. "A Spy in Grub Street." *The Literary Underground of the Old Regime*. Cambridge, Mass., and London: Harvard UP, 1982. 41-70.

Dart, Gregory. *Rousseau, Robespierre and English Romanticism*. Cambridge: Cambridge UP, 1999.

Durant, W. Clark, ed. *Memoirs of Mary Wollstonecraft, Written by William Godwin, and Edited with a Preface, a Supplement Chronologically Arranged and containing Hitherto Unpublished or Uncollected Material, and a Bibliographical Note.* London: Constable / New York: Greenberg, 1927.

Emsley, Clive. *British Society and the French Wars, 1793-1815.* London and Basingstoke: Macmillan, 1979.

Favret, Mary. *Romantic Correspondence: Women, Politics and the Fiction of Letters.* Cambridge: Cambridge UP, 1993.

Goodwin, Albert. *The Friends of Liberty: The English Democratic Movement in the Age of the French Revolution.* London: Hutchinson, 1979.

Grimsley, Ronald. *Rousseau and the Religious Quest.* Oxford: Clarendon P, 1968.

Holmes, Richard, ed. and introd. *Memoirs of the Author of a Vindication of the Rights of Woman.* By William Godwin. With *Letters Written during a Short Residence in Sweden, Norway, and Denmark.* By Mary Wollstonecraft. Harmondsworth: Penguin, 1987.

Jacobus, Mary. "In Love with a Cold Climate: Travelling with Wollstonecraft." *First Things: The Maternal Imaginary in Literature, Art, and Psychoanalysis.* New York and London: Routledge, 1995. 63-82.

Jones, Vivien. "The Death of Mary Wollstonecraft." *British Journal for Eighteenth-Century Studies* 20: 2 (Autumn 1997): 187-205.

Jump, Harriet Devine. *Mary Wollstonecraft: Writer.* Hemel Hempstead: Harvester Wheatsheaf, 1994.

———, ed. *Wollstonecraft. Lives of the Great Romantics III.* Vol. 2. London: Pickering and Chatto, 1999.

Kelly, Gary. *Revolutionary Feminism: The Mind and Career of Mary Wollstonecraft.* London: Macmillan, 1992, reprinted, 1996.

Locke, Don. *A Fantasy of Reason: The Life and Thought of William Godwin.* London: Routledge and Kegan Paul, 1980.

Luria, Gina M. "Mary Hays: A Critical Biography." Ph.D. thesis (New York University, 1972).

Marcus, Laura. *Auto/biographical Discourses: Criticism, Theory, Practice.* Manchester and New York: Manchester UP, 1994.

Marshall, Peter H. *William Godwin.* New Haven and London: Yale UP, 1984.

Myers, Mitzi. "Godwin's *Memoirs* of Wollstonecraft: The Shaping of Self and Subject." *Studies in Romanticism* 20 (Fall 1981): 299-316.

Nicholes, Eleanor L. "Mary Wollstonecraft." *Shelley and his Circle, 1773-1822.* Vol. 1. Ed. Kenneth Neill Cameron. Cambridge, Mass.: Harvard UP, 1961. 39-66.

——. "The Death of Mary Wollstonecraft: Excerpts from Godwin's Journal." *Shelley and his Circle, 1773-1822.* Vol. 1. Cambridge, Mass.: Harvard UP, 1961. 185-201.

Nussbaum, Felicity A. *The Autobiographical Subject: Gender and Ideology in Eighteenth-Century England.* Baltimore and London: Johns Hopkins UP, 1989.

Nyström, Per. "Mary Wollstonecraft's Scandinavian Journey." *Acts of the Royal Society of Arts and Sciences of Gothenburg, Humaniora* No. 17 (1980).

Paul, Charles Kegan. *William Godwin: His Friends and Contemporaries.* 2 vols. London: H.S. King, 1876.

Philp, Mark. *Godwin's Political Justice.* London: Duckworth, 1986.

——, ed. *Memoirs of the Author of a Vindication of the Rights of Woman.* By William Godwin. *Collected Novels and Memoirs of William Godwin.* Vol. 1. London: Pickering and Chatto, 1992.

Pollin, Burton R. *Godwin Criticism: A Synoptic Bibliography.* Toronto: University of Toronto P, 1967.

Schama, Simon. *Citizens: A Chronicle of the French Revolution.* Harmondsworth: Penguin, 1989.

Scott, Joan W. "The Imagination of Olympe de Gouges." *Mary Wollstonecraft and 200 Years of Feminisms.* Ed. Eileen Janes Yeo. London and New York: Rivers Oram P, 1997. 36-45.

Swaab, Peter. "Romantic Self-Representation: The Example of Mary Wollstonecraft's *Letters in Sweden*." *Mortal Pages, Literary Lives: Studies in Nineteenth-Century Autobiography*. Ed. Vincent Newey and Philip Shaw. Aldershot: Scholar P, 1996. 13–30.

Taylor, Barbara. "For the Love of God: Religion and the Erotic Imagination in Wollstonecraft's Feminism." *Mary Wollstonecraft and 200 Years of Feminisms*. Ed. Eileen Janes Yeo. London and New York: Rivers Oram P, 1997. 15–35.

——. "Mary Wollstonecraft and the Wild Wish of Early Feminism." *History Workshop Journal* 33 (1992): 197–219.

Todd, Janet. *Mary Wollstonecraft: An Annotated Bibliography*. New York and London: Garland, 1975.

——, ed. *A Dictionary of British and American Women Writers: 1660–1800*. London: Methuen, 1984.

——. "Mary Wollstonecraft and the Rights of Death." *Gender, Art and Death*. Cambridge: Polity P, 1993. 102–19.

Tomalin, Claire. *The Life and Death of Mary Wollstonecraft*. Harmondsworth: Penguin, 1977.